THE PHILOSOPHY OF RIGHT

*****

Rights in the Family

ANTONIO ROSMINI

THE PHILOSOPHY OF RIGHT

Volume 5

Rights in the Family

Translated by
DENIS CLEARY
and
TERENCE WATSON

ROSMINI HOUSE
DURHAM

Translated from
Filosofia del Diritto
Vol. 2, Intra, 1865

Typeset by Rosmini House, Durham
Printed by Bell & Bain Limited, Glasgow

ISBN 1 899093 15 X

Note

Square brackets [ ] indicate notes or additions by the translators.

References to this and other works of Rosmini are given by paragraph number unless otherwise stated.

Abbreviations used for Rosmini's quoted works are:

AMS: *Anthropology as an Aid to Moral Science*
CE: *Certainty*
ER: *The Essence of Right*, vol. 1 of *The Philosophy of Right*
OT: *The Origin of Thought*
PE: *Principles of Ethics*
RGC: *Rights in God's Church*, vol. 4 of *The Philosophy of Right*
RI: *Rights of the Individual*, vol. 2 of *The Philosophy of Right*
SP: *Society and its Purpose*, vol. 2 of *The Philosophy of Politics*
USR: *Universal Social Right*, vol. 3 of *The Philosophy of Right*

Foreword

The preceding four volumes of the English translation of Rosmini's *The Philosophy of Right* have dealt with the essence of right (vol. 1), individual rights (vol. 2), the principles underlying social right (vol. 3) and the application of these principles to theocratic society (vol. 4). In the present work and the following volume, Rosmini continues to apply these principles to the domestic and civil society, the other two societies necessary for 'the perfect organisation of mankind'. The first of these societies is natural to the human race and essential to its well-being; the second is the inevitable consequence of even minimal development as mankind increases in number and improves its native talents.

According to Rosmini, every human right is based upon some fact understood in its perfection. Consequently, the description of right(s) in conjugal society depends to a great extent upon correct comprehension of the nature of marriage. The author's first task, therefore, is to set out a definition of conjugal society based upon a thorough understanding of the union possible to man and woman. The fullness of this union, first at the level of humanity and then according to the characteristics proper to male and female, comprises the object of the mutual promise of self-donation which the spouses make to one another at the beginning of their life together as husband and wife. It is Rosmini's view that from this promise flow all the duties and rights which the couple have in their new society. The promise itself, although an act requiring freedom on the part of the couple, is not arbitrary; it is not within the power of the spouses to vary the promise, the elements of which are prompted by the human nature of man and woman. Permanence, for example, a self-explanatory element of the fullness of union between man and woman, cannot be gainsaid at will; unicity and fidelity, also self-evident characteristics dependent upon the nature of this total union, equally form part of the marriage promise and cannot be forsaken without damage to rights in one's spouse and neglect to one's own duty.

Permanence, unicity and fidelity in marriage are equal rights and duties in both spouses. Other aspects of the fullness of union between the couple need not be equal. In fact, the specific fullness of union proper to marriage, and far more dependent on spirit than matter, requires the inequality of complementarity between male and female with their different psychology, corporeality and attitudes. Right and duty in marriage will be based on these differences also, and give rise to the kind of disparity which perfects rather than hinders the fullness of union possible to the couple. It is at this point that Rosmini, having already set his face firmly against the moral possibility of divorce, draws further conclusions about married life wholly contrary to attitudes which, nascent in his own day, have gradually become prevalent in Western, post-Christian understanding of marriage. These conclusions need careful examination, not least because Rosmini offers reasoned arguments to the exaggerated demands of those whose only basis of opinion is either unreasoned reaction to past abuse, or misunderstanding of past situations when present-day economic and educational opportunities were totally unknown and quite impossible.

The same considerations can be applied to the development of conjugal society, which originates with the conception of children. Parental society, in which father, mother and children all have a part to play, gives rise to inalienable rights and duties on the part of spouses and their offspring. As persons, all the members of the family must be considered as ends and respected absolutely; as parents and children, their rights will differ and indeed change as children grow and become more responsible for themselves. Rosmini provides a fascinating description of this change based upon immutable principles which, applied to conditions in various ages, enable us to reach conclusions very different from his own.

DENIS CLEARY
TERENCE WATSON

Durham,
June, 1995

Contents

SECTION TWO

PARENTAL SOCIETY

Contents   xiii

SOCIAL RIGHT

SPECIAL-SOCIAL RIGHT

Part 2

RIGHT IN DOMESTIC SOCIETY

[INTRODUCTION]

969. The family is a union of individual human beings. Most authors divide it into three interconnected societies: conjugal, parental and seigniorial.

970. I noted that the relationship between bond-servant and master is not a *social* relationship (cf. *Universal Social Right*, 24–30). Aristotle, St. Thomas and many others had made the same observation.

971. My intention in repeating the observation is not to exclude this relationship as such, but to exclude it from *social Right* and assign it to *individual Right*, where I have already dealt with it.

972. Furthermore, although master and bond-servant live only *communally*, without forming a *society*, they are, as human beings, associated in a natural theocratic society and, as Christians, in a supernatural theocratic society (cf. *Rights in God's Church*, 541, 653, 664–667, 726, 785–788, 800–801).

973. The *social bonds* which necessarily bind bond-servant and master limit and temper the *seigniorial bond* between them. Thus, the state of servitude, moderated by the state of larger society, becomes compatible with human dignity (cf. *Rights of the Individual*, 243–244).

974. The harshness and injustice of servitude lie in the following causes:

1. A partial view, which considers only the seigniorial relationship of *master to bond-servant* without simultaneously considering the social relationship between one human being and another.

This exclusive view provided the logical cause and legal justification for pagan slavery.

975. 2. Non-recognition, through ignorance, or impious exclusion of a supernatural relationship which binds all human beings effectively to God in a sacred, intimate society.

When supernatural society is excluded, the only remaining bond is that of natural society. It is the weakness of this society that causes harshness and inhumanity. We see this ever more frequently in the seigniorial relationships present in regions where Protestantism and schism have hardened human hearts.

976. 3. Sensism, which tends to destroy natural theocratic society by removing from humanity the common possession of truth and moral virtue.

977. Sensism has caused great suffering to the lowest class of society, even amongst Catholics. The upper class, while claiming to help the lower, have so often tried to suppress it.

978. Hence, although the relationship between bond-servant and master, considered abstractly, is unsocial, I do not exclude it from Right. This does not mean that I justify the kind of servitude which is harsh and repugnant to human dignity, nor do I say that the moderation which makes it upright and jural springs from within itself. Any moderation and uprightness in servitude comes from outside, from its co-existence with a society essential to the human race. No human being, whether master or bond-servant, can justifiably opt out from this society or force others to do so. It has as its immovable foundation human intelligence, and as its glorious crown, divine grace.

979. I believe I have dealt sufficiently with the nature, titles and limitations of servitude in individual Right (cf. *RI*, 128–133, 239–244, 528–863, 1560–1613, 1995–1999) and have further confirmed and defended those limitations in my exposition of *theocratic Right* [cf. *RGC*].

980. Nevertheless, in this book on Right in domestic society and in the next book dealing with civil society I will need to refer occasionally to the relationship between bond-servant and master. I will add everything necessary to what has already been said in order to clarify the connection between the social and the seigniorial bond, which are mixed in different ways in the two societies. I will also describe the tremendous struggle that so often flares up between the two bonds.

981. Once the relationship incorrectly called 'seigniorial society' is excluded from domestic society, the other two societies remain as the subject of this book, which will be divided into two sections corresponding to the relationship between spouses and the relationship between parents and their children. These two interconnected societies form that body of persons living together known as the 'family', and are called, as we said, 'conjugal' and 'parental' society.[1]

982. In my work I have always tried to keep before my eyes good human nature, carefully separating it from anything wayward. This is more than ever necessary in the section dealing with domestic society. Nature alone, not the siren voices of corruption, must be my faithful guide in the investigation of human rights and duties. The sole purpose and task of the science of family Right is to determine and describe accurately 'that which is accepted by many, and by upright persons, and according to nature,' as Michael of Ephesus says.[2]

---

[1] The science of Right must not be confused with the science of family government, which we have called 'Economy' (cf. *Preface to the Works of Moral Philosophy*, *Principles of Ethics*, pp. vi–xvi). *Economy* teaches how a family is to be governed, guiding it to its perfection; in a word, it is the politics of family. In this science we certainly have to speak about *bond-servants* who are an animate instrument for such an end. On the other hand, the sole purpose of the science of social Right is to expound the jural duties and the rights of persons composing society. The possible jural relationships of society with persons outside it pertain to *individual Right* (*USR*, 1–20).

[2] *Ad Nicom.*

[981–982]

SECTION ONE

CONJUGAL SOCIETY

CHAPTER 1
The nature of conjugal society

Article 1.
The concept of the two natural societies structured for the
unification of the human race, according to the Creator's plan

983. The object of every right is some good,[3] and the value of
every good is ultimately a gratifying feeling.[4] The object and
matter of every right therefore is a pleasant feeling in human
nature. This explains why right is called 'natural'.

What then is the pleasant, natural feeling to which the rights
of conjugal society are referred?

984. Human beings are not sufficient to themselves;[5] they
continually feel the need to unite to themselves beings different
from themselves. They do this in their own feeling, in which
they themselves are the feeling principle. This FACT, furnished
by interior observation, can be stated as follows: 'Human beings
seek to unite to themselves beings different from themselves.'
Because every human being is one and identical, we see in each
human being a continual tendency to reduce plurality to unity.
Plurality reduced to unity pleases the contemplating *understanding*, relative to which it is called 'beauty'; plurality reduced
to unity in the *feeling* pleases the feeling, relative to which it is
called 'eudaimonological good'. Beauty is plurality reduced to

[3] *Essence of Right*, 252–255.
[4] *ER*, 332–339.
[5] Cf. *Saggio sulla speranza* in *Apologetica*.

unity in the world of ideas; eudaimonological good is plurality reduced to unity in the world of reality.

985. We want to unite with ourselves in the simplicity of our essential feeling all beings without exception. They can be classified as follows.

986. Some are simply things; others, persons and intellective natures. Uniting things to ourselves produces the particular fact of *ownership*;[6] uniting persons to ourselves produces the particular fact of *society*, especially conjugal society. Marriage unifies not things but natures and human persons. The character of this unification receives light from the following considerations.

987. Morality can tend only to intelligent objects. As human beings we communicate with God and our fellow human beings; both therefore are the objects of our moral duties.[7] These divine and human intelligent natures, the objects of morality, are also the natures we ceaselessly seek in many ways to unite to ourselves completely in order to make ourselves greater and achieve happiness. Union with the divine nature and its appurtenances constitutes theocratic society; the complete union of human beings with their fellows is the end of conjugal society. In both societies there is a feeling of happiness or of special contentment.

988. Granted this, we must compare these two societies and show how theocratic society, although absolute, allows for conjugal society on earth, and how, according to the Creator's plan, a very close association of the human race had to be formed through both.

Article 2.
The relationship between theocratic and conjugal society

989. How can theocratic and conjugal society, two basic societies arising directly from human nature, exist together?

990. The *common good* of theocratic society is universal being.

When joined to the spirit in the constitution of human beings, being is light. In it, everybody possesses the identical truth and

---

[6] *ER*, 332–339.

[7] *Principles of Ethics*, 215–227.

the identical rule for reasoning and living. But this natural light, resplendent in all people and constituting their rule of thought and life, does not, despite its supreme dignity, proffer a real-infinite good. Consequently, society, which is founded in the community of this good, is initial and incomplete (cf. *RGC*, 668–678).

However, God wanted human beings to enjoy a complete society. For this purpose he graciously gave them a kind of perception of himself, raising them to himself and transposing them into a region superior to all nature. *Being*, as known by us by nature, that is, *being* solely in its ideal form, became feelable by us through grace, which is *being* in its ideal-real form, God. Hence, all those who receive this gift which is not only *divine* (like the first) but also *deiform*, possess in common the supreme good. In this way theocratic society attained its completion; the kingdom of God was founded (cf. *RGC*, 694–711). A true society was established between God and mankind.[8]

991. God, the infinite good, could certainly communicate himself to human beings so completely that all their activity would be absorbed in him. In this case, no other society would be possible. Human beings would find in God not only every hoped-for, final good but every immediate, present good. This is precisely what God does in heaven. Consequently conjugal society, which cannot be fully fused into deiform society, ceases; a human being in heaven is like an angel of God.[9] The Creator however did not wish to accomplish this all at once; on the contrary, because he wanted to communicate himself to human beings by degrees, he first placed them in a wayfaring state on earth.

992. Nevertheless, even on earth we see that whenever God

[8] St. Thomas justifiably attributes the *society* of mankind with God to the supernatural order: 'Nature loves God above all things in so far as he is the beginning and end of natural good. Charity loves him in so far as he is the object of bliss, *and* IN SO FAR AS MANKIND HAS A CERTAIN SPIRITUAL SOCIETY WITH GOD' (*S.T.*, I–II, q. 109, art. 3, ad 1). Catholic theologians quite correctly therefore refer the *friendship* between God and human beings to the supernatural order. For example, Domenico Bainez expressly supports the thesis that 'the only real and proper friendship between God and human beings is supernatural friendship' (*Comment.* in II–II, 23, 1).

[9] Mt 22: 30.

communicates more of himself to human beings, conjugal society becomes less necessary relative to its material consummation; out of respect for deiform society it withdraws, as it were,
from human beings. In the earthly paradise where God was
close to humanity, the man did not feel the need to consummate
his union with the virgin given him as companion. Similarly, in
the Church of JESUS Christ, as soon as God had once more
abundantly communicated himself to human beings, great
numbers of them, of both sexes, magnanimously and with pure
intention, made themselves eunuchs for the kingdom of
heaven.[10] Conjugal society is possible only on earth because
God does not spiritualise human beings sufficiently by communicating himself completely to them. Although he makes
himself present to the intellect in a feelable way, he does so as in
a mirror or enigma.[11] In this condition and state, human beings
are united in their higher part to God while remaining material
in their lower part. With the former they can adhere to theocratic society as to their end; with their lower part they can
adhere to conjugal society, which, by offering many opportunities for practising virtue, becomes the meritorious means for
their fullest union with God.

993. *Conjugal society* can in another way become a means for
completing *theocratic society*. It is the source of the growth of
the human species which, by consummating conjugal union,
comes to subsist in many individuals. So the human race comes
into being, and human nature enters, or can enter, into theocratic society with all the individuals in whom this society is
destined to reveal and actuate itself. Thus, marriage contains
something elevated that moved the Redeemer of the human race
to raise it to the dignity of a sacrament.

Article 3.
In its first institution, the human race was to have been a single, divine-human society

994. According to God's intentions, as he has revealed them,

[10] Mt 19: 12.
[11] 1 Cor 13: 12.

the human race would not have been subject to death if it had not sinned. In this case, mankind, as first planned, would have formed not only a single, theocratic society, but a single, domestic society, a very suitable means to the theocratic society with which it would have ultimately merged, like a river flowing into the sea.[12]

Article 4.
In conjugal society there is a union common to all human beings and a union proper to the two sexes

995. Let us examine more closely the nature of conjugal society. I said that its foundation is the total union of one human being with another.

The union of one human being with another is the foundation and object of every friendship, even between persons of the same sex. But between persons of different sex, a fuller and altogether special union is possible. This union, effected exclusively between human persons of different sex, forms the object of love and the end of the conjugal society which results from it.

996. The intimacy and fullness of the union between one human being and another, as realised in conjugal society considered in its perfection,[13] is better clarified if we see that in it:

[12] Although we can mentally conceive various results if Adam had not sinned, we must note that my reference to the *first plan* can be deduced only from the best we can think of happening to human beings created innocent by God. This best, this ideal, not only excludes the sin of Adam and his descendants but in some way supposes that Adam would never have entirely left his children until transported with them into the beatific vision at a time fixed by God, no matter how long any of them might have lived on earth. However, with St. Augustine we can also suppose the opposite, that is, Adam would have been glorified before his children (cf. *De Genes. ad litt.*, bk. 9, c. 6; *The City of God*, bk. 14, c. 10), whether many families remained on earth or only one at a time. We can also conceive as possible that fathers, even after passing to eternal beatitude, could reveal themselves to and rule their children living on earth (as Christ did after his resurrection until his ascension into heaven) until all these were finally taken up into the same state of happiness.

[13] Plato acutely observed that in order to know the intimate nature of things we must always consider them stripped of all their accidental defects. Aristotle, and many others, made the same observation.

1. All the friendship and union possible, according to upright nature, between human beings of the same sex is first presupposed.

2. The intimacy and greater union which is possible between human beings of different sex but not possible between people of the same sex is added to the previous union. This final manner of union becomes the specific, characteristic difference of conjugal society.

Let us investigate both these elements.

§1. *The first element of conjugal society, the fullness of union common to all human beings*

997. According to upright reason, husband and wife are two human beings who unite with all the fullness realisable between persons of different sex. This is the true concept of marriage.

998. We note first therefore that sexual union, of itself, does not constitute conjugal society; sexual union requires and presupposes every other union possible between human persons.[14]

999. In order to understand clearly the exalted nature of conjugal society and have a correct, complete notion of it, we must use upright reason to examine the total extent of the union between two persons of different sex. In my effort to do this, I will first investigate the bonds which can bind one human being with another, even of the same sex; this will indicate the first necessary, preliminary element of marriage. I will then investigate the nature proper to the union of the sexes.

1000. Legitimate affections which bind human beings

[14] To avoid misunderstanding, the reader should note that *de facto* conjugal society is not the same as *obligating oneself* to conjugal society. The person obligated to conjugal society, that is, already married, must live in conformity with that society and realise it in fact. Anyone failing this obligation (for example, a husband who does not love his wife, or viceversa) does not in any way cease to be married. To be married means 'to have contracted the obligation to live in conformity with the demands of conjugal society'. Hence, spouses who fall short of the depth of union proper to the concept of marriage, do not lose their society *de jure*, although, through their fault, it remains *de facto* unfulfilled (cf. *RGC*, 638).

together can be fittingly classified into two groups: 1. inborn or *spontaneous*, which are calm and constant; 2. *aroused*, which are vehement and subject to change. Although we may hardly be aware of the first kind, they are sometimes suddenly aroused; for example, when someone who is the object of our habitual affections is in danger, we begin to feel our love: the thought of what may happen, the fear of loss, makes us reflect upon ourselves and we become very much aware of what we have, compared with what we may lose. *Spontaneous* affections are therefore the foundation and root of *aroused* affections. If the latter are not founded upon spontaneous affections as a development and further actuation of them, they flare up and die, or are the hypocritical, false product of selfishness; they are no longer generated by the great faculty of love, the modest mother of all true affection. I will list the *inborn*, spontaneous affections, therefore, in which *aroused* affections are included in embryo.

1001. The first good that human beings have in common is ideal being. From this being we are all free to deduce the same concepts, the same principles of reasoning, the same knowledge (cf. *RGC*, 641).

Furthermore, although this common good produces some kind of society of intellects united in identical truth, the society of human persons begins only when their wills are uniform in the same good (cf. *RGC*, 664–667).

Every human soul, however, has an inborn tendency to love known being, so that every entity becomes a degree of good for the soul.

Because we all have in common the knowledge of being, we all have love for it in common, and because *loved being* is a good for the one who loves it, all human beings have the same first good as object of their inborn affection.

In this way, as we said, an initial divine society is formed between all human beings. It is a divine society because the bond forming it (the light of truth) is divine.

The first foundation of conjugal society (cf. *RGC*, 662–663) therefore must be love of identical truth which reigns equally over the intellects of the spouses. Contrariwise, a will that opposes truth destroys the first golden link in the conjugal union.

1002. Human souls possess the same source of truth. This

means that they have the same rules for making judgments and governing their lives, and can have the same knowledge. It is natural therefore for them to agree in their judgments about, knowledge of and affections towards known beings in proportion to the value of the beings. Diversity can arise in the way they deduce truths from the same identical first source and in the knowledge resulting from these deductions. But if, however, they strive uprightly and honestly for their intellectual and moral development as they should, no contradiction whatsoever is possible in their cognitions, affections and desires. Uniformity of thoughts and opinions together with agreement of affections and desires is for the soul a treasure of inestimable value. It is impossible to estimate the peaceful joy that can come from the possession of such a rich, totally spiritual treasure, or to realise how much minds and hearts may be intimately united in it.

1003. If this complete agreement, dependent simply on the fact that souls are united in this way, diffuses in them warmth of affection (pertaining to what we have called *inborn and spontaneous* affections), it is clear that people with this warmth and affections can nurture and increase them without limit, and change them into *aroused* affections, as we have called them, which form a second golden link uniting the spouses prior to their final union.

1004. Inborn, spontaneous affections are therefore necessary to conjugal society. *Aroused* affections, on the other hand, properly ordered, are good for it as accidental ornaments, and help in a wonderful way to increase the perfection and felt happiness of conjugal togetherness.

1005. Although human beings have the same source of truth in their minds, and in their hearts the same tendency to love everything, two or more individuals may not only differ in knowledge and affections (which does not however destroy their uniformity of thought and love) but contradict each other in opinions and affections. This makes full agreement impossible. The general cause is false reasoning which, instead of simply following the dictates of truth, acts waywardly and follows the dictates of passion. It is clear therefore on the one hand that *virtue* is necessary to conjugal society, and on the other that all vice and immorality harms, wounds or even tears apart this society which seeks the fullest union of two intellect-ive, moral creatures.

1006. To understand this more deeply, we must recall that reason is guided by the will, as we have shown elsewhere. If the will is simple and pure, it leads reason to discover truth; if sunk in evil passions, it leads reason to invent falsehood for itself.[15] Reason (called 'practical' in so far as it is moved by the will), generates of itself reasonable or unreasonable affections, and initiates good or culpable external actions. But because truth is one, and falsehood multiple, the legitimate course of reasoning unites spirits in agreement, while the illegitimate divides them by disagreement. Every moral defect and evil desire that vitiates reason prejudices the loving character of conjugal society which, as the most intimate and full union of two intelligent creatures, requires or tends to full agreement. Conjugal society therefore needs the state necessary for this agreement, that is, it needs uprightness in the wills which direct the understandings. From all this we can justly infer that conjugal society is essen-tially moral, and that whatever deviates from virtue reduces or removes the union between the two intellective beings.

1007. A person who with his will, that is, with his whole self, adheres to known beings in accord with their comparative worth, feels peace and has pure enjoyment in beings. Moreover, he feels himself enhanced by such simple, ordered affections. With his assent he receives into himself the order of beings, and lovingly conforms himself to it. His sharing in and love of this order, this innermost enhancement, is called moral dignity. All these good things which we acquire by practising virtue form therefore a new bond for two souls who posses them in com-mon. Indeed, the thing that two virtuous souls possess in com-mon is the same *order of being*, to which they adhere with their whole self. This order according to which they love beings is *identical* and therefore a unifying bond. On the other hand, the awareness of their uprightness together with the *peace* and *joy* that arises and, as it were, wells up in them from love of *real beings* in accord with the *ideal order* are not, properly speaking, identical good things because the feelings of one soul are, we

---

[15] Cf. *Certainty*, 1247 *ss.*, and *ER*, 94–107.

must acknowledge, numerically distinct from the feelings of another. Nevertheless they are good things of the same species and are therefore enjoyed in common, in intimate society, according to their species. The same must be said about the *moral dignity* acquired by an intelligent creature through the practice of virtue.

1008. But this is not sufficient: these good things proceeding from virtue are indeed common in their species to virtuous friends, and proper numerically speaking to each friend, whose virtue produces them for himself. Lovers, however, have another way of enjoying them in common, whether these goods are considered identical, or proper to each lover (although they do not enjoy them in the same way). Here, we have something of great virtue and almost a miracle of love. As we have seen, intellective nature brings with itself a universal faculty of love, a faculty which relates to every being which, as being, is essentially lovable to the person who knows it. Consequently, it is clear that two intelligent beings can love each other. In this love, each loves all that is in the other, every part and every endowment of the other; every good and pleasure of the other is loved, together with the peace, joy and dignity proper to the other. All these things are loved in the beloved according to their intrinsic merit, that is, limitlessly. Hence, the love for one another's virtue and the resultant affections become the principle of the *moral esteem* found in lovers, and particularly in spouses, who are perfect lovers. This *moral esteem* is another sweet and powerful bond uniting their souls.

1009. All these tender bonds between human creatures proceed naturally from the possession of truth and the practice of virtue. The more they intermingle and strengthen each other, the greater the increase of the soul's willing adhesion to all *real beings*. This adhesion is in proportion to the comparative value of the real beings, which is revealed by comparing them to the *order of being* contemplated by the intelligent soul in the idea. Moral virtue is reduced to this adhesion. But among *real beings* there is a supreme being, relative to which all the others are nothing. Neither intelligence alone nor nature gives us direct communication with this being. Intelligence indicates it only negatively, as the necessary but totally inaccessible cause of the universe. But if it comes down, draws close to us and makes itself perceptible, we can really adhere to infinite Being. God becomes a completely social good, common to all, and those who possess him become one in the enjoyment of this good.

Here we have the religious bond, the complement of the previous bonds. Its function is to bind two human creatures who, united to one another by every possible union, finally fuse in the single union called marriage. Supernatural religion therefore elevates marriage above nature, binding spouses by the supreme bond, that is, by charity, and divinising their union. Through this bond God himself enters as a third member into their society: God becomes the common good both of himself and of the spouses. In this way, and granted the sublimity, nobility and consistency of the charity of Christ, the words of the great teacher of Hippo are justified:

> With this love we love one another and God. Nor could we truly love one another without God. If we love God, we love our neighbour as ourselves. If we do not love God, we do not love ourselves.[16]

St. Augustine then adds that St. Paul makes charity a fruit of the spirit:

> He sees the other things as issuing from and bound with this fruit: joy, peace, long-suffering, benignity, goodness, faith, gentleness, continence, chastity,[17]

each of which is an invaluable good in Christian marriage.

Because the Christ of God came to give human beings the precept of charity and strength to fulfil it, it was also fitting that he should elevate to the nature of a sacrament the society intended to realise but unable to attain perfect love; it was fitting that his charity should divinise conjugal society and adorn it with sublime virtue.

Being (truth), the order of being as the rule of the affections (moral law), and God as perceptible to human beings are each a good of infinite value. People who love them in common are more united in soul than they are by mere accidents. Their souls, in their intellective and volitive parts, have a common centre,

16 Tract. 86 *in Jo.*
17 Tract. 87 *in Jo.*

where intelligences have their true place. But communion in finite good also binds human persons together.

1010. First, human beings love themselves with subjective love, which reveals to them both what human nature is, and the goodness of that nature in others. They then love human nature as an object, which is always known as good wherever they see human nature, that is, in all their fellows. This second love is objective, evaluative love. But they love the human nature in their fellows also subjectively and instinctively, that is, they love their own likeness in them, they love themselves. This subjective love of others is spontaneous and natural; it colours and as it were gives flesh to the first love which is moral and virtuous. Hence, there is a double love, composed of the affection and virtue which we call 'humanity', and the Greeks, φιλανθρωπια.

1011. If 'humanity' means the affection human beings have for others in general, that is, if we limit the object of this affection to human nature considered in its essence and in the totality of its parts, the affection is unique and specifically different from all others.

1012. If however we group under 'humanity' all those affections whose object is everything in human nature, including what is purely accidental, humanity is a multiple affection and applies not only to the whole of human nature in its totality but to individual parts. In addition to nature's essential conditions, *humanity* also loves what is accessory, that is, its acquired embellishments; it is, as it were, a trunk whose branches are different affections that reach to all the different parts and endowments of human individuals.

1013. An affection exists therefore which relates to the essence of human nature, common to all individuals; it is *humanity* in its strict sense of fundamental affection. There are also affections relative to the natural or acquired accidental endowments of human nature, either of soul or body, or of the whole human being composed of soul and body. These are *affections stemming from humanity*.

1014. The accidental endowments of soul and body, rather than simple human essence, provide matter for more excellent, stronger affections, because all the endowments meriting greater evaluation and love (even the moral virtues themselves) are simply endowments accidental to nature.

1015. *Moral dignity*, which we have already discussed, is one such endowment; it originates in either natural or supernatural virtue. The human being embellished by supernatural virtue shares in the infinite worth of God himself, and becomes worthy of divine love, compared with which other affections disappear like stars before the light of the sun. This explains St. Augustine's acute observation, quoted earlier, that 'anyone who does not love God does not love himself.' Those who love God have within themselves an object worthy of true love, because it is not a means to another love; they can love God in themselves with ultimate love. On the other hand, those whose only love is humanity, have such a miserable object that their affections cannot legitimately find satisfaction in it; they are compelled to search elsewhere for a more worthy end. Hence those who do not love God do not love themselves, precisely because their affection cannot, according to reason, find satisfaction in themselves. They love their fellows still less therefore, because they are accustomed to loving them simply as they love themselves.

1016. Hence, if conjugal union must be the maximum union resulting from all possible unions between two human beings, the spouses must also be united by the affection and virtue of *humanity* throughout the trunk and branches; each must love in their consort human nature and its endowments whether these are already in the consort or in order that they may be there.

1017. In these and the previous *affections* we must distinguish between the levels of *inborn, spontaneous* affections and *aroused* affections. Indeed, every being together with its endowments, that is, human nature with its endowments, attracts and sets in motion a first level of affection solely by presenting itself to the human spirit through experience and knowledge, provided the human being is not perverted or wayward, nor posits an impediment. As we said, this level of affection is *spontaneous*.

Aroused affection is the fire ignited from this first spark: just as a great blaze can be made by blowing on smouldering embers, so spontaneous affection is aroused, intensified and increased infinitely.

We must carefully note however, as I have already said, that this kind of effected arousal, which affects the human heart so diversely, so tenderly, so powerfully and sometimes so forcefully is not necessary to the concept of conjugal society. All that is necessary is the first level of affection, aroused of itself according to the law of spontaneity to which human nature is subject. All additions to this are what distinguishes the different levels of feelable happiness produced by the union of the spouses. Often, however, these additions present the gravest dangers to human weakness by disturbing the tranquillity of reason; the weakness of the understanding is incapable of guiding the ship borne along by strong winds.

1018. We must speak about another class of affections, *pure love*, by which I mean love that loves itself. This is love at its most exquisite and consummated in the order of affections.

1019. Love loved by itself is passive and active, because the loving being loves to be loved, and to love.

The sweetness experienced by the lover aware of being loved by the beloved is inexpressible. But clearly its degree depends upon the greatness of the love with which the lover knows he is loved in turn, upon the greatness of the being by whom he is loved, and upon the love borne for that being.

1020. Loving to love, the lover becomes beneficent. This most noble affection continually induces him to diffuse good, to produce again and again lovable enhancements in others, for the very purpose of increasing for himself the objects of his love and the possibility of greater love. Both *benevolence* and *beneficence* derive their power from this source.

1021. Speaking of beneficence, we must distinguish between giving others the *good of existence* and the *good which perfects them*.[18] We can be drawn to give *existence* to a being by the inborn affection which makes us want to provide an object for our own love (this is the origin of the affection of *philogeniture*). On the other hand, when there is no question of giving existence to a being who already has it but *of perfecting it* (an accidental good), we are drawn by the natural love we have for subsistent being, or more accurately for its *essence* contemplated in reality, which shows us what is needed for its final endowment.[19] Because we naturally love every being, we naturally love that a being, or the essence we love in the being, attain the final state

[18] Cf. *PE*, 52–57, 197–199, 207–211.
[19] *Ibid.*, 52–54.

to which it is destined, without defect and with all its endowments.

It seems therefore that we are drawn by good nature to help and perfect beings in two ways:

1. By natural, essential love, which draws us to adhere spontaneously to all the entities we know. Hence our desire that the beings we know conform to their *archetype*, a desire which is accompanied by our effort and industry to bring them to their most perfect form, that is, to help them.

2. By our desire to have in them objects more worthy of our love, that is, more suitable for being loved by us, granted our connatural inclination as affective beings to love as much as possible.

1022. But these reasons which initially seem two are in fact one when considered more deeply. As we have indicated, the tendency to love proceeds from the ontological relationship between beings and spirit according to which 'all beings are naturally lovable to intelligence'. This explains the general tendency, which however manifests itself under two forms: 1. the tendency to love already existent beings, and 2. the tendency to want them perfect, that is, more complete in their entity so that they are more lovable. Both these tendencies are reduced to the general tendency for loving or, as we have called it, our love of active love. Hence, two human beings who seek to be united in the most perfect, fullest union of all possible unions must be joined by this most pure affection considered under both forms, this affection which moves us to love solely for the sake of loving.

1023. Summarising all the kinds of affection we have discussed, we can reduce them to three branches, all drawn from a single source as follows.

Being is in itself lovable to the affective, intellective spirit to which it communicates itself. This relationship, which we have called ontological, makes being 'good'. Being, however, has three primitive, inconfusable forms: ideal, real and moral. Hence the three basic tendencies and fundamental branches of all human affections.

1024. These basic forms however, although categorically distinct, are united in being itself. This explains the intertwining and mingling of the three different kinds of affection, which in turn generates other complex affections whose object is being, actuated in all its forms.

1025. Ideal being is *truth* and the source of:

1. The tendency to truth (ideality).

2. The tendency to knowledge (known realities).

3. The tendency to virtue (adhesion of the spirit to known realities according to the order of ideality).

1026. Real being is *feeling* and the source of:

1. The tendency to love ourselves in a felt way, and to love ourselves in proportion to our worth. Hence the capacity to love others in a felt way, which is founded in the capacity to love ourselves.

2. The tendency to love our fellows (humanity), and to love them in proportion to their likeness to us (affection for those who have fellow-feeling with us), and in proportion to the endowments they have (moral evaluation, etc.).

3. The tendency to love beings greater than ourselves, and to love infinite being known through the *way of eminence*.[20]

1027. Moral being is *feeling regulated by truth*. It is love in all its purity: universal, passive and active. Hence fellow-feeling, benevolence, beneficence, etc.

1028. Finally, absolute being is simultaneously ideal, real and moral. It takes up in itself the perfection and summit of every affection of intellective, volitive creatures. In Scripture it is called CHARITY.[21] It is the most sublime bond, the most exquisite union of human wills, which binds, perfects, and consummates all others.

---

[20] The *way of eminence* is the method of reasoning in which we strip our endowments of their limitations and ascend from them to knowledge of the divine endowments — cf. Leibniz, *Theodicy*.

[21] *Deus caritas est* (1 Jn 4: 16).

§2. The second element of conjugal society, the fullness
of union proper to the two sexes

A.

Three kinds of inevitable variations in the condition of human
bodies — first: natural defects which *per se* lessen the union;
their remedy

1029. The affections discussed so far can be said to be of
rational origin, although they consist of feelings whose effects
reach down to animality through the wonderful identity, in
human beings, of the intellective and animal principles.

Considering only the rational origin of affections, we could
suppose the possibility of *full consent* and a *perfect uniformity*
of thought between two human beings.[22] Now however we
must consider affections of another nature, in which human
beings cannot be equal and work in unison, as it were. Indeed,
the accidental variations in our bodies depend not on us but on
nature itself, and lack an immutable, uniform condition. It is the
affections originating from the body that we now wish to discuss.

Human bodies certainly have a similar design and nature,
making them all a single human species. But they also have
many accidental variations: differences of sex and, within the
same sex, of organisation, temperament and perfection of life.
These variations, especially if further developed by education,
alter the character, degree and composition of tendencies and
inclinations common to the human race, and to some extent
appearances. They also exercise extraordinary influence in the
formation of the different characteristics in people. But do these
variations, these instinctive, and as it were, contrary feelings
among human beings necessarily reduce the intimacy of their
union?

---

[22] Difference in education modifies human development and results in
different opinions and customs even in the rational order. These differences
however, unlike physical differences, do not depend on nature but on human
will. A description of the *ideal* union of two human beings can therefore
prescind from them.

1030. We must distinguish. These differences, which stem from the physico-moral condition of human individuals, divide into three classes:

1. Those contrary to nature: *defectiveness*.
2. Accidental *limitations* to which nature is subject.
3. Those according to nature, that is, the different *endowments and conditions* of nature itself.

1031. If the differences among human beings are contrary to nature, they certainly do harm to others and consequently reduce *per se* the closeness of the union between people.

1032. However they do not always have the effect of reducing *love*. We must recall *pure love* which we discussed previously. We called its function 'love of active love', which is itself either a *merely spontaneous* or an *aroused* affection. Clearly, defects in nature reduce love in those individuals who have only spontaneous love, but not always in those who have pure, *aroused* love. Aroused affection acquires indefinite virtue; thus, the lover can love the defective person with compassion, benevolence and beneficence in the person's very defects. I say 'in the person's very defects' because such love finds an opportunity of exercise in the defects, for which it shows compassion and seeks a remedy.

1033. We see therefore how pure love is indispensable to the conjugal union, if the union is to be full. From such love the union derives mutual tolerance of and support for defects. This is often required by the mutual duty of human beings who must, and do wish to live together for the duration of life.[23]

---

[23] We are speaking here about involuntary defects, because in the ideal union under discussion willed defects are excluded. Nevertheless, we can also see the necessity of this generous, pure love which bears and tolerates among Adam's descendants the many defects resulting from the weakness of moral forces and even from malice in the will.

B.
The second kind of natural variations: *accidental limitations
of nature*, which can lessen or increase the union

1034. Accidental *limitations* considered on their own and taken individually tend to diminish love.

1035. This is not always the case if they are distributed differently between two individuals. Differences of limitations can cause discord, but also harmony. When two people unite, the differences harmonise excellently if what is lacking in one is present in the other and can be enjoyed by both. This can happen even when defects are present. For example, we can see the advantages when a blind person carries a cripple: the cripple indicates the way to the blind person who helps the cripple to walk. This can make them very close friends. A collective person therefore can sometimes be made perfect even when composed of imperfect individuals. The good possessed by one individual becomes a good for them all, and the gifts of some reciprocally correct the defects of others. This must indeed be the principal reason why human beings sense the need and value of human society. Divine Providence unites human beings by the variety of their gifts so that they are mutually helpful or necessary to each other.

1036. It seems therefore that it is this diversity which principally causes the hidden attraction shown between certain persons which makes one person happy to be with another, but not with everybody. Those concerned cannot explain the happiness to themselves because their extraordinary harmony is the result of many little endowments and defects which escape their consciousness. This harmony and affinity of feeling, when established between two persons, is produced by the combination of many other causes. The following are a few.

1037. Different needs require suitable objects for their satisfaction. If everybody had the same need, sufficient objects might be lacking. People would be unhappy together, stressed and suffering. On the other hand, if needs are different, no one commandeers the object required by another; individuals live peacefully together. For example, two dishes are prepared. One appeals to a particular person, the other to another. Both people

[1034–1037]

are in total agreement because their appetites differ. If they both liked and wanted the same dish, and rejected the second, they would have to be satisfied with only half a portion each. Human feeling, we see, senses very early and, as it were, foresees the presence of an infinite number of very small defects or satisfactions in the company it may encounter; above all it would sense the presence of the mortifications and satisfactions of its self-love. These minute presentiments are present in the natural choice, affinity or harmony (or whatever we call it) of the feeling under discussion.

1038. The following is another cause of this preferential choice. As we have said, a relationship of *appropriateness*, not *uniformity*, exists between needs, and the objects suitable for satisfying the needs. A subject's disposition to enjoy a thing (tendency) or avoid a nuisance (need), and thus possess the relative object, presupposes a difference rather than an equality between the subject's defect and the object needed to remedy the situation. *Appropriateness* does not usually exist between equal but between unequal things which harmonise, just as a convex body fits into and is contiguous with a concave body. This is the case between two human beings made for each other. If one is to find himself in the other in such a way that his needs are satisfied, the other must possess certain qualities which, although different from those of the first person, must be proportionate and adapted to them. Thus, in things of the spirit, a person who wishes to command must derive pleasure from humble people ready to be commanded. On the other hand, those who feel the need to be directed by others are naturally content that someone more zealous and wise should command and direct them. Equivalent harmonious differences can be observed in animal tendencies: a strong person is more likely to be matched by a gentle person than another strong person, just as the gentle find more pleasure in the strong. The same can be said about other affinities and relationships; although arising from accidental differences, they are mutually appropriate.

[1038]

C.
The third kind of difference: various conditions integral
to human nature

1039. Agreement and disagreement can be found at different times among the variations caused by natural *accidental limitations*. As I have said, this results principally from feelings of propinquity or repugnance between individuals. However, some exquisite appropriateness is always present between variations *integral* to human nature. All these variations are directed by nature to uniting the persons who possess them.

Hence the different ages of human life temper each other very well. It is delightful to see old people join in the games of the very young, and have the comfort of robust maturity.

Sex is the chief amongst these different, natural conditions which make one person very suited to another; I must speak about it now.

Article 5.
The union proper to the two sexes

1040. We have distinguished between affections of *spiritual* origin and those of *animal* origin. We examined the former one by one, but limited ourselves to noting that the second vary, and made a summary classification of their variations. We wanted to speak more specifically about them when dealing with the principal affection to which Providence has entrusted the maintenance of the human species.

§1. *Three classes of affections of animal origin*
in the human being

1041. Affections that are partly or wholly of animal origin can be reduced to three classes: 1. *feelable*, 2. *sensuous* and 3. *sexual* affections.

1042. We reduce *feelable affections* to all those that combine something spiritual with something animal. The animal part, however, is so small that we are hardly aware of it. The spiritual part therefore is more dominant.

1043. These affections are:

1. Affections of pleasurable admiration generated by bodily beauty.

2. Affections aroused whenever we see in another's appearance or movements, as if in a mirror, a beautiful soul, dignified virtue, and loving, noble feelings. This kind of affection is nurtured particularly by courteous speech, which indicates more clearly the gifts of spirit shining through bodily forms, and by refined, humbly dignified, gracious manners. Affections produced by the attraction of 'grace' pertain to this class.

3. Affections which are sometimes suddenly enkindled between two people through a kind of mysterious attraction drawing them to love each other without their being able to explain this attraction to themselves. They quickly feel a hidden, reciprocal appropriateness in each other. They feel themselves bound by tender emotions and conquered by a fusion of delicate, indiscernible feelings which are suddenly aroused by apposite, harmonious and sympathetic dispositions. Some of these affections belong to the two previous classes of 1. beauty (although relative, partial beauty, because one can fall in love even with deformed people) and of 2. the reflection of a beautiful soul seen in the features of the body.

1044. When all these mixed affections change from inborn *spontaneous* affections to *aroused* affections and reach a certain degree of intensity, they are called 'love' in the strict sense, and constitute what has been called 'platonic love'.

1045. This kind of love is certainly harmful to the perfection of virtue because, in the present human condition, it binds the soul, taking away from it the freedom to give itself to *good* wherever good may be. Instead, it restricts itself to a single object, and, blinded to better objects, fixes itself exclusively on it, as Petrarch observed about himself:

> Although I gaze attentively and fixedly
> on a thousand different things,
> I see one woman only, and her lovely face.[24]

[24] P. 1, *canz.* 23.

1046. This affection is caused not only by people of the opposite sex, but even by those of one's own sex. It explains the Greeks' esteem for love of children. This kind of love, even if considered safe from impurity (although it can easily become impure), is always defective, as I have said; it is a passion that clouds the understanding and binds the will unjustly to some small good. The lover of Alexis quite rightly exclaimed: 'Ah! Corydon, Corydon, what madness has seized you!'[25] When such love becomes incontinence, forsaking its first genuine form, it is totally detestable to human beings.

1047. *Feelable* affection is co-terminous with *sensuous* affection. Consequently, when the former reaches a certain degree of intensity, the human being passes very easily to the latter.

1048. I call 'sensuous' the affection engendered by mutual proximity and innocent physical contacts of persons of the opposite or same sex when in conversation with each other, or by their imagining the pleasure from such situations. The affection is reduced therefore to a desire or tendency to renew such pleasures.

1049. Not every pleasure caused by bodily contact is referred *per se* to the generative organs. In fact we can see that movements relative to generation are entirely *sui generis*. The animal arouses them in itself through a kind of spontaneous activity different from every other kind, so that the purely physical and mechanical movement of the sexual organs can sometimes be separate from the generative, organic movement, while at other times it is united with and serves it, according to the nature of the internal activity or the external force producing it.

1050. We clearly see therefore how this principle of generative activity, residing in the imagination, would be subject to the dominion of free will, granted that the human being is in an integral and perfect state in nature (even if he were not raised to the supernatural state). In this state, no external stimulus suitable for moving the genital parts physically could excite any

---

[25] Virg. Ecl. 2, 69. — It must indeed be a cause for wonder how such a fine author as Giuseppe Taverna can praise the Greeks for their love of boys, as he does in his *Lezioni morali a' giovanetti tratte dalla storia*. This is one example of the defects I would like to see purged from a book so full of good, succinct instruction.

generative movement against the will of the person himself. Such a person would not be prevented from carrying out all other necessary bodily movements, which would be incapable of causing disorder in him. I find evidence for this in the experience of continent persons who know very well how the dominion of their will can frequently not only deny consent to base sensations but very often directly obstruct the sensations themselves. The fact that people can sometimes, but not always, achieve this demonstrates that a dynamic, physical bond of seigniory and dependence obtains between the will and the generative movement. Because this connection is rather weak in the state of fallen, corrupt mankind, we must attribute to the original infection the present diminution of the power which the energy of the human will has over the lowest parts of our animality.[26]

1051. Bodily contact can of its nature give pleasant feelings different from sexual feelings, and the movement producing them need not pertain to generative movement. Acts of this kind are touches of the hand, embraces, innocent kisses, etc. There is mystery and communication of life in a kiss, but this is not the place to investigate it. We must carefully observe however that, although the above-mentioned sensations do not of their nature involve generative movement, they harmonise with it in such a way that they easily arouse its active principle to produce it, granted, as we said, the weakness of the superior part of the human being in his present fallen and feeble state. The path from *sensual* to *sexual* affection is therefore highly slippery, and sometimes inevitable.

1052. Whenever sensual affection (which is possible even between persons of the same sex) reaches a certain degree of intensity, it is called 'sensual love' and is really a preparation for sexual or *physical love*. The preparation can in fact be so proximate that it generates the need for physical love, to which it stimulates the human being to blindly give way. Hence, between persons of the same sex it is disordered and wrong. It is also

---

[26] It seems certain that some strong women, overcome by men, have sometimes prevented generation taking place solely by the force of their resistant will.

disordered and wrong between persons of opposite sex, unless they are bound or bind themselves by legitimate marriage.

1053. Finally, *sexual affection* unites the two sexes with the intention of generation. This affection is so proper to them that it is physically impossible between persons of the same sex.

1054. Every sexual movement therefore that does not have generative union between spouses as its immediate end is an opprobrious disorder, contrary to the intention of nature and to the Creator's will. It is abhorrent to *human instinct* itself (when this has not been debased and become degenerate) and is reproved by human and divine law.

1055. It may be objected, but vainly, that pleasures which are naturally possible must sometimes be allowed because they are established by a wise Creator who did not make anything useless in nature. I reply:

1. For the *upright human being* there are no sexual pleasures outside marriage. There may be pleasures for the animal, but not for the *complete human being* who is not only animal but principally rational and moral, and to whom every disordered pleasure is supremely hateful, abominable and painful. The hatred and pain overcome the pleasure so that they remove the nature of pleasure and make it a torment: as I said, every disordered pleasure is rejected by the *moral-human instinct* which loves the contrary virtue above everything else. Those who seek such pleasures are distorted and drawn outside their own nature.[27]

2. *Sexual pleasures* between persons of the same sex (which an upright person will never want) are a sort of necessary consequence of the sexual tendency, whose legitimate mode of satisfaction is however in honest marriage. This consequence results from the limitation inherent in animal nature. But, as we said, all the defects of this consequence considered physically are opposed in a human being by the existence of intelligence and of noble instincts, instincts which intelligence is born to produce and does produce, provided the human being is not damaged. In animals, however, who lack reason as a brake and

---

[27] The pagans themselves sensed this. The Pythagorean philosopher, Hipparchus, thought 'immoderate desires were AGAINST NATURE' (*De animi tranquill., apud Stobaeum*).

moderating influence, the Creator provides that the sexual instinct does not suffer any misuse, except rarely, through some infirmity or damage to their physical inclinations.

§2. *The nature of sexual union*

A.
Sexual union is an act of the soul

1056. According to the Creator's most wise dispositions, the chief of all the different conditions of human nature is the difference between the sexes. The character of this difference is such that, far from impeding the full union of two human individuals through lack of uniformity, it accomplishes the union through diversity of form. The Creator has predisposed a wonderful appropriateness of form and organisation of one body to the other. The immediate cause of this cannot be found in a principle of reason but solely in the fact of animality, which according to its eternal concept is necessarily subject to such law and determination.

1057. The nature of sexual union, for which human nature is suitable in its lowest part, is not, I repeat, material, as if it could be achieved by the mere mechanical union of material parts. It is rather an activity of the active animal principle. This certainly operates in matter but with an action of its own that differs greatly from any mechanical operation.

1058. I remind the reader of what I have said elsewhere: the animal principle is simple, and is the soul itself.[28]

The act of sexual intercourse, in which generation takes place, is an act of the soul operating in bodies and through bodies.[29]

---

[28] *Anthropology as an Aid to Moral Science*, 92–134.

[29] We should note the following words of St. Thomas where he is referring to much older teachings about generation: 'Just as the parts of a human being are set in motion by command of the will, so a son is set in motion by the father through the generative power. Hence the Philosopher says that the

The soul does not act through particular parts to the exclusion of others; the whole animal contributes to the act, especially the whole nervous system stimulated by the soul. The ancients themselves knew this.[30]

B.
The union of the sexes is a mutual communication of life

1059. In *Anthropology as an Aid to Moral Science* I gave as my opinion that the sensations (at least those of touch) which we have from an animate body are specifically different from those of an inanimate body. From the former we receive a communication of the soul itself which gives life to the body that produces the sensation in us.

1060. Individual life, it must be noted, has an expansive force communicable to the bodies it is able to invade. It certainly has a power to make them one with itself, as we see in nutrition and other phenomena.[31] We can have no great difficulty therefore in conceiving and admitting that a kind of communication of life takes place between two living bodies when they make contact; one body feels the very soul of the other body. This is particularly true in the case of lovers, where each would fuse totally with the other, if possible. The channelling and communicating of life in this union is aided, or rather produced, by the spontaneous consent of the wills, that is, by the effort of the souls, the principles of animation. Sexual intercourse is certainly the most

father is cause of the child AS MOVER (*Physics*, bk. 2, com. 29). Bk. 2 of *De generatione animalium* states that in the seed there is A KIND OF MOVEMENT FROM THE FATHER'S SOUL which forms the matter into the conceived child' (*De Malo*, q. 4, art. 6).

[30] It is sufficient to read Aristotle's *De generat. anim.*, 1: 17–19; *Phis.*, 2; *Problem.*, 4: 21. Hippocrates claimed that the σπερμα [sperm] was a distillation of all parts of the body, but principally of the brain (*De genitura*). Gallenus followed the same opinion. It is said that Plato made the spinal marrow the source of the sperm; Pythagoras, the most liquid, vital part of the blood, and Alcmaeon, the brain. This last opinion is followed today by Laurent (bk. 8, c. 2). Epicurus thought it was composed of soul and body. Cf. Plut., *De placitis Philos.*, bk. 5, c. 3.

[31] *AMS*, 323–349.

intimate of bodily unions: the two fundamental feelings seem for a moment to become one, so that the feeling of one is reciprocally the feeling of the other. No words can express this more effectively than those of Scripture which define marriage as: 'And the two shall be in one flesh.'[32] Here the unity of the flesh must be understood as the unity of life by which the flesh is vivified and in which both individuals share. The union of the sexes is therefore a vital not a material union. In the act, which can last only a moment, life exercises the function by which it joins two living bodies in the way the parts of a single animated body are joined together: for example, the brain and heart of the same human being intercommunicate through organic, vital functions and make a single animal out of both.

§3. The ordering of marriage to sexual union is the specific difference distinguishing it from other unions.

1061. Although the other unions in marriage are presupposed and have even greater nobility, the sexual union is the final completion of marriage. The ordering of marriage to this union is the specific difference between it and all other unions possible to human beings.

1062. Ancient traditions said that the first parents of mankind were ανδρογυνοι[33] [androgynes] who were later separated. It was in fact logical that the propagated human species should consider its parents in the very act of generation, because in this act they are precisely ανδρογυνοι [androgynes], and generation and paternity begin.

[32] Mt 19: 5–6 [Douai].

[33] Plato, *Conv.* — *Censorin.*, 4 — The same idea is found in Indian traditions. In the Mânava-Dharmasâstra, bk. 1: 32 we read: 'When the sovereign lord divided his body into two parts, one half became male, the other, female.' The sovereign lord is Brahma in human form and represents the first human being.

Article 6.
Generation, effect of the sexual union

1063. According to the eternal idea, the Creator so ordered animal nature that at the moment when sexual union reached its greatest degree of intimacy and the feeling soul of one partner tended with greater impetus to invade the bodily parts of the other, some particles should separate from the body of each, move towards one another and meet in a place suitable for maintaining their life. In the act of detachment, these particles are not only alive but at the highest degree of vital stimulation and, as it were, animated by double life.

After union they do not cease to live, even though partly divided from the individuals to whom they belong and from whom they were drawn by impetus of the souls that wished to unite. Through this division, the feeling preserved in them is no longer part of the feeling of the two individuals. They constitute therefore the first rudiments of a new animal destined to become a new human individual through communication of the light of God's face.[34]

1064. There is no more apt way of expressing this mysterious fact of generation than the phrase of divine Scripture in which the son of the parents is called their 'spark'.[35]

Article 7.
Inconfusability of persons

1065. Conjugal society is a perfect union in accord with nature, a union between two human individuals of different sex. But one thing remains distinct in them: *person*. The spouses unite to form one *nature* out of two, but cannot form one person out of two. When God defined marriage saying that the

---

[34] Cf. what I said at greater length about *generation* in *AMS*, 323–349, 812–831.

[35] Thecua's wife calls her son this, in the Second Book of Kings, claiming that they wish to kill her remaining son, she appeals to David: 'They seek to quench MY SPARK which is left, and will leave my husband no name, nor remainder upon the earth' (c. 14: 7 [Douai]).

spouses must be one flesh, he said simultaneously that they will be two in the one flesh, 'THEY WILL BE TWO'.

1066. It is true that a kind of *personal* communication also exists between lovers, and therefore between spouses, in so far as one enjoys the personship of the other. But this kind of transfusion of persons neither intermingles them nor excludes their proper, inalienable being.

1067. If the affection we are discussing changes from a *spontaneous* to an *aroused* state, it produces a special loving phenomenon; it goes outside itself to the loved object. Petrarch indicates this:

> Sometimes in the midst of sad tears
> A doubt assails me: how can these limbs
> live so far from their spirit?
> But Love responds: Don't you remember?
> This is a privilege of lovers
> freed from all human qualities.[36]

Article 8.
Conclusion

1068. It is a mistake therefore to see in marriage only the lower, sexual part of the union. The good sense of ancient peoples had understood very well the totality of the union between two persons of different sex, that is, of marriage. The Romans wisely defined it: 'The union of male and female, the sharing of all life, the communication of DIVINE and human right,'[37] and said that the wife 'is accepted as companion in human matters and in the DIVINE HOUSE.[38] With wonderful foresight, the Romans included in marriage that divine society about which we have spoken and which we have posited as the foundation of marriage.

[36] P. 1, Son., 13.
[37] D., bk. 23, t. 2, 1. Modestinus' definition, bk. 1, *Regul.*
[38] C., bk. 9, t. 32, 4.

CHAPTER 2
The act placing conjugal society in being

1069. We have described the nature of conjugal union. We now have to examine the act by which it is placed in being by the two persons of different sex who wish to form it.

Article 1.
Conjugal society is placed in being through a contract

1070. The concept of *full union* between two human individuals indicates the necessity of a contract if conjugal society is to be placed in being.

1071. If the union is full, it must result from all the natural bonds which can come about between two human individuals. These bonds have a hierarchical order corresponding to that of the faculties of which they are the equivalent acts. Higher bonds embrace and contain lesser bonds.

The highest bond capable of drawing together two rational beings is that formed by their personal will, the supreme human faculty, which possesses the power and reason enabling these persons to move all other faculties.

Moreover, the bond of will can contain other bonds subject to itself because they can in fact be ordered by the will. In marriage, this must be the case if different bonds are to preserve their natural order, which requires them to be governed, as it were, by the consensual action of the two personal wills.

The first bond, therefore, which puts into being and embraces all others in conjugal union, is necessarily that of the two wills, that is, their mutual desire, the free consent of the parties; in other words, the act which associates them.

1072. Natural light alone had taught this to the Roman legislators who expressed the matter very clearly in Ulpian's words: 'Consent, not a common bed, makes marriages.'[39]

---

[39] Dig., bk. 50, tit. 17: 30. Consequently, even when marriage was not consummated but only consented to, married couples were considered to possess any rights which came to them on condition that the marriage had taken place. Cf. *Dig.*, bk. 35, tit. 1: 15.

1073. This explains why conjugal union can be called 'society'. It is such because it comes about with the consent of the parties, that is, through a *contract* or *social pact*.[40]

1074. What is the character of this pact? Is it arbitrary or natural? It is certainly *arbitrary* in the sense that no individual has any jural obligation to enter such a society with any determined person.

1075. But its object is not arbitrary. The object of the contract is not and cannot be other than the *full, de jure union* between two persons of different sex which we have described above.

Article 2.
The object of the marriage contract is not arbitrary, but determined by nature. It is the full union described above

1076. A *moral necessity* requires that the object of the marriage contract be the full union we have described, not some less full union.

1077. It cannot be said, however, that any *jural necessity* requires the two persons to unite in such a full manner. If both of them were happy with a less close union, they would not be doing one another any injury, according to the principle: *no injury is done to one who consents* (cf. *RI*, 134–138).

1078. Injury would be present only in the case of *violence* done by one person to the other either to constrain external consent or to force physical union.

1079. Injury would also be present in the case of *seduction* provided that the seduction had not gained victory over the other's will. *Injury* is immediately removed if the will cedes, although the crime remains (cf. *RI*, 166, 168).

---

[40] Everything was subject to controversy. People went to the extent of denying that marriage was a contract, although Placido Boeckhn (*Comm. in Decret.*, bk. 4, tit. 1, part 2, n. 6 and 9) rebutted the objections. Moreover, Roman laws wisely considered the *marital contract* as synonymous with *marital affection*. They stated that marriage comes about as a result of either a *contract* or *affection*. Justinian says that marriages are contracted not with dowries, but affection (*Cod.*, bk. 5, t. 17, 11. — *Nov.*, 22, c. 3; and 74, c. 4). This explains why in this article we have considered 'contract' as the final, most noble act of rational affection between spouses.

1080. We still have to show, therefore, how the moral law forbids union between the sexes, which is the specific difference of conjugal union, if sexual union does not take place as part and completion of the greater, full union between two individuals in which, as we have said, marriage consists.

1081. We have to start from the *moral system* placed at the beginning of this work [*ER*, 93–143] if we want to provide such a demonstration.

This system shows that:

1. Respect for the human person is the principle of the entire branch of morality which has human beings as its object;

2. Consequently the whole of human nature must be respected because it is united with person, which it serves as its end. It forms a single thing with person in such a way that when the nature belonging to person is injured, person itself is injured. Nature shares in the dignity itself of person through the intimate connection it has and must have with person.

Respect for *person*, and respect for *human nature* in so far as it is united with person, means in the last analysis to act in thought, affections and actions in such a way that:

1. the natural needs and tendencies of person and human nature are not opposed by *disorder* caused in them and by the damage inevitably connected with disorder (do no evil to them);

2. the natural needs (the natural and hence well-ordered tendencies) are followed (do good to them).

The order, the natural need and the interior tendency of human nature is *unity*. — The human being is one; his order consists in being one. Every division, every split amongst his tendencies is an imperfection and often a cause of his degradation.

It is of the essence of person to be above all the other powers, each of which in acting waywardly detracts from the natural power of person, and inflicts some injury on person.

In the same way nature, which receives its dignity only from its submission to person, is degraded as soon as it rejects this submission. Every human faculty destined to obey person, yet disobedient to it, is an evil opposed to the intrinsic order of human nature.

Consequently the union between two individuals of different sex must be carried out in such a way that it does not cause any kind of separation between the various parts which make up humanity. Unity, personal dignity and the subordination of powers depend upon this.

Limited union rather than full union between two human individuals can take place in two ways. 1. The individuals are united only at the level of the higher affections (affections of a rational character) as in friendship, mutual esteem, etc. This union does not constitute marriage whose specific difference is, as we said, directed to the union of the sexes. 2. They are united by means of their lower, baser parts without the intervention of the union dependent on the higher, more noble faculties. This is against the moral law.

It is against the moral law because it is opposed to the exigencies of human nature and to the exigencies of the individual persons, each of whom acts against their own and the other's dignity.

It is opposed to human nature because sexual union consists in a substantial, vital communication which forms one body from two. Nature requires, therefore, that each of the two persons loves the other as they each love their own body and soul. The nature of each has in fact become the nature of the other. If, then, the order of nature is such that the soul is united in the fullest possible way with its own body that it never wishes to be separated from it, but loves and favours it as much as it merits, the natural order equally requires that the soul should love the individual with whom it enters into vital communication in the way that the individual should be loved, and therefore as person.

1082. God made this understood from the very first institution of marriage when he took woman from the rib of man. The same truth was expressed by the first husband when he saw his wife and immediately exclaimed:

> 'This is bone of my bones and flesh of my flesh;
>> she shall be called Woman,
>>> because she was taken out of Man.'[41]

This law of perfect union, required in sexual union by the order in human nature, then became an immutable foundation

---

[41] Gen 2: 23.

of divine legislation about marriage. It was repeated and re-stored by Christ in the new law.[42] St. Paul, too, spoke about it in the following way: 'Even so, husbands should love their wives as their own bodies. He who loves his wife loves himself. For no man ever hates his own flesh, but nourishes and cherishes it.'[43] There is no more appropriate concept than this to express the intrinsic order of human nature.

1083. According to nature, each human individual is most intimately united with his own body in such a way that it would be against nature to desire separation from it or to desire the dissolution of the natural bonds which hold the body united to the soul. The same must be said about the union of the sexes; it draws in its wake every other full union of individual with individual. The contrary is opposed to nature because it means acting against nature, against the order of nature, against na-ture's complete, perfect instinct. In other words, it means acting against the moral law which requires respect for human nature.

1084. We said that the union of the sexes, when unaccompan-ied by other unions of a rational nature, is opposed to the requirements of the dignity of both the persons who engage in intercourse.

In fact, each person does an injury to the other because each uses the other solely as a means. This is the case whether the purpose in intercourse is one's own sexual pleasure or a desire for children. All this is against the nature of sexual intercourse which, as we saw, is vital intercourse, brought about by the soul. In human beings the soul not only feels, but feels and under-stands; it cannot be used as a mere instrument and means for a human being without its dignity being subjected to defilement and extremely serious injury. Hence the opprobrium felt by good sense at all times and in all places for prostitution. An individual of one sex cannot, therefore, have intercourse with an individual of another sex without loving that individual as an end, that is, as another self with whom there is that full union for which all peoples have reserved the proper, honorific name, *marriage*.

1085. In merely sexual intercourse, human persons despise

[42] Mt 19: 4–6; Mk 10: 6–8.
[43] Eph 5: 28–29.

self; they sin against self, against their own dignity. This is done in several ways.

First, they *disorder* in themselves the natural gradation and correct chain of affections which are organised in such a way that the superior affections link with and communicate movement to the lower, as we have seen. The lower affections have to be a consequence and kind of completion following upon the higher affections. The union of the sexes should therefore come about as a natural accessory to rational love, which tends to union. In intellective individuals such as humans, who are also animals, this union involves the lowest, less noble parts of animality so that there may be total union. Union, as we know, is the indispensable law of love. If, however, the principal love (of intellective origin) ceases, the series and order of affections is broken. Human beings no longer act as human beings, but as brutes. They offend against the moral law which imposes on them respect for human nature and, for this end, the maintenance of the order with which nature embellishes itself and rises above other, irrational things.

1086. This destruction of the proper, natural order of human affections can be seen in the use of sex which is unaccompanied by the higher affections, even if the end of the individuals using sex in this way is of itself decent, as in the case of the procreation of children. The decent end does not in fact excuse the base action; evil cannot be done for the sake of good. Such a disunion of human affections so contrary to nature, such denial of full affection to the partner who makes himself or herself a continuation of the other, is a clear, blatant injustice, a disavowal of that which is, a refusal to grant the practical esteem due to the person who is another self. At the same time, the individual, making use of a double measure, reserves all esteem for self.

1087. Second. If, in addition, the end itself is disordered and the aim is only sexual pleasure, the disorder introduced into the natural affections and parts of the human being is immensely increased. There is open rebellion by the lower part against the higher; the human being, tyrannised and debased by the flesh, would rather obey than command it.

1088. Modesty is the alarm aroused in the noble part of human beings when they feel or foresee that their lower part threatens to overcome the higher part. It is also the shame felt by humans when they imagine that this offensive threat has been noticed in them by others. In fact, the attack is always made with strong forces on the rebel side, compared with the few, weak forces, born to command, on the higher, rational side. If the threat alone brings shame, if people blush when the part which threatens, or could threaten, is simply exposed naked to the eyes of others, actual giving way to sexual enticements outside decent, marital union is rightly said to be 'filthy' vice and held abominable by the whole of humanity. When people are in search of this pleasure alone, they feel themselves degraded to animal level; all human superiority seems already lost.

1089. Hence Krause[44] rightly declares that love, this noble, human affection, is the principle of marriage, and deduces the moral and jural laws governing love. Rotteck also states rightly that the union of the sexes is ennobled and rendered worthy of humanity by feeling.[45] Pabst in turn, considering that marriage *h*as been elevated to the sacramental level, describes it as the mysterious veil which covers and enfolds the per se impure, animal act of generation.[46]

[44] *Fondamento del Diritto naturale*, Jena, 1803.

[45] We must note, however, that if Krause's and Rotteck's statements about *love* and *feeling*, are to be true, they must be understood of love and feeling which are *spontaneous* (rationally operative), not *stimulated*. Stimulated love and feeling can add sweetness to the marital partnership, but they are not necessary for the essential ennoblement of the union.

[46] *Adam und Christus, Zur Theorie der Ehe*, I. H. Pabst. Vienna, 1835, in 8°. — This mysterious veil, under which intellective nature feels the need to hide the act of generation, was signified in ancient times by the actual rite of veiling new brides. This explains why the Romans called the marriage of citizens *connubium*. The rites and very different ceremonies which have always accompanied weddings in different peoples and at different times are natural effects and spontaneous indications of internal feelings. Feelings have the power to lead people to act spontaneously in harmony with them, and to express and exteriorise them through sensible signs. The Romans, in calling the marriage of their citizens *connubium*, wanted to show that in more noble persons there was a more acute feeling inducing them to veil the lowest element of marriage. Only the women were veiled, however, because the feeling of modesty is stronger in them. The greater strength of modesty in women shows that while this human being feels her own intellective, personal dignity, she also feels her own weakness and the danger of giving way to the lower part. Moreover, because she is passive in the use of sex *fear* is natural to her; she fears the thought of the possibility, and has a vague presentiment,

Article 3.
Nature of the consent forming marriage

1090. The consent forming conjugal society must have, for validity, all the qualities necessary in the formation of other contracts. We have explained these qualities in *individual Right* (cf. *RI*, 1112–1165), but they will receive greater light as we examine the defects which render consent null in the formation of marriage.

1091. For the moment, we note:

1. Merely external and legal consent is not sufficient for validity; consent must be *natural.*

Consent which is merely external and legal through the fault of the person who gives it produces an obligation to provide a true, natural consent which will supply for the deficiency (cf. *RI*, 1153).[47] If this is impossible,[48] no marriage has taken place.

that violence could be done to her because the noble acts of person and freedom are active, not passive. The more passive an action, the less noble it is, and the greater embarrassment it produces for human beings.

[47] This principle is admitted by ecclesiastical laws in several particular cases. For example, a man may have married a woman while, unknown to her, his wife was still alive. After the death of his wife, he may wish to separate from the second woman, whom he has married invalidly. But he cannot do this; he is obliged to give a new consent and convalidate the marriage. Alexander III wrote of a similar case (1180 AD): 'It is not right that this man, who knowingly acted against the Canons, should profit by his deceit' (*Decret.*, bk. 4, tit. 7, c. 1). Again, we may consider the case of a marriage which is null because extorted under serious fear. Because the nullity cannot perhaps be proved in court, the marriage appears valid externally, and the person who suffered the fear is obliged to cohabit. This person is then violated despite opposition. Later the party who caused the fear wishes to abandon the marriage; the other person, however, no longer wishes to separate on account of the shame. The guilty person is obliged to remain and to convalidate the marriage. The reason, given by Alexander III, is that there should be no benefit from deceit: 'Although the person inflicting the fear is not obliged by the force of the contract, he is obliged because of the injury', as the moralists say. — Lugo, *De Contract.*, d. 22, a. 119, v. 4.

[48] A person marrying a second wife while the first is still alive is obliged to abstain from the use of marriage, even though he cannot prove that he was already married, and his second marriage appears legitimate before the courts (*Decret.*, bk. 4, tit. 21, c. 2). In this case, the second marriage is seen as *legally legitimate*, although this is not in fact the case. Legality, therefore, is not sufficient to form marriage; consent must be *natural*. In the case mentioned,

2. Because human beings have been placed by the Creator in a supernatural order, marriage also receives a supernatural character. It must, therefore, be approved by God, the head of theocratic society. But because the Church of Christ holds the place of God, the *natural contract* must be sanctioned and recognised by the Christian Church in the name of God if a true marriage is to exist for Christians who belong to the perfect theocratic society.

1092. 3. Moreover, people who unite in civil society can oblige themselves not to contract marriage except under certain conditions and according to certain norms; and there is nothing to prevent the legislators, who act on their behalf, from establishing these laws. However, if these human regulations are violated in the formation of marriages, the citizens involved, although forsaking the obligation that all have of obeying the law, are validly married provided the contract is not defective before the natural law and has been sanctioned by God, whose representative is the Catholic Church. It is written: 'What God has joined together, let not man put asunder.'[49] If, however, the Church herself requires the observance of these civil laws as a condition for God's sanctioning the marriage, the laws become essential for the marriage contract of Christians. One example is *legal relationship* or adoption. Of its nature this is a civil, human matter, but has been accepted by the Church as a diriment impediment to marriage.

Note that in every sacrament a divine operation intervenes which cannot be nullified by human disposition or power. When the Church, the depository of the sacraments, consents to the contract between spouses as sacramentally existent, their marriage acquires by that very fact an absolute indissolubility which cannot be dissolved or weakened by any human reason or faculty.

---

consent cannot be supplied because the first wife is still alive.

[49] Mt 19: 6.

Article 4.
Distinction between marriage and the use of marriage

1093. Sexual union is something passing; the contract with which two individuals oblige themselves to conjugal society induces a stable, lifelong obligation.

1094. Consequently, the proximate object of this contract is that *full union* which we described relative to spontaneous affections. Relative to the real union between the sexes, the proximate object is only the *right* to union, the right which each of the contracting parties confers on the other.

1095. Actual affections are closer to the class of *stimulated affections*; habitual affections to the class of *spontaneous affections*. The latter, as we said, are essential to the fullness of conjugal union; the former are not. Sexual affection, if considered in potency, is indeed necessary to marriage; but it is not essential that this potency, and the right to the union, be put into act (actual intercourse). Hence, the power or *jural faculty* which one spouse receives of using the body of the other with marital affection is precisely the specific right which brings the marriage contract into being.

1096. There is a distinction, therefore, between marriage and the use of marriage which corresponds to that between a right and the exercise of the right. This distinction is common to every right: the exercise of a right is not essential to the existence of the right.

1097. On the other hand, the *human union* between two persons can be completely full even if they do not have intercourse. The fullness of the union consists in the fullness of *possession* that one has of the other. It consists in the fullness of affection enabling them to rest totally content. I would remind the reader that I have already shown how *contentment* is a personal,[50] not a physical act. Certain determined pleasures, and sexual pleasure amongst them, are not at all necessary for contentment. All that is necessary is the act of person, the most noble and elevated part of human beings.

The same can be said about *full love*. Full love is that which remains totally *content* with the beloved person, whom it enjoys

---

[50] *SP*, 516–523.

with all its soul as its own proper good. Love, therefore, is what we may call contentment of soul.

1098. In fact:

1. Love does not always require sexual pleasure.

2. Even when love does require intercourse, a much more sublime and tender desire can prevail. It is possible to love, in the beloved and in oneself, heavenly continence much more than carnal delight because continence has an infinite attraction for pure souls. In this case, union can be greater precisely because it does not entail physical union. The essence of loving union is found ultimately — let me say it once again — in the soul. Physical union is only a kind of adjunct which can very well be compensated by a greater degree of virtuous union between spirits. The moral bond is immensely increased through the sacrifice of the physical bond.

Article 5.
The distinction between marriage and the fulfilment
of marital obligations

1099. Because marriage is brought about through a contract, it is easy to see that its essence consists in a mutual obligation which the parties assume in order to put into effect the *union* forming the object of the contract. *Conjugal society*, therefore, is a *promissory contract* (cf. *RI*, 1104–1108) which is valid even though the parties neglect their duty to fulfil what they have mutually promised.

1100. The conjugal society and state is a group of rights which the contracting parties transmit to one another. These rights, reduced to a single complex, can be defined as: 'The right to have from one's consort bestowal of the *full union* which is the object of the contract.'

1101. The conjugal society and state are not formed, therefore, by positing *in act* the union we have described, but by the union considered only *in potency* under its concept of right. In a word, it is 'the jural-moral power which each of the two partners acquires for real, actual union, together with the jural-moral duty that each has to contribute their own part to it.'

CHAPTER 3

Christian marriage is a sacrament

1102. Conjugal society between individuals who belong to the perfect theocratic society is divinised by the divine Head of this society and receives the nature of a sacrament (cf. 752, 906–907, 1089, 1091–1092).

The love of Jesus Christ for his Church is communicated to Christians when they unite in marriage. It perfects their natural love, as the Council of Trent says.

1103. The love which Christ bears towards his disciples affects the union between spouses and renders it purer, fuller and more indissoluble. This is the grace of the sacrament.

The Council states:

> Christ himself, who instituted and put into effect these venerated sacraments, merited for us with his passion the grace which PERFECTED THAT NATURAL LOVE, confirmed its indissoluble unity and sanctified the spouses. St. Paul refers to this when he says: 'Husbands, love your wives, as Christ loved the Church and gave himself up for her', and adds immediately 'This mystery [sacrament] is a profound one, and I am saying that it refers to Christ and the Church.'[51]

Marriage, therefore, acquires a new and greater kind of indissolubility. The sacramental union is formed by God himself, and human beings, as we said, cannot impede or weaken divine operations, nor impede or annul their effect.[52]

---

[51] Sess. 24.

[52] St. Alphonus Liguori explains this teaching in the following way: 'St. Augustine (*L. de Bono Conjug.*, c. 24) shows that marriages are ratified because they are sacraments where he says: "For the pagans the good of marriage lies in the way it leads to generation; for the people of God its good lies in the way it leads to holiness." Again (c. 8): "In our marriage, the holiness of the sacrament is of greater worth than fertility of the womb." "This," as he says in c. 7, "explains the indissoluble bond. Marriage amongst the faithful would not have such firmness if the notion of sacrament were not included. I do not think it could be of such worth without reference to some kind of sacrament. Nor, indeed, except in the city of our God, is there such relationship (namely the indissolubility of the sacrament) with one's wife." This is shown more clearly in c. 4, *De divort*. where Innocent III says: "Even though

CHAPTER 4

Necessary conditions for placing conjugal society in being

Article 1.
Impediments in general

1104. It will help if we summarise here. In the first chapter, we considered marriage as a full *union* between two people of different sex; in the second, as a *contract* that puts such a union in being; in the third as a *sacrament* which consecrates the concept and the union which is its object. Christian marriage has all three qualities. The conditions required to bring it into being are, therefore, all those which are needed in order that the following may come into existence:

1. the union,
2. the contract and
3. the sacrament.

1105. The lack of one or other of these conditions is normally called an *impediment*.

The *impediments* to marriage are, therefore, divided into three classes: Some make the *union* impossible, some the *contract* and some the *sacrament*. Every impediment of each of these classes makes marriage between Christians impossible. Christian marriage must be, at one and the same time, full union, valid contract, and sacrament.

1106. These are called *diriment* impediments because they render marriage not only unlawful, but also invalid if they precede it.

1107. There are however other *impediments* which render marriage unlawful but not invalid. These are *prohibiting* impediments.

1108. To understand how a marriage can be valid even though it is unlawful, we need to recall the teaching already explained

true marriage exists amongst the pagans, it is not ratified. Amongst the faithful, marriage is both true and ratified because the sacrament of faith, which is admitted once, is never lost but makes the sacrament of marriage ratified (note) so that marriage lasts in the spouses as long as the sacrament lasts"' (*Tract. de Matrim.* c. 2, dub. 1).

about the *lawfulness* essential to a right. We said that the lawfulness essentially required to constitute a right regards only the *title*, the *object* and the *activity constituting the right* itself. In other words, if the *title*, or the *object* of the right, or the *activity* constituting the right is immoral, the right cannot subsist because it is intrinsically vitiated in its constitutive elements (cf. *RI*, 1124–1126). On the other hand, the subject can act immorally in acquiring a right without necessarily infringing the act of acquisition. In this case, the immorality of the act does not fall on the constitutive elements of the right.

For example, a man who, after his betrothal (an accepted promise of marriage) with one woman marries another, certainly does something unlawful and unjust. Nevertheless, the woman to whom he made the promise, and whose right (the right arising from the promise of marriage) is injured by his action, can no longer claim marriage with him. Her right was concerned only with the future conjugal contract. It was a *right to action* which did not, however, bring any *right in the thing itself* (in the conjugal union) (cf. *RI*, 1087). Because the *thing* (the conjugal union) was not yet in the ownership of the engaged woman, it could still become the ownership of another through a contract of marriage. The first woman has no possibility of claim because the man is no longer the owner of what has been promised. *Betrothal* is considered, therefore, as a *prohibiting impediment* and as such leads to an obligation to compensate the injury (cf. *RI*, 1181), but it is not considered as a *diriment* impediment.

1109. We can now take up the thread of the argument. According to natural Right, the diriment impediments which render marriage invalid are reduced to three classes, that is:

1. Impediments which render the *union* null. These are two: *impotence* and *natural relationship*.

2. Impediments which render the contract null. These can be reduced to three: the *object of the contract has already been alienated*; *error* in the person giving consent; *lack of freedom* in the consent.

3. Impediments which *directly* render the *sacrament* null. These can be reduced to five: *one of the parties does not belong to Christian society*; *spiritual and legal relationship*; *affinity*; *justice proper to public decency*; *clandestinity*; and *crime*.

1110. If the *union*, or the *contract*, or the *sacrament* is null, the *conjugal society* of Christians is null. As we said, Christian marriage requires for its formation all three elements as its essential constitutives.

We shall now say something about each of these impediments.

Article 2.
Diriment impediments

§1. *Diriment impediments which render the conjugal* union *null*

A.
Impotence

1111. A person lacking the faculty for sexual intercourse cannot contract marriage because the specific object of the contract is missing.

1112. But if this faculty is present when marriage is contracted, even though lost immediately afterwards and perhaps before the consummation of the marriage (for example, through enforced castration), the marriage is valid, and full union is obligatory even though the union cannot descend to generative intercourse, which is its least part.

1113. On the one hand, therefore, the *actualisation* of this least union is never necessary to constitute conjugal society and the state of marriage (cf. 1093 *ss.*); on the other, the *possibility* of such a union is necessary only at the moment of the contract. This union is in fact the *specific object* of the contract,[53] and no contract of any kind loses its validity because a part of its object ceases to exist immediately after the contract has been established through the handing-over of the right (cf. *RI*, 1080–1087).

---

[53] Lack of the *possibility* of sexual union can occur because the individuals have not yet reached puberty. Consequently, too tender an age is counted amongst the diriment impediments of marriage when it renders intercourse impossible. — Ecclesiastical laws fix puberty at fourteen years for males and at twelve for females.

1114. In our case, only a part of the object of the contract is lost because the total object is full union (cf. 1094). The right to sexual union, although it makes this contract specifically different from all others, is the extreme part and consequence. The contracting parties, despite their loss of this part, retain the rest and the best part of their union which remains as full as it can be according to nature and reason.

B.
Relationship

1115. According to the *Summa Pisanella*, 'there are three kinds of relationship: carnal, called *blood-relationship*; spiritual, called *spiritual relationship*; and legal, called *adoption*.'[54] Here we shall speak of blood-relationship only. The other kinds will be dealt with later.

1116. Blood-relationship is between ascendants and descendants, or in the lateral line. We shall speak first about

I.
Relationship in the direct line

1117. Mankind judges that marriage between ascendants and descendants is abhorrent because the *full union*, in which the essence of marriage consists, cannot be effected between them.

1118. As far as natural law is concerned, this can easily be understood by reference to the *moral-human instinct*,[55] which

---

[54] Maestruzzo (1: 75), quoted by the *Dictionary*.

[55] In *AMS* (683–686), I spoke about *human instinct* in so far as it is opposed to *moral reason*. Considered from this point of view, *human instinct* arises from *merely subjective feelings*. But there is also a *feeling* which reaches the contemplation of objects. This can be called *objective* (moral feeling); from it flows a *moral instinct* which is certainly human, and indeed supremely human. This *moral sense* will be understood better by reference to the *intellectual sense* of which I spoke in the *Lettera a Don Pietro Orsi* (in *Prose*, p. 266 ss., Lugano, 1834) and to *subjective* necessity of which I spoke in the *Moral System* (cf. *ER*, 132–147). Here I call this instinct *moral-human* rather

repudiates full union of this kind. We shall indicate the fact, and then analyse it.

a)
The fact

1119. Luigi Pasquali writes:

> The deep love a father has for his daughter makes him abhor intercourse with her, and gives him a profound respect for her chastity. The same is true for a mother in the case of her son. And the deeper the love between these blood-relations, the more it is opposed to purely carnal love.[56] These two loves are very different in nature. I am not sure how to express the matter, but I hope the truth is well understood. Love in a blood-relationship includes esteem and reverence for the very body of one's blood-relation. Carnal love is directed more to the body than to the whole person of the beloved. Hence the opposition between these two loves. We see, therefore, that the first kind of love excludes intercourse, marriage and conjugal society between blood-relations because of a kind of sensation and moral feeling that is more easily understood than expressed. Any rare example of such intercourse amongst human beings in society is looked upon with extreme condemnation and horror by all. There are indications that it is disproved also by universal agreement,[57]

than simply *human* to help the reader understand that I am not speaking of an instinct arising merely from subjective good. Objective good produces subjective good which in turn generates moral feeling and the *moral instinct* that forms part of the *human instinct* generally considered.

[56] This observation was also made by Xenophon (*Cyropaedia* 5).

[57] This universal agreement is not lessened by the earlier or actual presence on earth of a few monstrously perverted people who choose to follow, or even support, not nature but the corruption of nature. The cynics Diogenes and Crisippus, who denied that blood-relationship was an impediment because it was not found amongst the Gauls, belonged to this class. (Cf. Laertius, bk. 7: 71, 187). There are also a few extremely decadent nations which either ignore incest altogether or think very little of it, as Xenophon (*Memorabilia*, 4: 4, §19, 20) and Philo (*De special. legibus.*) tell us about the Persians. The same crime was frequent amongst the Medes, Indians and

which certainly uncovers motives repugnant to nature and true human happiness in an occurrence of this kind.[58]

1120. This is the undeniable, universal fact. Once it has been ascertained, it is clear that there can be no *full union according to nature*, that is, marriage amongst ascendants and descendants. If there is a *natural* repugnance to a part of the union between two persons and if this repugnance falls on that precise part of the union which constitutes the specific difference of conjugal union, it is clear that according to nature marriage cannot take place.

Nevertheless, we shall examine the hidden reasons which produce such repugnance to sexual union amongst blood-relations in the direct line.

b)
Analysis of the fact

1121. First, I suspect that within animal nature itself there lies a hidden law which to some extent impedes sexual communication between ascendants and descendants, at least to a certain degree and with certain limitations. Ancient naturalists have maintained this about some animals such as the horse and the

Ethiopians, according to St. Jerome (*Contra Giovin*, bk. 2). Lucanus (bk. 8, 401§410), Dion of Prusa (*Orat.* 20) and others (Augustine, *In Levit.* c. 18., Eusebius, *Prae. Ev.*, 6: 8) say that the Parthians practised it. Dion puts it down to their bad education. — Cf. Alessandro d'Alessandro, *Genial. Dierum* 1: 2; and Selden, *De J. N. V.*, 11). For the barbarians in general, cf. Euripides in *Andromaca* (v. 173 *ss.*) and Ovid (10 *Metam.*). Note however that such crimes were rare and abhorrent even amongst the barbarians. The claimed *right* of the Persians of which Xenophon speaks, seems to have been a *religious right*, that is, introduced by pagan superstition which was wont to sanctify horrendous things that were always contrary to nature. As Catullus tells us, they believed that magi were born of such incest (*In Epital. Pelei et Thetid.*), and permitted incest to their magi (Laertius, bk. 1).

[58] *Diritto naturale e sociale, e principi del Diritto delle Genti, dedotti dall'analisi dell'uomo, ossia dal senso morale e dal comun consenso di Ragione*, Padua, Bettoni, 1815.

camel.[59] A Roman tragedian illustrates this opinion when he makes Phaedra say:

> Beasts themselves avoid the AWFUL venereal CRIME;
> Unconscious modesty preserves the laws of generation.[60]

1122. However, we can leave aside these hidden laws of animal nature (if there are such), to deal with what is proper to human nature (animal-intellective-moral). We need to explain, or rather to analyse, the repugnance we have indicated by observing other particular facts which form elements producing it.

1123. The act of generation unites two opposite qualities. One (that of producing an intelligent being) is extremely noble; the other (the animal act considered without reference to the laws of reason) is extremely ignoble. The latter, by drawing to itself the whole human being, degrades him; at that moment, he is no longer a rational being in control of self. Such degradation and debasement, the momentary loss of the noble faculties that lift the human being above the stars, is the evident origin of the shame with which he seeks to conceal the generative act from the eyes of others, and of the modesty with which he covers the parts which share in the act.

---

[59] Aristotle (*De Histor. animal.*, bk. 9, c. 47; and *De Admirabil.*); Pliny (*Hist. N.*, bk. 8, 42); Antigoneus (*De Admirabilibus*, c. 59); Oppianus, (*De Renatu*, bk. 1); Varro (*De Re Rustica*, 2: 7); Elianus (*Var. Hist.*, 3: 47); Cf. also Selden (*De jure nat. et gentium secundum discpl. Haebreor.*, bk. 1, c. 7); and Carpzov (*Crim.*, p. 2: 9, 72). It is truly extraordinary, if Pliny and other ancient authors are to be believed, that a stallion, first blindfolded in order to make it mount its mother, then immediately unblindfolded, goes wild when recognising the mother and hurls itself over a precipice. This happened not once, but several times, according to these authors. If this is true, it would show how instinct simulates intelligence, although the conclusion reached by the Roman naturalist is improperly expressed when he says: 'They (horses) understand what the relationship is.'

[60] In *Hippolytus*, act 3, verses 914, 915. We find the same in *Oedipus*, verse 638:
> 'Whatever way animals do things
> They scarcely ever generate siblings for themselves.'
Arnobius (*Adv. Gentes*, bk. 5), speaking about this ancient view of things, reproves the Gentiles for adoring a Jove who did not find intercourse with his own mother abhorrent. Even some beasts dread it, and Arnobius calls this fear 'that normally ungenerated sense'.

[1122–1123]

On the other hand, the nobility and the dignity included in the fact of being the author of an intelligent being like oneself is at least the origin of the act's special mark of dignity, even if it is not the source of paternal authority.[61] At the same time, it is the source of the reverential feeling placed by nature in the heart of children.

These two feelings are opposed to one another in the way that the two elements contained in the generative act, from which they spring, are mutually opposed. Any feeling for which we have some love produces abhorrence of its contrary, opposing feeling. We want to preserve and increase the precious feeling we love, and isolate it from every alien as well as inimical feeling so that it may live and dominate on its own. The genitor who feels his dignity as father — a very precious feeling because it exalts and enhances him — naturally abhors everything that could oppose or destroy something so precious to himself, to his children who are its object, and to all mankind. But there is nothing more opposed to the dignified feeling of fatherhood than the turpitude and baseness contained in the act of generation and in the members used for that purpose. Consequently, consciousness of paternity sets in motion the will to hide all such things from the child, and to prevent the child's perceiving or even thinking about them.

1124. The child does not have the same shame relative to his parents. Nevertheless, he finds it totally repugnant if his parents debase themselves in his presence by uncovering that which is most ignoble and shameful in human nature. It is natural that integral human nature requires in the child the greatest reverence and honour for the authors of his being and that the child's filial feeling be gripped by extreme horror solely at the thought of sexual communication with his parents.

1125. This irreconcilable opposition of feelings and the extreme abhorrence and shame which, according to nature, renders sexual union impossible between parents and their children, is vividly expressed by phrases used in Scripture to forbid such intercourse: 'You shall not uncover the nakedness

---

[61] We derived paternal authority solely from the fact of being the author of a child without reference to the nobility attached to the act by which one becomes the author.

of your father, which is the nakedness of your mother; she is your mother, you shall not uncover her nakedness.'[62] The Roman legislators also assigned this shame, or rather horror, as the reason for their laws 'because, in contracting marriage', as Paulus says, 'natural right and MODESTY are to be considered.'[63] This most holy modesty is so delicate that when offended it inspired Noah to curse his own descendants. It arouses fierce remorse and atrocious feelings in the person who has violated it. Such feelings caused Oedipus to tear out his own eyes and Jocaste to cut open her womb. Nature, when wounded to this extent, shows the enormity of the affront: 'Nature can tolerate no greater crime than this',[64] screams the unhappy mother of Laius. The same cry has been heard wherever human beings have existed.

1126. Another element of the moral instinct which leads parental love to reject sexual love is to be noted in the natural development of the sexual act. It begins naturally with the vague desire of union with a person of the other sex. This desire, at first obscure and mysterious, does not remain stationary. It is endlessly restless and wants to draw from the beloved person ever-increasing delight. It extends further and further until it descends finally to wanting to add sexual union to the other bonds. But, when this union has been consummated and a child conceived, the lively desire can go no further. Fulfilled, it has arrived at its final term.

The child is, therefore, the final term of the natural activity of

---

[62] Lev 18: [7].

[63] *D.*, bk. 22, t. 2: 14.

[64] *Oedipus* (verse 272): The poet makes Jocaste speak of the conflict between the opposing feelings that arise from her opposite conditions as *mother* and *wife* (act 5, verse 1038):

> My spouse lies under this knife.
> Can you truly call him spouse? He is your father-in-law.
> O right hand of mine, seek out this womb
> Which has been home to a son and his father.

The same confusion between mutually repugnant feelings is expressed in another tragedy, the *Thebaide* (act 1, sc. 1, verse 130 *ss.*); and in *Agam.* (act 1, sc. 1). A similar struggle is described by Statius, *Thebaide* (bk. 4); by Ovid (*Metamorphoseon*, bk. 2, fab. 2, and bk. 10, fab. 9); by Catullus (carm, 58). Cf. also St. Augustine (*The City of God*, bk. 2, c. 4; bk. 15, c. 16; *Confess.*, bk. 2, c. 4).

sexual love which ceases at this term precisely because emergent love is totally released.

Such development shows that it must be against nature for sexual love to begin at the very point where nature brings it to an end, that is, in the child. Note that the child is loved by the parents as the precious fruit of their love; love has passed from them to the offspring. This is indeed the character of parental love; it reminds the spouses of their final contentment and of the extinction of their sexual affections. According to the law of nature, therefore, the genitors love in the child their rest from the work of generation. Carnal love, as long as it is not complete, is restless and troublesome rather than sweet. When this disturbance ceases[65] through realised and natural satisfaction it brings its own peace and pure enjoyment.

This is the intimate reason why parental love is most chaste, dignified and tranquil of its nature, and why people abhor returning to the tumult and fatigue of carnal appetite at the place where they possess, seek and find delightful rest and restoration from the appetite. A sailor who reaches port after a dangerous voyage has no desire for further adventure. If, in parents, sexual love returns between them or with other persons, the parents neither see in these others the consummation of their love, nor do they love them as the fruit of such love — fruit in which they possess and hold dear the totally special delight which follows the fatigue of love.

1127. The two elements of the instinct that we are analysing arise from the laws to which human beings are subject as *real beings*. If we go on to consider human beings as *moral beings*,[66] we find that *moral reason* also directly forbids marriage between parents and children. This moral duty, felt immediately by us through our *moral sense*, generates and strengthens in us the instinct that repudiates similar unions.

1128. This element of human instinct deduced from moral reason is found in the collision between the duties of parents and spouses, of children and spouses. The clash is manifest in the

---

[65] Sophocles claimed that he was subject to a hard master. This explains why love has been called 'tyrant' by all the poets.

[66] Man is not *ideal being*. Human beings are *real, intellective beings*. As intellective beings they receive the *law*; as real beings, they constitute its *titles*.

incompatibility between the reverence owed by children to parents, and the homeliness and equality between spouses. It is even more clear when we consider that the parents together form a single person, according to nature, and have the right and duty of ruling and governing their children. Children on the other hand have the duty to allow themselves to be ruled, and to obey. These duties are so contrary to one another that they cannot be present, without self-destruction, in the same subject towards the same person. If a parent marries one of his children, he has already destroyed his *patria potestas* by the new relationship; someone equal to him in everything cannot be inferior to him in everything. In the same way, other duties are frustrated and as such frustrate family order. But to cause confusion in family order is to ruin it; and ruining the family is condemned at the highest level by the moral law.

1129. What we say about parents and children can easily be applied to all ascendants and descendants.

1130. A similar argument is valid in the case of step-fathers and step-mothers. According to nature, parents form a single person, granted the *full union* of marriage. Uniting oneself with the wife of one's father means uncovering the shame of one's father (to use a Scriptural phrase). The other reasons used above are also valid when applied to the true mother.[67]

1131. Nature itself provides a bulwark against human corruption even in the greatly different age normally present between ascendants and descendants. Certainly, disparity of age weakens the affection that naturally arises between contemporaries and people on the same level, and makes marriages unhappy. All this helps to show more clearly what nature intends [*App.*, no. 1].

---

[67] St. Paul (1 Cor 5) detests such unions as naturally impure even in the eyes of the Gentiles. The laws of Charondas declare as infamous the person marrying his step-mother. Incest is the object of detestation in the discourse of Lysias, and is considered detestable by Cicero (*Pro Cluentio*, c. 6), Virgil (*Aeneid*, 10, verse 389), Ovid (*Epistolae Heroïdum*, 4), and Seneca in *Hippolytus* (verse 712). Cf. also Plutarch in *Life of Metrius*, and Tertullian, *Adv. Marcionem*, 5.

II.
Relationship in the transversal line

1132. If, in considering relationship in the transversal line, we take into account only *human instinct*, we may find there is no absolute repugnance to conjugal unions between siblings or other relations. In this case, marriage between them cannot always be said to be opposed to nature, or at least not to the extent that it is amongst blood-relations in the direct line.

1133. It can be said, however, that *human instinct* considered in its perfection strongly inclines people to unite with someone with whom they have no relationship, that is, someone with whom common ancestry is so distant that it can no longer be recalled.

1134. This is explained by the fact that the common descent is vividly present and remembered. In these circumstances the common ancestor seems to be reproduced in the children. Contemplating the paternal image in them, it almost seems as though we contract marriage with a common father when we contract it with a sibling or a cousin in whom the general imagination beholds a rejuvenated father or grandfather.

1135. It will be useful to recall here how rights are founded in a feeling, and how they are lost or abolished to the extent that a feeling, and the memories that maintain the feeling, fade more quickly amongst the community of mankind (cf. *RI*, 1047–1049). The same teaching must be applied to the feelings which impede the formation of marriage amongst blood-relations.

1136. As descendants grow more distant from the common stock, the memory and image of the ancestor gradually weakens. Sooner or later it is lost altogether (there are innumerable circumstances to account for this). Hence the different extension, in various peoples and at various times, of degrees of relationship considered as impediments to marriage.

1137. One example of these circumstances is the shorter retention of paternal memories and traditions in peoples of less noble race. Amongst these peoples, the degree of relationship forbidding conjugal unions is more restricted.

1138. When Mexicans and Peruvians were first encountered, it was found that marriage was forbidden only in the first degree

[1132–1138]

of lateral consanguinity, that is, amongst siblings. The brevity of line along which people were forbidden marriage was sufficient to show their lack of development, their low intelligence or certainly the broken, degenerate state of their family life.

1139. On the other hand, it is worth noting how the ancient Indian laws took impediments as far as the sixth degree of relationship for the first three castes. This shows the vigour with which domestic society flourished amongst those peoples, and the strength of the continuity in domestic traditions [*App.*, no. 2]

1140. At the same time, it also shows an exaggerated prevalence of domestic society, which impedes the progress of civil structures. A middle way is present amongst developed peoples where civil society develops freely on a par with domestic society. In other words, marriage is impeded to the fourth degree, the very degree at which generally the remembrance of the ancestor is completely forgotten amongst these peoples [*App.*, no. 3].

1141. We should note that marriage amongst close blood-relations can only continue without serious prejudicial consequences amongst undeveloped, primitive peoples [*App.*, no. 4]. As society develops, and even begins to enter a corrupt stage, an obvious need grows for rigorous laws which impede unions amongst overly close relatives. These impediments, although issuing from public authority, have their just foundation in rational Right, that is,

1. in the need to obviate the crime of incest between parents and children;[68] and

2. to preserve decency in family life.[69]

1142. Yet another good derives from these laws: the diffusion

---

[68] St. Augustine says of the marriages of early Christians with their cousins: 'It was not customary, although it could have been done lawfully. Even the divine law did not forbid it, nor was it yet forbidden by human law. Nevertheless, the lawful fact was held in abhorrence because of its propinquity to what was unlawful' (*The City of God*, 15: 16).

[69] The Hebrew teachers also ascribe the dispositions of Leviticus to the need for domestic decency (c. 18). Moses Maimonides, in his book *Halath*, adds as another reason the natural modesty between blood-relations and between people joined by affinity. This is universally recognised as a cause of non-marriage in these circumstances.

of friendships and the greater breadth of society between human beings.[70]

1143. It can be seen from all these things that conjugal unions between collateral relations do not find the same intrinsic, absolute repugnance in an immovable feeling of nature as the unions between ascendants and descendants. Instead, they are subject to various modifications according to changes in feeling which repudiates them to varying degrees, and according to the needs appearing in society and provoking the formation of public laws.

1144. These laws have a triple level which should be noted. Indeed

1. positive laws begin to sanction that which first appertained only to natural law and to custom;[71]

2. the prohibition is gradually extended from a greater to a lesser degree of relationship;[72]

3. marriages, once considered unlawful for certain degrees of relationship, are later considered invalid.[73]

1145. From all these observations we can also see the reason why circumstances rendered such marriages legitimate at certain times (as, for instance, amongst Adam's first children) and why, after laws were established against them, rare exceptions and dispensations were found within the limit that competent authority had prescribed for itself.[74]

[70] Cf. Plutarch, *Quaest. Rom.*, q. 108; St. Augustine, *The City of God*, 15: 16.

[71] 'From the beginning it was neutral whether a brother slept with his sister or not. But once the law against such intercourse was made, it was immediately relevant whether it was observed or not' (Michael of Ephesus, *To Nicomachus*, bk. 5).

[72] The opposite is seen in decadent peoples. Amongst the Romans, permission to marry a niece accompanied licentiousness. According to Tacitus: 'We have new marriages by which uncles marry their nieces, marriages which were solemnised amongst other peoples without their ever being forbidden by law' (*Ann*, 12, c. 6).

[73] In the Apostolic canons (can. 18), a person who married two sisters one after the other, or a niece, was excluded from the clergy. However, this does not seem to have been considered a diriment impediment.

[74] The maintenance of families, the preservation of wealth within a family and the public good were the three principal causes recognised by ancient laws as efficacious in granting dispensations for the closer degrees of relationship. It

III.
Affinity

1146. When we consider the nature of marriage, which makes two human beings one, we see clearly that the blood-relations of either spouse have to be considered as relatives of the other.

1147. The same considerations which led us to discover the intrinsic motives forbidding marriage between collateral blood-relations can therefore be applied to in-laws.

1148. At the same time, we should reflect that although this explains why the blood-relations of one spouse are said to be in-laws of the other spouse, the notion of affinity does not hold between the blood-relations of the spouses. In-laws do not form a single person with the blood-relations of the other spouse. Hence the rule: *affinity does not engender affinity*.

IV.
Adoption

1149. *Adoption* also provides an intrinsic reason for impeding conjugal union.

1150. Adoption is not simply a fiction of civil law. It can take place through a contract between people still at the level of the state of nature. One person takes in another whose rights and duties are those of a child; the former thus obliges himself to fatherly affection and duties. The other person spontaneously attributes paternal rights to him, and takes on the affection and other duties proper to children.

1151. This contract produces in both parties feelings, duties and rights similar to those present between father and child. Marriage, therefore, is impossible between them because it involves other feelings, duties and rights directly opposed to those inherent in the relationship between child and genitor. We have

was the first, for example, which enabled a brother amongst the Hebrews to marry his widowed, childless sister-in-law for the sake of raising up offspring to the brother's sibling. Special laws were made in almost all the Greek legislations to provide for inheritance.

to apply to the connection established by adoption that which was said about the impediment resulting from relationship in the direct line.

1152. Adoption recognised by civil laws is called *legal adoption*.[75]

V.
Spiritual relationship

1153. In perfect theocratic society, that is, in the Church of Jesus Christ, human beings are reborn in baptism, which is strengthened and completed by the sacrament of confirmation. The person who administers these sacraments becomes in the supernatural order the father of the person receiving them.

1154. Moreover, the Church has established godfathers and godmothers who assist those who are baptised and confirmed, and assume in their regard the office of spiritual fathers and mothers. This is a kind of adoption.

1155. Such sacred relationships give rise to very serious and chaste feelings between the person conferring the sacraments and those who receive them, and between the godparents and the baptised or confirmed person. These feelings are similar to those arising from the relationship of natural fatherhood and childhood, except that they receive a greater degree of dignity and holiness from the supernatural order whence they originate and to which they belong.

1156. This *spiritual relationship*, as it is called, is, therefore, a diriment impediment to marriage because of the incompatibility of feelings and duties[76]

[75] Imperfect adoption, as it was called, in which the person adopted does not come fully under the *patria potestas* of the *adopter*, is not properly speaking *adoption*.

[76] This explanation, which depends upon mutually repugnant *feelings* and *duties*, pertains strictly speaking to *natural Right*, and for this very reason is sanctioned by the Catholic Church. Some *feelings* and *duties* come to human beings from human nature itself, others are the result of their *condition as Christians* or members of the perfect theocratic society. But whether they spring from nature or from the Christian condition, their *formal reason* as

§2. *Impediments which render the* contract *null*

1157. Impediments which render the conjugal *union* null necessarily render the *contract* null. In these cases, matter suitable for the contract is lacking.

1158. There are, however, other impediments which vitiate the contract as such. We have reduced these to three headings. People who form a contract must 1. own the thing alienated; 2. know what they acquire through the contract; 3. enjoy the necessary freedom to make the contract (a contract is an essentially free act). The contract is therefore rendered impossible and null

1. through lack of ownership of what is alienated;
2. through lack of knowledge of what is acquired;
3. through lack of freedom.

impediments to marriage is always the same. The sole distinction is that the former pertain to *natural Right* and the latter to *supernatural Right*. These two Rights have to be distinguished (as we have said several times). The second is the complement and perfection of the former. The Church's prohibition of solemn nuptials from Advent to the Epiphany inclusively, and from Ash Wednesday to the octave of Easter inclusively (Council of Trent, sess. 24, c. 10, *De Ref. Matrim.*) is dependent upon the same notion of opposition between feelings and duties, although this is not a case of diriment impediment. Note that the joy and festivity that accompany weddings is considered by the Church as opposed not only to the feeling of penance nurtured in Advent and Lent, but also to that complete heavenly, pure joy and festivity found at the Lord's birth, at the Epiphany and at Easter. The Church forbids solemn nuptials at these times because she prefers Christians to rejoice at these moments with a totally chaste, heavenly happiness undisturbed by base, carnal thought. According to this spirit of the Church, certain dioceses maintain the praiseworthy custom of not celebrating marriages at all during these holy times, at least not without licence from the bishop. This is the case, confirmed by the last diocesan Synod of Cardinal Morozzo, in the diocese of Novara (p. 134). and because of the other reasons which render marriage morally and jurally impossible in the case of natural relationship.

A.
Lack of ownership of what is alienated

I.
Bond

1159. It is clear that a person already married has no owner-ship, as long as his partner lives, over the right with which the conjugal contract is conferred on another. This is a case of diriment impediment (*bond*).

1160. But if a person had only promised a future marriage with another who accepted it (*betrothal*), the object of the contract would not be alienated, as we saw. If one of the engaged persons contracted a marriage with a third party, the promise would certainly be broken, but the object of the contract could not be reclaimed.[77]

II.
Vow of chastity

1161. The vow of chastity is also a diriment impediment to marriage if it is accepted as such by the Catholic Church. This is the case when people receive the sacred order of the subdia-conate or make the vow in a religious order with an act that incorporates them in it as true religious [*App.*, no. 5] (*votum*). The vow, when accepted by the Church, contains a contract through which the person making the vow deprives himself of the right to marry by sacrificing the right to God; the Church, in the name of God, accepts such a right offered in sacrifice.

1162. If this acceptance by the Church does not take place, the vow is not a completed contract which alienates the right to marry, but only a promise that a person makes to God of sacrificing to him for a time or forever his chastity. This kind of vow does indeed render marriage unlawful because it is a viola-tion of a promise made to God. It does not annul the matrimon-ial contract, however, because the object of the contract still lies

[77] Cf. *RI*, 1088–1103, for the obligating force and the jural effects of accepted promises.

within the sphere of the right of ownership of the person making the vow. The Church, as the earthly procurator of God himself, has not accepted the vow.

B.
Lack of knowledge of what is acquired

1163. Contracts are invalid if there is substantial error about their object (cf. *RI*, 1156–1157).

1164. Error about the object of the matrimonial contract may be related to *one of the persons* or the *qualities of one of the persons*.

1165. If error falls on a person (if, for example, someone thinks he is marrying Rachel but is given Lia), the contract is invalid through lack of consent. This would be the case even if the person deceived would have been disposed to marry Lia, knowing that it was she. The validity of the contract requires actual consent, not a mere disposition to consent.

1166. If error falls on personal *qualities*, several kinds of qualities have to be distinguished. These are the person's
1. free or servile condition;
2. material well-being;
3. internal or external gifts and defects.

1167. If, in the case of true slavery (*mancipia*), error occurs about a person's servile condition, the marriage is null.[78]

1168. Slavery is indeed an extreme injustice (cf. *RI*, 128–133), but granted this first error in civil laws, it follows necessarily that there cannot be marriage between bond-servant and master, but only *contubernium*, as the Roman laws called it.

1169. There can be no marriage from the point of view of the contract nor from that of the fullness of union between a man and a woman. Not from the point of view of the contract because bond-servants cannot by nature make a contract, nor can they be the subject of rights (they are simply 'animated instruments', as Aristotle defined them); nor from the point of view of the union because there is no *communion of right*

[78] *Decret.*, bk. 4, tit. 9, c. 4.

[1163–1169]

between bond-servant and master. A bond-servant cannot, therefore, become a single jural person with the master, nor possess in communion with him all worldly goods; the bond-servant cannot have power over the body of the master nor attain the *equality* which is indispensable for full union between two intelligent creatures; the bond-servant cannot be end, but only means.

1170. When Christianity came into the world, such marriages were therefore considered as illegitimate and null. They remained such at least until the time of St. Leo, who noted that the *equality* of which we have spoken was a necessary element of marriage.[79]

1171. The reason for considering them null was lack of consent. The free party, although living with the bond-servant, did not have the intention of uniting with the other party in a full, perpetual conjugal union, nor of granting to the other person the freedom necessary to give spontaneous, jural consent.[80]

1172. These unions, which were always denominated *unjust*,

---

[79] 'The marriage contract between those born of free parents and BETWEEN EQUALS is legitimate and was constituted by the Lord long before the beginning of Roman right' (Leo the Great, Ep. 90, *ad Rustic. Narbon*).

[80] This full, perpetual union in Christian society is the symbol of union between Christ and his Church. Thus St. Leo writes: 'Hence, because the society of marriage was constituted FROM THE BEGINNING to contain the sacrament of Christ and the Church, as well as the union of sexes, there is no doubt that marriage is impossible for a woman in whom, it is taught, no nuptial mystery has been present' (*ibid.*). The Pope is speaking here about the primal marriage instituted by God between the first spousal couple in whom there was, despite the certain absence of sacramental grace, the prophetic sign of the future marriage between the Saviour and the Church. This sign, called by St. Leo 'sacrament (the sign of a sacred thing) and nuptial mystery', consisted in the perpetuity and fullness of the union. This is why I think Sebastiano Berardi gave an excellent interpretation of this passage of St. Leo when he wrote: 'My own opinion of what I have explained until now is that Leo only wished to point to what is necessary in the intention of the individual for expressing the beginning of marriage, whether marriage comes about secretly or in sight of the Church. The nuptial mystery, that is the sacrament of Christ and the Church, is contained in the declaration of this intention, in so far as man and wife profess that they will remain together perpetually, just as Christ promised never to leave his Church' (*Gratiani Canones genuini ab Apocryphis discreti* etc., p. 2, c. 42).

that is, not carried out according to legal justice, gradually began to be forbidden by the civil law.[81]

1173. The Church could never recognise the *unjust element* of ancient servitude, and from the beginning used its own maxims to assert the *freedom essential* to all human beings. Amongst Christians the nature of servitude changed *substantially* as soon as the Gospel was promulgated; only its *just element* remained after the removal of what was unjust. However, the language of the ancient Roman laws and exterior, social customs could not be swept away all at once. It was sufficient, nevertheless, to destroy the *unjust element* of ancient servitude, as we said, through the profession of the Christian faith and thus open the way to true and perfect marriage between masters and bond-servants. With the removal of the inhuman element, all human beings were substantially *equal*; they were brothers in Christ, made free in his baptism, even though they retained the outward appearances and title of bond-servants.

The Church recognised marriage contracted between a free person and a bond-servant as true marriage provided the condition of the bond-servant was known to the other party when the marriage took place. The only impediment still attached to the *servile condition* was that of *error*, when the free party was ignorant of the servile state of the other. This did not mean that the bond-servant was such in the ancient, unjust sense, and therefore incapable of marriage, but that even the name, customs and external aspect of servitude, together with the abuses to which it was subject, served to maintain between the parties such an immense difference in the temporal order that only an extraordinary love, which could not normally be presumed, would have been equal to the situation. Lack of consent had to be presumed in the party ignorant of the other's servile condition at the act of celebration of the marriage.

1174. Another good arose from admitting and recognising true marriage between bond-servants and free people. These marriages were a means for promoting the abolition of that part of servitude and servile burdens which still remained. This part,

---

[81] Constantine forbade them to centurions under very severe penalties in an endeavour to prevent the deterioration of this rank. His law is also found in the *Code of Justinian*, bk. 5, tit. 5: 3.

although not unjust in its concept absolutely speaking, was immensely hard, and easily became unjust in fact. This was caused by the concept of ancient servitude impressed in the mind (masters used the concept as a rule of conduct with their bond-servants) and by the lack of protection afforded by laws of the city for bond-servants against the abusive and reprehensible inhumanity of the masters. Christian marriage, which of its nature did indeed make spouses equal and life-long consorts, necessarily freed the party that had previously suffered servitude.[82] This also happened if the master gave in marriage to a free person his male or female bond-servant, and the free party was ignorant of the condition.

1175. Moreover, bond-servants acquired along with Christianity the faculty of marrying even in opposition to their masters provided they continued to give the service proper to upright servitude after the marriage.[83] This was a great step forward on the road to their complete emancipation.

1176. No other servitude, except that of bond-servants, invalidates marriage if it remains unknown. It simply enters as one of the common circumstances determining or specifying the quality of the person. Two of these circumstances, as we have seen, are temporal well-being, and the internal and external gifts and defects of the person.

---

[82] Cf. the theologians of Salamanca, *De Matrim.*, n. 35.

[83] 'According to the Apostle (Gal 3), as in Christ JESUS neither free man nor bond-servant is to be kept from the sacraments of the Church, so marriage amongst bond-servants is not to be forbidden. Marriages contracted despite the opposition and unwillingness of masters are not to be dissolved on this account. Nevertheless DUE and customary service must be shown to the masters' (Pope Hadrian, 790 AD, *Sext.*, bk. 4, tit. 9, c. 1). Note that this is one of the ways in which JESUS Christ freed human beings from servitude. He gave TO ALL AN EQUAL RIGHT OF SHARING IN THE SAME SACRAMENTS. This already constituted an immense freedom given to mankind. Moreover, marriage was placed by Christ amongst the sacraments. He gave TO EVERYONE, therefore, THE RIGHT TO DOMESTIC SOCIETY. This right involves a group amongst whom there exists not only society, but government. The divine, spiritual power in the Christian system essentially influences the temporal order, in which it rectifies all the distorted, unjust and unbecoming elements placed there by mankind. We have here an example of the greater attracting the less, of the accessory following the principal. There is no half-way house: we either recognise this or renounce Christianity.

[1175–1176]

1177. These circumstances do not, when ignored, *per se* invalidate marriage even if the error is the result of deceit by one of the parties and avoidable by the other. The substantial object of marriage is the person, and no contract is dissolved unless error falls on the *object*, even if it falls on the *motive* for the contract (cf. *RI*, 1156–1157). The argument is stronger still if we consider that consent was freely given, and that the person giving it could and should have informed himself fully about the matter. Nor does it help to say that the person contracting marriage would not have given his assent if he had known the truth. The question is not about what someone else might have been able to do, but about what one person actually did. It does not help either to say that the person making the contract was looking as much or more to the accessory qualities of the other person than to the other person, as too often happens. This does not change the nature of things; the person truly remains the substantial object of the contract. Consequently, consent has to be considered as given whenever there was no error about the person, except in the case where it can be proved that 'consent was conditioned by the presence of some quality.'

1178. In this last case, that is, if the contracting party who has been deceived shows fully that he gave only a consent conditioned *by the qualities* of the person (which are not verified), and did not confirm his consent in words or fact after he came to know the actual *qualities* present, the marriage is null through lack of consent.

1179. However, the marriage must be held valid until the lack of consent has been *proved externally*. In the meantime, if consent has not in fact been given, the person withholding consent may abstain from cohabitation. If it cannot then be proved that the consent was conditioned, the party concerned is obliged to cohabit with the other and, in this case, to first renew the consent and thus convalidate the marriage. Proof of conditional consent will depend upon arguments:

1. suitable in the state of nature for convincing the other party and arbitrators;

2. suitable in the state of society for convincing competent tribunals.

If these external arguments are lacking, consent will appear absolute and lead to the consequences we have indicated.

[1177–1179]

1180. What are the arguments that must reasonably convince the other party, or whoever stands in for him, that consent was conditioned to certain *qualities* which afterwards were found absent in this party?

They are:

1. The direct expression of the condition. — It is clear that no consent is present when the *condition*, expressed in the formula with which the consent was given, remained unverified.

2. The condition was expressed indirectly, but indubitably. — The formula expressed the quality of the person so clearly that it was at least an essential part of the principal object of the consent, although not perhaps the object itself. For example: 'I want to marry a rich woman, and therefore I want Teresa.'

3. Indetermination in the case of the person. — If the formula expresses an individual quality of the person, for example: 'I want to marry Matilda, the Spanish King's first-born child.' In this case, if Matilda is not the first-born child of the king of Spain, there is a presumption of error about the person determined both by the name and the description. If, however, the name determines the person in one way and the description in another, the person remains indeterminate unless one can prove that a slip of the tongue or the pen has been registered.

4. Grave error altering sexual union and its consequences. — After the contract has been made, and before the consummation of the marriage, some very serious defect may be found, prior to the contract but deliberately hidden and relevant to generation. The error would seem sufficient to annul the ratified marriage if this defect is such that on the one hand the party ignorant of it would never have married the defective party if such knowledge had been available and, on the other, that it must naturally and reasonably be abhorrent to generate, through such union, children who would probably be defective and unhappy. In fact, sexual union is ordered essentially to the procreation of children and includes the *tacit condition* that there is no great error opposed to the ordinary state of nature and relative to this object essential to the contract.[84]

---

[84] I noted a case of such an impediment in *AMS*, 676.

C.
Lack of freedom

1181. Consent suitable for forming a true contract must be *free*. We have already discussed the conditions of such freedom (cf. *RI*, 1127–1138). Violence, therefore, and fear inflicted[85] for the purpose of extracting consent to marriage dissolves the marriage through lack of consent when the violence and fear are unjust and so serious *relative to the person* concerned that he thinks it a lesser evil to accept the hated marriage than to submit to the evil threatened or even initiated in fact.[86]

1182. Tribunals, however, cannot always know with certainty the gravity of the fear relative to the person, and consequently require an unjust and generally serious fear, that is, 'fear which affects a resolute person'.[87]

1183. Fear unjustly inflicted, besides rendering the *contract* null if it is the cause of the marriage, is also opposed to the *union*

[85] Many authors distinguish *violence* from *inflicted fear*. However, the spirit which must give consent suffers fear only, not violence, as the Roman jurisconsults noted. 'The praetor says: "I do not consider ratified what was brought about by fear". Once upon a time, the phrase used was "caused by violence or fear". "Violence" was mentioned because of the necessity imposed contrary to the will, "fear of present or future danger" because of mental trepidation. Afterwards, however, violence ceased to be mentioned because whatever came about through atrocious violence was also considered to come about through fear' (Ulpian, *Dig.*, bk. 4, t. 2: 1). This passage also shows the natural progression of ideas in Roman laws.

[86] 'Labeo says that fear is to be taken not as any fright, but fright of a greater evil' (Ulpian, *Dig.*, bk. 4, t. 2: 5). *Majoris malitatis*: Haloando and others read *majoris mali*.

[87] Nevertheless, Roman laws do consider the gravity of the fear relative also to the person, as we can see from the quotation from Ulpian. Brunnemann, speaking of the phrase 'which affects a resolute person', says: 'The extent [of the fear] is explained by the quality of the person involved. Fear, therefore, is also considered relative to a resolute woman. The same fear is not required in both sexes, and should be left to the decision of the judge according to bk. 3, *ss. ex quib. caus. maj.* — Again, there is a great difference amongst males themselves. Graver fear is required in a soldier than in a literary person. Some men are by nature more meticulous than others who have no fear whatsoever. Age must also be taken into account.' He quotes Sanchez (*d. d. tert. numer. secund.*) and Fagundes (*de I. et I. L., prim. cap. quint. num. decim.*). *Comment. in Pandect.*, bk. 4, t. 2, bk. 6.

which, as the product of perfect love (cf. 995) has a character contrary to that of the feeling of such fear.[88]

1184. *Abduction* is reduced to violence and fear. Positive laws presuppose that the woman always loses her freedom as long as she is in the power of the abductor who cannot therefore validly marry her until she is returned to a place of freedom.

§3. *Impediments which remove the matter of the sacrament*

A.
Lack of religious faith

1185. Two causes prevent marriage from being a sacrament:
1. lack of baptism;
2. lack of the conditions placed for validity by the Catholic Church upon the matter of the sacrament.

1186. Marriage cannot be a sacrament for those without faith because they have not received the sacramental *character* conferred with baptism (cf. *RGC*, 906–907) which makes possible the reception of the sacraments.

1187. In the first centuries of the Church, when disparity of cult was still not an impediment, the Christian partner received the sacrament, the other did not. Nevertheless, the other partner also intervened as the quasi-minister of the sacrament, just as an unbaptised person can baptise.

1188. But if both parties are unbaptised, *lack of religious faith* is not numbered amongst the *impediments* because these are understood simply as defects which render the marriage of Christians null

---

[88] This reasoning is put forward by St. Alphonsus de' Liguori who makes the following noteworthy comment in his *Teologia Morale*: 'Marriage is a perpetual bond of mutual love between spouses, as we see in St. Matthew (c. 19): "A man shall leave his father and mother and be joined to his wife." — If marriage is contracted from fear, therefore, it must *per se* be null. No man adheres to anything which he holds against his will' (bk. 6, tract. 6, *De Matrim*, c. 3, 1054).

[1184–1188]

B.
Laws of the Church

1189. An intrinsic moral evil can be present in human actions either through their own culpability or through the culpability found in them when considered in their relationships.[89]

1190. The act of generation has no culpability of its own; it is good or bad according to its relationships.

1191. This act cannot be completely good unless it is truly the consummation of the full union called marriage which we have described. It must therefore first possess this *relationship of completion* with the noble affections of two persons of different sex. If not, the act is wayward.

1192. Other relationships are also necessary, however, if the act is to be fully upright. These depend upon the state of societies in which several families find themselves bound together, that is, civil and theocratic society. Marital unions must be formed without substantial prejudice to the end of these two more extensive societies whose governments, therefore, have the power to make laws regulating marriage, provided that rational Right is safeguarded. Indeed, such laws must be ordered to rational Right alone.[90]

1193. The government of civil society can certainly make laws regulating marriage provided that natural freedom is not restricted. Government must limit itself to regulating the *modality* of the exercise of natural freedom, without prejudice to the end of the greater, theocratic society. Civil government can also intervene to punish those who do not observe its law about marriage. Of their nature, each of these laws is a *prohibiting impediment* which all the members of civil society must faithfully observe.

1194. In the absence of Christianity, or in a case where neither

[89] I am speaking of actions furnished with all that is necessary for their subsistence, in other words, of what I have called a *full species* of actions (*OT*, 509, fn. 14). If I were dealing with an *abstract action*, I would have to distinguish three, rather than two things in it: 1. the *substance* of the action; 2. its *accidents*; 3. its *relationships*. There could be an intrinsic moral evil in each of these three things.

[90] For the force of *positive, human* laws, cf. *Conscience*, 175–187.

spouse is subject to the Church, civil government can, for grave reasons of public good, attach penalties to certain of its regulative laws on marriage. It can decide that ratified,[91] but not consummated marriage, is null when its laws are broken. In this case only the *promissory contract* is dissolved, not the *union*, which is still incomplete. Civil law can in fact place just conditions to the validity of contracts.

1195. It cannot, however, dissolve for any reason whatsoever the consummated marriage of those who may have violated its laws on this matter (although it can punish such people), provided that the marriage substantially conforms in other respects to natural laws. *Positive law* can never set itself up in opposition to *natural and rational law*, which it can only assist. It is contrary to natural and rational law that full, consummated conjugal union between two persons should ever be dissolved. Such union is of *its very nature* perpetual precisely because marriage is a *full, natural union* between man and woman, as we have defined it. The parties to a dissolved marriage of this kind would find themselves in a state altogether against nature. Nor can the contract be invalidated by this accidental reason. It is joined to the union, of which it forms a part, and indeed the causal, formal part which, if lacking, should be posited for the sake of rectifying the marriage, granted its consummation.

1196. Things change, however, when Christian marriage is in question. The Church can lay down impediments which invalidate consummated as well as ratified marriages. There is no *full conjugal union* between Christians unless it is made and concluded by the sacramental bond.

1197. The Church's power does not directly concern the *contract*, as the civil power does; it is directly concerned with the *union* and only indirectly with the contract.

1198. The union of Christian spouses possesses a natural and a supernatural part. The *natural part* is the natural union, the supernatural part the *supernatural union*. Christians are human beings raised to a supernatural state. Their union is not full if they join together as natural beings only and not as supernatural

---

[91] Here, *ratified* means marriage formed by the natural consent alone of the parties. I do not take the word 'ratified' here in the sense it has when we say that the marriage of pagans is a *true*, but not *ratified marriage*.

beings. In this case, the best part of their union would be lacking. It is necessary, therefore, in their regard, that the grace of Christ 'perfect the natural union and confirm the indissoluble unity', as the Council of Trent says.[92] The opposite is the case with persons in a merely natural state: because they are not capable of greater union, their union is absolutely full when it is full according to nature alone. If 'marriage is the full union between man and woman', there can indeed be an entirely true marriage between unbaptised people without the presence of the sacrament, but not between baptised persons. These would lack the sacred bond which is the most intimate and precious part of the union of which they are capable.

1199. The Church's power is supernatural. It directly regards the *supernatural part* of the union, that is, the sacramental bond. The Church has, moreover, received from Christ the power to determine the matter of this sacrament, which is the *natural union*. She can, therefore, place on the *natural union* those conditions which in her divine wisdom she judges necessary for the good of the perfect theocratic society. All Christians belong to this society, which they must serve if their *natural union* is to be capable of constituting suitable matter for the sacrament.

1200. This power of the Church is proved ineluctably with the same theological reason which shows it flowing necessarily from the whole system of the Christian sacraments.

1201. The principal operand in the sacrament is Christ. But Christ operates through the hand of the Church, and the Church through the hand of her ministers who, relative to marriage and according to the most common opinion, are the simple faithful who contract the marriage. The Church intervenes to form all the sacraments with her authority, her faith, her will, so that the ministers in forming the sacrament must always have the intention of doing what the Church intends to do. Every time the Church posits a diriment impediment, however, she no longer intends that a sacrament should come about

---

[92] Sess. 24. Although sin puts an impediment to grace, the sacrament does not cease either to contain grace or to act with a tendency to communicate grace. Thus, when the impediment has been removed, the effect of grace revives just as movement takes place as soon as the obstacle impeding living forces has been removed.

through the marriage contract that two Christians might otherwise be able to establish. She declares that the sacrament is not present and thus becomes impossible for the ministers themselves, who cannot have the intention which the Church herself does not have.[93]

Positing a diriment impediment simply means determining the *matter* of the sacrament. It means placing certain conditions and limitations which form the object of the ecclesiastical legislation on this subject. Finally, it means requiring that the conjugal union preserve those relationships which render it fully upright.

1202. Consequently, when a contracted marriage has on the other hand all that is necessary for validity according to natural and divine Right, except the intention and the law of the Church which posits a positive impediment, the Church herself can also convalidate it with her own authority simply by adding the intention which she first denied. In this way, she removes the *positive* impediment imposed by her own authority. The spouses, ignorant of the impediment, have no need to renew their contract because this is presumed to persevere habitually — in other words, the contract was not revoked before the dispensation was given. This is the power present in those dispensations given by the Holy See to convalidate invalid marriages. Such dispensations are said by theologians to be *at the root of marriage*.[94]

---

[93] 'These ministers DO NOT ACT IN THAT SACRED FUNCTION ON THEIR OWN ACCOUNT, BUT IN THE PERSON OF CHRIST. Thus, whether they are good or bad, provided they use the form and matter which the Catholic Church has always preserved as Christ's institution, AND INTEND TO DO THE SAME AS THE CHURCH DOES IN HER ADMINISTRATION, they truly bring about and confer the sacraments, etc' (*Catechism of the Council of Trent*, part 2, c. 25). The intervention of the Church in the confection of the sacrament of marriage is also expressed by the words of the priest: 'I join you in marriage in the name of the Father and of the Son and of the Holy Spirit. Amen.' When this rite is not fulfilled, the Church supplies for it with her authority, faith and intention which, in addition to the minister, is necessary. As we said, the minister must refer, in the sacred function he exercises, to the intention and faith of the Church, and bring his own faith and intention into line with hers.

[94] Benedict XIV says of them: 'These dispensations, said to be *at the root of marriage*, are sometimes granted in special circumstances. They remove the necessity for the renewal of consent, according to the teaching of the

1203. The object of this part of ecclesiastical legislation are certain relationships and requirements that the Church sees as necessary in Christian matrimony for the good of Christian society.

1204. Without these relationships and requirements, the union would be damaging to this society. Hence, although the union would have no intrinsic evil in itself, it would have an intrinsic evil if considered in these social relationships.

1205. The aim of the Church's dispositions in placing these impediments is the good of Christian society. She does not therefore invalidate matrimony every time some defect is present, but is often content simply to forbid it. She does this in all those cases in which invalidity would bring more evil than good to Christian society in general. In this case, she permits the lesser, particular evil because she sees in her wisdom that she could not remove it without occasioning a greater, universal evil.

1206. Hence, the Church recognises as valid, although unlawful, marriages contracted while the parties are in sin, or in a state of excommunication, or marry heretics, or after making a simple vow of chastity, or have already contracted betrothal with another person, or are under an ecclesiastical interdict. Marriages infected by these defects are disapproved by the Church and condemned, but not rendered invalid, in order to avoid a greater evil, as we said. Those who contract these marriages receive the sacrament and are bound by it. God and the Church provide sacramental efficacy even for the wayward on the occasion of such marriages. If such people then repent of their misdeed and

authors and as we see from the apostolic letters of Clement XI beginning *Apostolicae Dignitatis*, 2nd April, 1701; and from other letters of Clement XII beginning *Cum Demum* which are to be found at n. 142, §3, t. 14 of the *Novum Bullarium*. Nevertheless, such dispensations, which validate marriages and legitimise their offspring, although granted for very grave reasons (when the union of the spouses seems externally a true marriage, and the sexual act has not obviously been fornication), are confined solely to cases where the impediment invalidating marriage takes its origin not from divine or natural right but from what we call POSITIVE ECCLESIASTICAL LAW, from which the Supreme Pontiff can derogate. He does this not by making the invalid marriage valid, but by removing those effects which brought about the nullity of the marriage prior to the dispensation and in the very act of contracting the marriage, according to the Clementine letter: *Quoniam de Immunitate Ecclesiarum*' (*De Synod. D.*, bks. 13, 21: 7).

[1203–1206]

obtain remission of their sin, the effect of grace, previously impeded and suspended through their fault, flows from the secret operation of the sacrament.

1207. If, however, the defect connected with the marriage is such that it is more harmful to the public good of Christians to validate than invalidate the marriage, the Church declares the defect a diriment impediment. Under this special title, she posits the following five diriment *impediments* in the present state of Christian society: 1. disparity of cult; 2. public decency; 3. affinity; 4. clandestinity; 5. crime.

I.
Disparity of cult

1208. In the first place, the Church invalidates the conjugal union which a baptised individual attempts to contract with a non-baptised person (*disparitas cultus*).

1209. This impediment, now in force, did not exist when the Church began. At that time she allowed the validity of such unions, judging it less harmful to Christian society to admit than to exclude it. It would certainly have been impossible to impede these marriages without extremely serious consequences. Moreover, they assisted the conversion of the world. As the Gospel spread, however, the good expected from such marriages was replaced by greater danger of subversion of the baptised spouse.

1210. In addition, granted that matrimony is a sacrament representative of the marriage between Christ and the Church, it was altogether fitting that such a holy union should be represented by holy people alone.

1211. Again, marriage is a full union. But this fullness is not present on the part of a baptised spouse who cannot put all his or her goods (chief of which are supernatural goods) into communion with the non-baptised spouse.

1212. The pagans themselves were able to deduce from the *fullness of union* that marriage required community of religion between spouses. Modestinus, for example, expresses this in a wonderful way when he defines marriage as 'the union between

[1207–1212]

a man and a woman, a sharing of one's whole life, A COMMUN-
ICATION OF DIVINE AND HUMAN RIGHT.'[95]

It follows from this that the *prohibiting impediment* with
which the Church forbids the marriage of Catholics and
heretics, although caused by the danger of seduction, has a more
intimate reason dependent upon the very nature of marriage. It
is impossible for Catholic spouses to believe themselves fully
united with heretical partners with whom they have no common faith or hope of eternal union.

II.
Affinity and public decency

1213. The preservation of good morals in Christian society
prompted the Church to remove from Christians their hope of
being able to contract marriage with their in-laws.

1214. If the marriage has already been consummated, it is not
possible to marry the dead spouse's blood-relations to the first,
second, third and fourth degree (*affinitas*).

1215. If the marriage has been ratified but not consummated,
it is still impossible to marry the blood-relations of the spouse
to the same four degrees (*honestas publica*).[96]

1216. Moreover, it is fixed by law in the Church that a person
who illicitly has intercourse with another, cannot validly marry
the blood-relations of the other person to the first and second
degree (*affinitas*). It is fitting that those who unite unlawfully
should make their carnal union decent by completing it through
marriage. The first union, therefore, is considered an incipient
marriage, as it were. If then marriage is impossible because one
or both of the accomplices are already married, it helps if their
hope of contracting marriage with blood-relations of their part-

---

[95] *Dig.*, bk. 23, tit. 2: 1.

[96] Because the purpose of this impediment is the preservation of good
morals, it arises even from an invalid marriage, provided the invalidity does
not depend upon lack of consent. Indeed, if consent is lacking, one cannot
presume the presence of the kind of familiarity with the other contracting
party that can be extended to near relations. In this case, the Church removes
the impediment.

[1213–1216]

ner are shattered. This should prevent further diffusion of this evil custom.[97]

1217. Finally, even bethrothal places an impediment to contracting marriage with blood-relations to the first degree, that is, with the parents, children, brothers and sisters of the person with whom the betrothal was contracted (*honestas publica*). The aim is to prevent the supposed familiarity with the other person from extending to near relations, with its consequent detriment to good morals.[98]

1218. The degrees of extension of the impediments of *affinity* and *public decency*, like the degrees of consanguinity, were established by the Church in keeping with the exigencies of the state of Christian society, and the public good expected from such enlargement or diminution.

III.
Clandestinity

1219. The impediment of clandestinity, posited by the Council of Trent, invalidates marriages not contracted in the presence of the parish priest (or his delegate) and two or three witnesses.

1220. The public good requires that all should know with certainty the identity of persons joined in matrimony so that no one may aspire to contract marriage with them. This would disturb domestic society and open the way to immorality.

1221. For a long time, the Church tried to avoid this extremely serious defect by severely condemning clandestine marriages and laying down various penalties for them, but without declaring them invalid. As soon as experience showed that this was not sufficient to prevent the evil, the Council of Trent invalidated them by creating the so-called impediment of clandestinity.[99]

[97] A spouse who has had intercourse with a blood-relation of the other to the first or second degree is punished by inability to request the marriage debt. Nevertheless, such intercourse after the marriage cannot dissolve the matrimonial bond which is of its nature indissoluble.

[98] This shows that the impediment of *affinity* arises from licit or illicit *intercourse*; the impediment of *public decency* from ratified marriage and betrothal.

[99] Sess. 24, c. 1.

IV.
Crime

1222. Murdering one's spouse invalidates marriage with the accomplice to such a crime if it was committed with the intention of marriage, or if this was the intention of one of the parties.

1223. If the murder of the spouse was preceded by adultery, it produces a diriment impediment to marriage with the adulterous party even though this party was not an accomplice to the crime, and the intention of contracting marriage was held by only one of the parties.

1224. Adultery alone, accompanied by a promise of marriage made during the lifetime of one's own spouse, results in a diriment impediment.

1225. Finally, a similar impediment arises from adultery accompanied by an attempt at marriage when both have been carried out during the lifetime of the spouse who has suffered from the infidelity. There is no impediment if they have been carried out during the lifetime of a second or other spouse.

1226. The end of such impediments is clear: the Church wishes to defend domestic society, the personal safety of the spouses and the preservation of the fidelity they have sworn to one another.

CHAPTER 5

Duties and rights of spouses

1227. So far we have discussed the nature of the union (cf. 983–1103), and how and under what conditions it is posited in being (cf. 1104). We pointed out that *marriage* and the *fulfilment* of its obligations are not the same thing (cf. 1099).

After this discussion of the nature and constitution of marriage, we must deal with the obligations accompanying it and founded in its intimate essence. After the *obligations* come the *relative rights*.

Article 1.
The spouses considered as a single person and as two jural persons

1228. We must first examine what, in domestic society, the spouses posit in communion and how they do so.

Because their union is full, everything is placed in communion, but in a limited way; the spouses retain their individuality as persons, or personal dignity. I say 'individuality as persons' or 'personal dignity' because these two expressions mean the same to anyone who really understands them. Personal individuality is itself dignity as person; in other words, individuality of person is constituted by the dignity human beings have from their communication with what is eternal and divine. Let us look at this in another way.

1229. Natural theocratic society, which is completed by supernatural theocratic society, precedes conjugal society. It is called 'natural' because it emanates from nature, from the essence of humanity. Human individuals are constituted in it by their natural, spontaneous will directed towards universal good whether they will this freely or not. All have a supreme duty to adhere freely to it.[100]

1230. Theocratic society is principally the society of the individual human being with God. Relative to nature, it is *initial* society; relative to the grace of the Saviour, *complete*.

The individual human being can have moral good in common with God, together with what precedes moral good (truth) and what follows it (happiness). He cannot renounce these goods except by violating his essential society with the divine being; this society constitutes him what he is, a human person. In fact the human person is an indivisible principle possessing truth and a (moral) activity with which it can adhere to truth.[101] The universal moral obligation is non-violation of this society.

This society precedes all others, constituting their possibility and uprightness. Without this first society (natural theocratic

---

[100] *SP*, 545–573 where I proposed the following formula when discussing the moral system of the Stoics: 'Making the *will of the human person* fully agree with the *will of human nature*' [573].

[101] Cf. *AMS*, 832 ss.

society), human beings no longer have rights or duties; social right no longer exists, and without social right, society does not exist. This first society therefore is that which renders all other societies possible. It also makes them upright and endows them with moral dignity, because moral dignity resides essentially in it. The first society therefore is also THE SOCIAL PRINCIPLE.

Hence, if two or more human beings associate, the first obligation of the social body they have formed is to acknowledge that 'every individual has a society immensely more honourable with the supreme Being.' Consequently, the first, fundamental obligation of the social body and of all its members is 'to acknowledge the personal individuality of every member', that is, to acknowledge that 'every member, before being a member, is an individual *per se* who possesses supreme, inalienable and intangible rights. Neither the society nor individual members can dispose of these rights. On the contrary, these rights must direct the society and its laws to maintain the rights themselves with a respect that has something infinite and final, like its object.'

Granted all this, how do spouses come together as persons in such a way that their union is full? Not by confusing their personal individuality, nor by destroying the society which each has *individually* with the supreme Being, but by enjoying together the individual good of the other (society of fruition) and promoting the society itself (society of moral action).

1231. Nevertheless, this good remains individual. At the same time, the consequent delight and interest that all take in the individual good of each becomes common. All desire to preserve and advance this individual good, and desire it to be individual. Its excellent nature consists precisely in this individuality.

1232. Love, by loving the individuality of the good, is pure friendship, and has a nobility beyond all loves because totally *unselfish* in its essence.

Friendship is something more than *society* (as we have observed elsewhere),[102] but produces a society of its own, because that good which can only be essentially individual is enjoyed in

---

[102] *SP*, 91–101.

common by all members; all equally rejoice in that good and its individuality.

God willing, I will speak about the mysteries of friendship and love in *Agathology*.

Article 2.
The double *series* of rights and duties of spouses: individual and social

1233. It is clear from what we have said that the fullness of the conjugal union does not destroy the individuality and personship of the spouses, which they enjoy in common in an entirely special way. Hence, their duties and rights can be divided into two *series*: those which they have as personal individuals and which exist *per se*; and those which they have as members of a society.

1234. This first division is important and I will make great use of it in all that follows. However, I do not think it necessary to classify under it the special rights and duties I intend to discuss. This would take far too long[103] and oblige me to divide the content, which I think is better kept as one in the mind of the reader. To do otherwise would mean imparting deformed and imperfect concepts.

Article 3.
COMMON and DISTINCTIVE rights and duties of spouses

1235. Let us set out an easier classification of the rights and duties of spouses. *Personship* makes the spouses distinct subjects of rights and duties. *Nature*, partly different in man and woman, gives spouses different *common* and *proper* rights and duties.

1236. As we have seen, every society implies *equality*. But we have also seen that if, in two intelligent individuals, one part is

---

[103] The duty of one spouse to respect the personship of the other is common to all human beings. Similarly, the duties arising from this duty are common, together with the relative rights. We have spoken about these in *Rights of the Individual*, to which they pertain.

equal, the other part can be unequal. Granted that the inequality is harmonious, it can give rise to that element of *appropriateness* which, far from impeding the union, makes it possible and gives it a character of its own. This is particularly true of the conjugal union.

In spouses one part (human nature) is equal, and the source of *common* rights and duties (communal Right); the other part is unequal (sex) and the source of *different* rights and duties (seigniorial, governmental Right in domestic society). We will speak about these two great classes of duties and rights of spouses.

Article 4.
Common rights and duties

1237. The principle giving rise to common rights and duties is the *fullness of* conjugal *union*, which can be formulated as: 'Spouses must preserve and make real the fullness of union which constitutes their marriage.'

1238. They can fail in this duty in two ways:

1. By performing acts which of their nature are opposed to the preservation and realisation of the union.

2. By not observing the right way of implementing the union, although on the other hand they intend to preserve and realise it.

These common duties and rights can therefore be subdivided into those concerning the union of the spouses and those concerning the manner of this union.

§1. *Duties and rights concerning the conjugal union*

1239. The fullness of union between the spouses has four consequences:

1. the indissolubility of marriage;
2. the uniqueness of each spouse;
3. community of life;
4. community of goods.

[1237–1239]

These consequences constitute corresponding duties and rights in spouses. I will say something about each one.

A.
Indissolubility

I.
The triple reason for indissolubility

1240. The *indissolubility* of marriage is founded on 1. natural Right; 2. primitive divine Right, and 3. evangelical Right grounded in the sacramental dignity of Christian marriage.

1241. *a*) Natural Right. — Marriage is the union of man and woman in all its fullness. The union would not be full unless it were indissoluble. Hence indissolubility proceeds from the nature of marriage.

1242. *b*) Primitive divine right. — When the first human being pronounced the solemn words with which he expressed the nature of marriage,[104] he spoke as legislator for all his descendants. The law he enunciated was rightly considered divine.

Properly speaking, it was *natural* law that was promulgated, which can however be called divine in so far as God is the author of nature and the source of the light of reason. It was also *divine-positive* law, because inspired and confirmed by God, and *human positive* law because the first human being, as head of the human race, had authority to make and promulgate universal laws.

1243. It was very fitting that the law of domestic society[105] should be promulgated immediately after the law of theocratic society, which consists in the obedience of the creature to the Creator and all his ordinances.[106] This guaranteed that the two original and essential societies of the human race were fully constituted and regulated. These two laws were in fact the first laws of society.

[104] Gen 2: 23.
[105] Gen 2: 23–24.
[106] Gen 2: 16–17.

1244. Adam's words contain no imperative; he says, 'This is bone of my bone, and flesh of my flesh. She will be called derivation from man because she has been taken from man. Therefore a man will leave his father and mother and adhere to his wife, and they will be two in one flesh.' This however causes no difficulty. Adam was indicating the nature of marriage, showing that the law enunciated by him was natural. Nor did he, who was created upright and perfect, need anything else for him to fulfil the law. A human being in the state of total rectitude never acts contrary to the nature of things. Hence God himself did not use a legislative formula to enunciate the law of marriage, but promulgated it by the very act of drawing the woman from the side of the sleeping Adam. This act was most suitable for expressing the relationship between man and woman, and was well understood and interpreted by Adam. God therefore promulgated the conjugal law by the fact of the production of woman from Adam's rib, and Adam promulgated it with the words which interpreted the divine fact. The law was thus shown to be founded in the reality of things, in the nature of man and woman, and in their mutual appropriateness, which drew them to their perpetual, full union.

1245. *c*) Sacramental right. — Finally, the Saviour unites Christian man and woman by the insoluble sacramental bond. With it, he gives them the power to remain perpetually united for as long as they live on earth, with a love similar to that which unites JESUS Christ with his Church, or God with humanity.

II.
The nature and force of the triple indissolubility

1246. We are now in a position to understand the nature and force of the triple indissolubility of marriage.

1247. *a*) Natural indissolubility. — From what we have said, we see that natural indissolubility has its *title* in the human being's *upright nature* subsisting in both sexes. Reason, based on sound principle, does not eliminate indissolubility. Its sole enemy is the corruption of humanity which alone alters and deforms the conjugal relationship.

1248. *b*) Divine-positive indissolubility. — We also see how the primitive divine-positive law of marriage confirmed the natural law which made marriage indissoluble. Indissolubility was greatly ennobled by God when he constituted the human race in a supernatural order.

1249. Man, placed in this sublime order, had indeed a greater obligation to conform himself to the laws of his upright nature. Any contrary act deformed him, insulting the grace conferred upon him by the supreme Being.

1250. Furthermore, the only dispensation which the divine-positive law allows and of which the Church is simply a mouthpiece and interpreter, comes from the divine legislator himself. Consequently, a stronger bond is added to the natural law of indissolubility.

1251. *c*) Sacramental indissolubility. — But the sacramental bond is much stronger. It is not simply *jural-moral*, like the previous two, nor does it consist simply in the obligation imposed on the spouses by *jural-moral* laws; these can be violated or broken by human free will. The sacramental bond, effected by *divine action*, is a *real* bond, the work of God himself, which unites the spouses supernaturally. It is neither lawful nor possible for any earthly authority to destroy the work of God. A legitimate authority may sometimes remove a bond consisting in mere jural-moral obligations, but no one can destroy the reality of facts. No *human power* exists which can divide Christian spouses validly united. No human power is greater than divine power; no power can undo what God accomplishes with his power.

1252. The divine action accomplished in the sacraments is the communication of grace. On the part of God, this action never fails in its efficacy, although the human recipients can impede its sanctifying effect by their sin. But, as we have said, the action remains potentially in them, so that the effect of sanctification takes place when the obstruction of sin is removed. When human beings, through their depravity, turn the grace contained in the sacrament into their own damnation, this terrible consequence itself shows how the sacramental bond is never without its effect in them.

1253. The bond gives rise both to the spouses' greater *obligation* not to disunite (the law of supernatural indissolubility) and to the *reality* of the sacramental union.

1254. Hence the crime of two pagan spouses differs immensely from that of two Christian spouses who in each case separate to enter another marriage. The former have only a jural-moral union, that is, the jural-moral duty and right to remain perpetually together. But the Christian couple, in addition to the jural-moral obligation, remain bound by the divine action. This action unites them in the love of God, even if they obstruct him, just as a heavy body gravitates to earth even though its movement is impeded by some other body. For this reason Canon Law usually calls pagan marriage, which lacks the sacramental bond, *true* but not *ratified marriage* — the 'Gloss' explains that it can be dissolved, and this is normally understood in the way I have explained.[107]

III.
The extent of the difference between the indissolubility of ratified and of consummated marriage

1255. Moreover, merely *ratified* marriage participates in indissolubility to a different degree from marriage that is also *consummated*. Here I understand 'ratified' in the general sense of *lawful* (and include the marriage of pagans) as opposed to *consummated*. It is indeed necessary that we examine the difference between the indissolubility of ratified and of consummated marriage with reference to the *natural, divine-positive* and *sacramental law*. From these three laws every kind of indissolubility comes.

1256. *a*) Natural indissolubility. — The following points demonstrate that *consummated* marriage shares more than *non-consummated* marriage in the indissolubility dependent on the natural law:

---

[107] 'Although TRUE MARRIAGE exists among pagans, it is not RATIFIED. Among Christians it is TRUE AND RATIFIED because the sacrament of faith, once admitted is never lost. This sacrament ratifies the sacrament of marriage so that the latter endures in the spouses as long as the former' (Innocent III, 1212 AD, *Sext.* bk. 4, tit, 19, c. 7).

1. The fullness of union is finally activated in the consummation of the marriage. As long as the only union is that brought about by the contract, the union is merely *in potency*; it is not *realised* and actuated. But a union in act is certainly a fuller union than the same kind of union in potency. In the former the notion of marriage is fulfilled, but not in the latter. Marriage, as I have defined it, is 'the full, appropriate union between man and woman'.[108]

2. In the marriage contract the *right* to union passes reciprocally between the contracting parties. There is jural but not *real union*: the handing over of the thing, accomplished in the exercise of the acquired right, is not carried out.

3. A third, stronger reason, the special nature of the act uniting the bodies, shows that the consummation of marriage renders conjugal union more indissoluble. As we have seen, the act is consonant with human dignity only as a consequence and completion of the fullness of union called marriage. If the couple should part after having had intercourse, their act would remain in its most shameful nakedness, because the veil of immortal affections which ennobles it, or at least hides what is unbecoming, would have been removed.

Any couple who, after carnal knowledge of each other, break up and enter other marriages, dishonour human dignity. All that remains to them of their transitory union is shameful impurity.

4. Finally, if children result from the consummation of the marriage, the parents' duties towards them make the stability of their union even more necessary.

---

[108] It may be objected that 'the fullest union can exist between two spouses without any use of the marriage right.' — It is true that I have said this myself, but we must note that a totally full union between two chaste spouses could not be mentally conceived unless their extraordinary virtue and the great love they share for eternal things united their souls in a wonderful way; this wonderful agreement and greater union of souls would advantageously supply for what is lacking in their union relative to their bodies. Here, we are dealing with an altogether extraordinary case, the intervention of a *love stimulated* to immortal good. Relative to ordinary cases and to what happens in the order of *spontaneous affections*, the things I have already said apply. — Furthermore, spouses who have souls so noble and distant from this earth that they dwell together like two angels do not dissolve the conjugal bond, rather they embellish it and consummate it more tenderly with the virtuous flame burning in their hearts.

1257. *b*) Divine-positive indissolubility. — When the first man and legislator of the human race pronounced the law of indissolubility, he made express mention of the carnal union in the solemn words, 'and they shall be two in one flesh.'[109] These words posited the end and reason for the previous words, 'Wherefore a man shall leave father and mother, and shall cleave to his wife: and they shall be two in one flesh.'[110] It has already been observed[111] that Christ in restoring and declaring the first law, described consummated marriage in the ancient words of Adam ('And they shall be two in one flesh')[112] *before* affirming the indissolubility of marriage ('What God has joined together let not man put asunder'). Similarly, the Apostle said, 'This is a great sacrament in Christ and in the Church', only after describing the consummation of marriage, using Adam's same words, 'And they shall be two in one flesh.'[113]

1258. As we have said, this divine-positive law of conjugal indissolubility is simply the same law of nature posited in reality by God, expressed in words by Adam, and confirmed by Christ's efficacious power. We must therefore conclude that, in accordance with the same natural law, indissolubility has two degrees, of which the higher degree is carnal union. This union is debased immediately it is separated from the total union of two human beings of different sex. Divine authority therefore does not make any change to the concept of indissolubility, or to its degrees; rather it renders them more honourable and sacred.

1259. *c*) Sacramental indissolubility. — Nor does the sacrament change the natural reason for indissolubility or its degrees, but reinforces it and raises it to a higher dignity.

1260. We can distinguish two parts in the sacrament: 1. the sign, and 2. the efficacy of the sign which produces the grace of the Saviour.

1. As *sign*, the sacrament of marriage when consummated represents a greater union and indissolubility than when simply

---

109 Gen 2: 2 [24, Douai].
110 *Ibid*.
111 Cf. Pignatelli, T. 1. *Consult.*, 148, n. 4.
112 Mt 19: [6].
113 Eph 5: [32, 31, Douai].

ratified. A ratified marriage represents the soul's union with God by means of grace, a union that can be severed by sin; a consummated marriage indicates the union of Christ with the Church, effected in an entirely indissoluble manner by the incarnation of the Word.

1261. The words of Pope Innocent III deserve mention here because they explain in a wonderful way the two degrees of sacramental indissolubility. He replied negatively to the query, 'Must a man who has taken as wife a widow who is still a virgin, be barred from sacred ordination as a twice-married man.' He argued as follows:

> There are two things in marriage: consent of minds and union of bodies. The first indicates the charity which exists in the spirit between God and the just soul, as the Apostle says, 'He who is united to the Lord becomes one spirit with him.'[114] The second sign signifies the conformity, which exists in the flesh, between Christ and the Church, of which the Evangelist speaks when he says: 'The Word became flesh and dwelt amongs.'[115] A marriage not consummated by the union of bodies cannot represent the marriage contracted between Christ and the Church in the mystery of the incarnation. St. Paul speaks about this when he quotes the words of the first parent, 'This is bone of my bones, and flesh of my flesh'[116] and, 'For this reason a man shall leave his father and mother and be joined to his wife, and the two shall become one flesh',[117] and he immediately adds, 'This, I say, is a great sacrament in Christ and in the Church.'[118]
>
> Now although it is forbidden for the twice-married man and husband of the widow to presume to be promoted to holy orders simply because he lacks the sacred sign (neither the widow nor the twice-married man has had only a one-to-one relationship with the other), it is also true that when the marriage between these spouses has not been consummated, the sign of such a sacrament has not been eliminated. Hence the person marrying a woman

[114] 1 Cor 6: 17.
[115] Jn 1: 14.
[116] Gen 2: [23].
[117] *Ibid.*
[118] [Cf.] Eph 5: 32.

once a spouse in a non-consummated marriage cannot therefore be impeded from promotion to the priesthood. Neither of them has shared their flesh with more than one person,[119]

and it is this sharing alone which prevents the re-presentation of the unique bridegroom, Christ, in marriage to the unique bride, the Church.

1262. Consummated marriage, therefore, even among pagans, can aptly serve as a symbol of the marriage between God incarnate and humanity, even if less worthily and completely, and without sacramental action. Thus Benedict XIV writes:

> Consummated marriage, even among pagans, signifies the union of Christ with the Church through the incarnation, as the Cardinal *de Laurea* acutely observed.[120] Vasquez[121] considered this so conformable to the truth that, according to his teaching, it could not be denied without error.[122]

The learned Pope apparently holds the opinion that a consummated marriage of pagans has an indissolubility greater than a marriage of Christians which is only ratified. We cannot legitimately infer that the Pope has the power to dissolve a consummated marriage simply because he has the power to dissolve a ratified marriage. As we said, not even the sacrament itself changes the reason and natural degrees of conjugal indissolubility; rather, granted indissolubility as foundation, the sacrament ennobles and consecrates it.

This natural *reason* consists supremely in the principle, 'The act of carnal generation is impure immediately it is separated from the more noble elements of the total union of two human individuals of different sex'. Granted this, we see that indissolubility begins when the *right to this act* is acquired through the contract. The right itself is unbecoming if separated from the

---

[119] Sext., bk. 1, t. 21, c. 5.

[120] *De Matrim., disput.* 16; art. 2, §6, num. 231.

[121] In 3 *P. D. Thom.*, t. 4, disput. 2, sub num. 57.

[122] *De Synodo D.*, bk. 13, c. 21: 4. — Lambertini held the same thesis in a discourse printed in vol. 4, *Thesaur. Resolutionum* of the Sacred Congregation of the Council. He gave the discourse relative to a case presented to the Sacred Congregation, 29th March 1727.

right of full, perpetual union. But when the carnal act itself is consummated, it only ceases to be impure by taking on the concept of *completion of the full union*. If the marriage is dissolved, this concept is lost.

If no carnal act takes place and only the right exists (ratified marriage), the marriage can be dissolved *per accidens*, provided the causes are such that the solution leaves nothing unbecoming in the human being. This happens in the case of a *solemn vow*, by which human beings consecrate themselves totally to God. There can never be any indecency in renouncing the exercise of the conjugal right for a greater union with God himself. By means of the vow, a human being truly enters into a special jural union with God, a union infinitely more noble than the abandoned union with a creature. Because the exercise of the right to carnal union is incompatible with the vow of chastity, the right whose exercise is rendered impossible ceases. As we have said,[123] a right does not exist if it is impossible to exercise it or profit by it. A solemn vow therefore indirectly dissolves marriage.

1263. It is clear that a ratified marriage can, for other very grave reasons, be dissolved by the authority of the Church, but not by the will of the contracting parties. Granted these reasons, the unbound man or woman lose no dignity, while Christian society acquires, by means of their dissolution, a more worthy and noble good than their right to carnal union.[124]

1264. [2.] Relative to sacramental grace, this certainly accompanies and sanctifies the two degrees of indissolubility we have described. Both are efficacious signs of something sacred.

1265. Ratified marriage brings with it the grace of charity between the spouses, mutual fidelity, peace in their domestic life

---

[123] *ER*, 252–255.

[124] Fr. Maurus von Schenkl speaks about some rights which German custom attributed to spouses who had performed a ceremony which simulated the consummation of marriage and was called 'thoral consent': 'Generally among the Germans, ratified marriage did not have civil effects unless there was thoral consent. Even today, in certain regions and cities of Germany, the communion of goods, the succession of spouses together with the statutory portion of goods, the dignity of the husband to be communicated to the wife and the bridegroom's gifts to the bride on the morning after the wedding are still in vogue' (*Institutiones juris ecclesiastici communis*, pt. 2, §665*).

together, fortitude in bearing each other's burdens, and mutual help and succour.

1266. The consummation of marriage brings with it the grace of conjugal chastity in the exercise of this office of nature, holy fruitfulness, the procreation of children of good character to increase the number of saints, and wisdom in educating them.

1267. Grace not only renders the bond more honourable, bestowing a greater obligation to respect it, but draws it much tighter by means of interior divine action and the will of the spouses to remain inseparably together.

1268. If ratified marriage (marriage merely of right) is dissolved by the authority of the Church, grace is not violated, granted that the causes of the dissolution redound to the glory of God. Grace received at the time the marriage was contracted is also not wasted; indeed it continues because it is an increase of charity and holiness, and able to make perfect the other elements of the union. Marriage, I repeat, is not simply carnal union; it supposes, as a kind of preamble to carnal union, every possible union between two human individuals of different sex.

IV.
Reprehensible customs contrary to indissolubility: concubinage and divorce

a)
Concubinage

1269. Concubinage is cohabitation between a man and woman for the purpose of satisfying the sexual stimulus outside the *fullness* of conjugal union. Sex used in this way does not receive from the fullness of union the dignity due to the actions of creatures who are endowed with reason. Consequently it is something impure.

1270. We must note that the word 'concubinage' was sometimes used to mean a true marriage, a full union, contracted however with a woman to whom civil society did not grant all the external prerogatives granted to wives. Such a purely civil disposition does not change the nature of the union, which, according to nature, can still be full.

1271. This distinction into wives of first and second order however is not at all natural. *Upright* human *nature* acknowledges only one kind of marriage and therefore only one kind of wife. Indeed the very expression, 'fullness of union', which the concept of marriage contains, demonstrates the simplicity and uniqueness of the union: what is full can be only of one kind.

1272. The distinction of marriages and wives into two kinds has its origin in the decadence of human nature, and in social laws, which normally conform to that decadence.

1273. The Church distinguished the essential constituents of marriage which she required uncompromisingly and without relaxation of any kind. Once they were safeguarded, her spirit, teaching and incessant exhortations were directed to perfecting the marriages of the faithful. She removed the difference between marriages and marriages, between wives and wives introduced by the imperfection of individuals and human societies. She continues this great work today, and will accomplish it only in the course of centuries.

1274. But even in her first task, that is, of making sure that no illegitimate marriages were formed but those only which possessed all the constituents of a true marriage, she proceeded with her accustomed wisdom. At first she left intact the language of society, and was content to remove any disorders expressed by such language. But once the disorders had been removed, the language had to fall, and did so of itself. By this natural and gentle means, the Church corrected behaviour and abolished Roman concubinage. Some observations about this wise conduct of the Church in abolishing Roman concubinage will not be out of place.

1275. The marriage called *justum conjugium* [just marriage] by the Romans had three forms, corresponding to its three relationships with *theocratic* society, *civil* society and the *state of nature*.

1276. In the first form, the solemn rites of religion were used. The Pontifex Maximus and the priest of Jupiter joined the spouses[125] by a sacrifice in which the bride presented a spelt cake;[126] hence the contract was called *per confarreationem*. The

---

[125] *Serv. Georg.* 1, v. 31.
[126] Arnob., bk. 4.

ceremony signified that the couple intended to communicate sacred things. Certain formulas were pronounced, and ten witnesses took part.

1277. This form was very ancient and recalled the original institution by God himself. The fact that marriage came from God and must be something sacred was an opinion impressed on the minds of all ancient peoples. The communication of divine things is certainly the noblest part of the conjugal union, the part that contributes the highest nobility and extends a heavenly mantle over all other parts.

1278. Moreover, people felt there was something divine in generation, and something ineffably great in perfect love.[127] But no love is fully great unless the lovers communicate something divine to each other.

1279. The second form of contracting marriage among the Romans was *per legitimam stipulationem* [legitimate stipulation], or *per coemptionem viri et mulieris* [ceremonial sale of man and woman], in a word, by a civil contract.

1280. The third form was called *per usucapionem*, that is, by living with a woman for a whole year. After this period of cohabitation or concubinage, the Twelve Tables declared the woman a legitimate wife, but without religious ceremonies or civil acts. It was presumed that after a year's cohabitation the couple wished to be husband and wife. Thus the marriage took place by tacit consent and was supposed by law.

1281. These three forms for contracting marriage deserve the greatest consideration. They show people passing through the various social states forced upon them by events.

1282. The first form pertains to people who were able to preserve a larger portion of the very ancient state of *theocracy*, or were at the mercy of less harsh events or, endowed with a fuller, more constant spirit, were able to rise above such events and to some extent preserve the original family.

1283. The second form pertains to those who, after the destruction of the original family or because they had left it to

---

[127] I have observed that anything beyond the understanding power of the human mind, or rather, beyond human imagination, was called God or confused with God, that is, it was divinised. Cf. *Frammenti d'una storia dell'empietà* in *Apologetica*, pp. 379–380.

follow their own purposes, united into bands of bachelors which then became civil associations.[128] As long as the earth was uninhabited, entire families, together with their family customs, could move from one region to another. But when, as armed groups of settlers, they left one populous region to go in conquest of lands already occupied, the family was an encumbrance in the solely military enterprise. Strong, bold young men confronted every danger on land and sea. And at the mercy of events, they succeeded in conquering a country or founding a city by the power of individual energy and thought, not on the basis of forgotten traditional and domestic practices. With the customs of their ancestors almost entirely lost, the thing that occupied their spirit was civil organisation. Thus religious marriages were the first to go, or rather there was no time to think about well-regulated marriages. However, when the pressing needs of war had ended, and settlement was sufficiently established, they felt the need to re-organise marriage after past neglect. New legislators drew up civil ordinances for it and introduced the civil form of contract.

1284. There was however another part of humanity, which had suffered ill fortune, or lacked understanding, energy or moral feeling: those who remained unattached and dispersed without attaining civil association. Hence, savages and the 'state of nature' as opposed to the state of society. In this state of disassociation marriage lost its religious forms and did not regain even the forms proper to the city. Generally, people had intercourse more or less at random; union was a fact rather than a clearly known right. Humanity however still remained, because certain of its feelings and of its mental conceptions are indelible and natural to it. Consequently stable unions between man and woman, as something totally in keeping with human nature, could never entirely disappear. Even in this state of degradation a kind of *de facto* marriage remained, although almost entirely without external forms. This kind of union, legalised by the city, gave rise to the third form of Roman marriage.

1285. We have to imagine a country where one section of the

---

[128] Cf. what I have written in *SP*, 371–391.

inhabitants live in a state of domestic or tribal society and preserve the customs and traditions of their fathers. Another section has become weak and has degenerated to a state of nature. Let us imagine that a band of warlike, enterprising young people arrives and settles in the country, subjugating the inhabitants and founding a civil state. It is clear that both sections, those living in a state of regular domestic society and those dispersed and degenerated to a state of nature, must be incorporated into the overriding establishment of the bold adventurers. The conquerors now wish to organise and increase the civil society they have founded. They apply themselves to making laws, and do exactly what the Twelve Tables did, that is, they recognise and legalise the three ways of contracting marriage: 1. the way proper to families that have preserved religion: *per confarreationem*; 2. their own way, *per stipulationem*, because they know no other organisation than that which they give to themselves through new civil laws; and finally 3. the way proper to the state of nature, *per usucapionem*. Hence, each condition of the human race brought its own element into Roman society which welcomed and legalised it.[129]

1286. The laws of the Twelve Tables, by legalising natural unions lasting more than a year, removed the impurity of these unions and changed them into true marriages. The laws however allowed concubinage to continue for the year;[130] they dared not impose on degenerate human beings the hard necessity of abstaining from every disorder [*App.*, no. 6]. This was not the

---

[129] Pliny calls the form of contracting by the communication of sacred things (*per confarreationem*) *conjunctio maxime religiosa* [a supremely religious union] (bk. 18, c. 4). This way however gradually decreased among the Romans. First limited to the marriages of priests, it was then totally abandoned, as we learn from Tacitus (*Ann.*, bk. 4, c. 16). This indicated the decadence of Roman society. Religious faith ceased in the family, and Roman society became totally absorbed by external things. In other words, it suffered a hidden, internal wasting and lost its dignified character together with the original traces of humanity.

[130] Children begotten in concubinage, that is, in the first year of these unions, are called *naturales*. They are distinguished from children called *injusti, illegitimi, spurii* who were born of adultery, that is, from the union of a married man with any woman other than his wife.

case in the Catholic Church — she dared all because she could do all.

1287. She censured every carnal union outside marriage as soon as it appeared on earth.[131]

1288. Although she always disapproved of the words 'concubinage' and 'concubine', which at that time were less offensive than today, she did not immediately prohibit them. But, by suppressing the year's experiment allowed by impotent human legislation,[132] she at least wanted concubinage to become true marriage. However, once the substantial disorder had been removed, the words themselves gradually fell into disuetude, and today, to Christian ears, they are abominable. Finally the Council of Trent completely removed every kind of clandestinity.[133]

---

[131] In the first Council fornication was forbidden by decree of the Apostles. They found it necessary to make a positive law because of the prevalent disorders permitted and justified by the social laws of the pagans. In this way they indirectly exercised the power of Christ which they received for the correction of human legislations.

[132] Hence in many places canon law permitted a man who had no other wife to have a concubine, that is, a true but clandestine wife; she was, as it were, a wife of second order — cf., for example, a canon of the first Council of Toledo (400 AD) found in the Decree (Dist. 34, can. 4; also can. 5). Christian emperors, taught by the Church and themselves subject to the holy laws promulgated by her to all the faithful without distinction, felt it their duty to correct civil legislation in conformity with ecclesiastical sanctions (cf. Justinian., *Nov.* 18, 5). The Church for her part willingly acknowledged all the formalities required by the civil laws for the legitimacy of marriages, provided she found them upright and helpful for the Christian people. Thus, through respect for laws recognised by the Church, St. Augustine himself does not dare call 'wife' a woman given away without the *dowry instruments* and other formalities required by the laws. But he does recognise the validity of these marriages lacking in formalities with a woman who retained the name 'concubine', provided the following three things were present: 'First, both must be free to marry; second, there must be mutual fidelity which excludes their union with a third party, and no aversion to procreating children; third, they both intend to remain in that state of life until death' (*De bono conjugali*). Every other kind of concubine who was not a true wife was totally forbidden by the Church. Furthermore, the Church reproved this kind of marriage if it lacked the solemnities required by civil and ecclesiastical law, and repeatedly applied sanctions to prohibit them (cf. *Causa*, 30, q. 6).

[133] When the politico-philosophical wickedness of the times boasted of its ability to guide Christian nations by a way different from that indicated by

1289. Nevertheless, the forms of marriage, practised mainly in Germany, called *ad morganaticam* or *ad morghengabam* seem to do some insubstantial harm to the fullness of the conjugal union (which implies perfect equality between the spouses). In these marriages, a nobleman marries a woman of lower family status on condition that her children, although legitimate, do not acquire the paternal status or inheritance, but remain in the lower status and are content to receive from the father sufficient for their maintenance.[134]

1290. As I said, this harm is not substantial, because it concerns only external condition and ownership, and must be attributed more to the weakness of social organisation than to individuals who unite in such a lesser union.

b)

Divorce

1291. It is clear that *full union* excludes not only concubinage but also *divorce*; if the union is full, it is perpetual. Those therefore who intend to disunite or believe they can revoke their union are never fully united.

1292. Why then were the Hebrews allowed to divorce? First, civil laws do not necessarily approve what they permit; *to permit* something is not the same as *to approve* it. Even evils are *permitted*, if greater evils are feared by their prohibition. But

the wisdom of the Church, the ancient evil laws of paganism re-appeared. Among the defects of the Napoleonic law on marriage, we must note article 181. This allows spouses to cohabit who have united without free consent, once the constrained party has obtained freedom, and nevertheless dissolve the marriage within six months. Here we have the restoration of legitimate concubinage under conditions worse than those of the Romans. We can make the same observation about articles 183–185.

[134] Cf. Dürr, *Dissert. de Matrimon. aequali vel inaequali personarum illustr. in german.*, Sect. 2, §9 in *Thesaur. Jur. Eccl.*, vol. 6, p. 567, where he condemns such marriages as contrary to *natural Right*, because they deprive the children of the inheritance. I do not think these marriages are contrary to *natural Right* for this reason (cf. *RI*, 1425–1448) but because they do some harm to the fullness of the union in its external consequences.

they do not cease to be evils, and the natural law which disapproves them preserves all its force.[135]

1293. Moreover we must remember what has been said about the immutability of rational law. In its principles, this law is immutable, which explains its name, 'eternal law', but considered in its consequences and application it produces no real obligation unless we grant the factual circumstances supposed by its ideal dictate. The *perfect union*, which forms the essence of marriage, is inferred from the supposed factual circumstance that the nature of man and woman is perfect enough for the perfection of union to be fitting for it.

If this is not the case, that is, if the nature of individual human beings is so vitiated that it can no longer absorb the *fullness of union*, which is required by perfect humanity and suggested to the minds of those who contemplate this union, some *indulgence* is possible. This indulgence permits human beings what in itself is defective. The defect however must be merged with and attributed to the defect of nature itself.

This indeed was the corrupted, defective condition of humanity before the Saviour. Christ says that for this reason the Hebrew legislator permitted his people divorce 'because of the hardness of heart',[136] that is, because their nature was greatly *defective* and incapable of perfect union. The union requires a wise soul and tender heart where the elevated, rational affection, which the blind impetus of the libido opposes, can take root. The nature of the libido, extremely selfish and capricious, seeks only its own delectation, the contrary of true affection which has a noble, altruistic, constant character [*App.*, no. 7].

1294. In the beginning however human beings were constituted perfect by God. Dissolubility of marriage was impossible. Moreover, after the Saviour had restored humanity, the moral element returned with such power that human beings could restrain their libido and nurture pure, rational, holy and divine affection. The Saviour then restored the original law of marriage, a law in keeping with perfect human nature, and still more in keeping with human nature raised to the state of grace

[135] For the difference between what is *permitted* by positive law and what is *lawful*, cf. *ER*, 256–261.
[136] Mt 19: 8; Mk 10: 5.

where human nature can emulate even the angels. In this way the new legislator recalled the marriage of Eden when he said, 'But from the beginning of creation God made them male and female.'[137]

1295. Moses therefore could permit divorce and in the name of God dispense the Hebrews from the rigour of conjugal indissolubility constituted by divine-positive law. He made himself interpreter of rational law by means of a constitution which permitted a writ of repudiation. As we have said, rational Right has various applications dependent on *humanitarian differences*, and does not always produce externally more than a part of the total *obligation* it contains deep within itself. The various applications thus make it give rise to external *titles*, the kind which give force to the law and make it effective.

1296. The re-introduction of the law of divorce into Christian societies is a clear sign of great deterioration of morals, and of a deplorable return to paganism. This law appeared in Europe together with heresy; once nations had renounced the religious faith of their fathers and divided themselves from the Catholic Church, they suddenly felt the need for divorce. Theocratic society and the family were simultaneously lacerated.

In France the law was passed in 1792. Later (1803) the *Napoleonic Code* took up the inheritance of philosophico-revolutionary depravation. The Code, the product of its time, revealed the profound ignorance of busy, confident men when it said with military frankness in the senate, 'It is not true that marriage is indissoluble. THAT HAS NEVER EXISTED.'[138]

1297. The degeneration of morals in England[139] and Prussia[140]

---

[137] Mk 10: 6.

[138] Cf. *Mémoires sur le Consulat*, Thibaudeau, p. 443.

[139] In 1779 the British parliament, shaken by the frequency of divorce (despite its very high costs) and of adultery (the only cause for which a divorce is granted in Britain), sought a way to contain it. Some, including the Duke of Richmond, favoured total abolition of divorce. But Parliament limited itself to making it more difficult, prohibiting divorced adulterers to re-marry within a year. This had no effect, and there were further complaints to Parliament to obtain new provisions.

[140] In the *Gazzetta Piemontese* (17 January 1843) we read the following under the heading: Berlin, 3rd January 1843: 'The Minister De Savigny has just presented to the Council of State the law on divorce accompanied by an

was for a time a cause of alarm to both governments. They were concerned and still are, with limiting or abolishing the laws of divorce.

1298. However, as long as these nations remain separated from the Church, to which England seems to be drawing closer every day, they lack the powerful supernatural principle to restore morals.[141] Hence the prohibition of divorce among them would be similar to the sumptuary laws of the pagan nations: it would be incapable of emending the general degradation.[142]

V.
The principles regulating the law on marriage in the *Napoleonic Code*

1299. I have spoken about the indissolubility of marriage, of the triple reason that determines it (natural, divine-positive,

order of the cabinet prescribing that only the consequences and particular dispositions must be discussed, not the principles of the law which must be held to be invariable. For some time now, it has been observed that requests for divorce have increased alarmingly. Every unhappy spouse wishes to profit from the short period left before the publication of the new law.'

[141] Cf. *SP*, 473–475 for the force of this kind of laws.

[142] An observation of the Viscount de Bonald, although very close to the truth does not actually reach it: '"From the time that supreme wisdom has been perceived by human beings," as J. J. Rousseau says, and the knowledge of one's natural relationships with others has been the basis of the Codes of societies, reason has become public, laws have attained perfection, and customs, far from being correctives to weak, disordered and variable laws, have found their rule in solid, immutable laws. It has thus become possible to overturn the ancients' maxim and say, "What are customs without laws, etc." Not the restoration of customs but the goodness of the laws was all that needed to be awaited' (*Du Divorce, etc., Résumé* §9). I said that this observation did not entirely attain the truth because it supposes that human beings can conform their customs to the best laws, granted they know them. The reason however why Christian nations can amend their customs in keeping with the laws is not because they know them but because the *moral virtue*, the practical force of their will, has grown. If this decreases, as it clearly has among heretics or among peoples guided by wickedness, the mind itself becomes darkened and no longer sees which laws are perfect. In fact, Bonald himself did not succeed in persuading his fellow citizens that the law on divorce was a very bad law, and it was passed.

sacramental), of its two levels (ratified, or ratified and consummated marriage), and of the serious defects which violate this most holy law of conjugal society. It will be helpful now to offer some thoughts about the system adopted by French legislators who claimed to split Christian marriage into two marriages: one before political authority and obligatory under civil law, the other before Church authority, not obligatory under civil law but left to the individual's conscience.

1300. I think I can reasonably state that the French system *splits marriage into two marriages* rather than *separates the ecclesiastical effects from the civil*, which is the phrase normally used to describe what occurs. In the eyes of the law and government, civil marriage is the *marriage itself*, not a complex of its civil *effects*; if not, *marriage* would be outside the law, which would deal only with its effects. Napoleonic law makes no distinction between marriage and the double series of ecclesiastical and civil effects. If it did, it would have to abandon marriage to nature and the Church, and thus acknowledge that true marriage takes place independently of the law. In this case and provided the conjugal bond was always safeguarded, the law could only determine its civil consequences, such as inheritances, protection of the mutual rights of the spouses, relationships with relatives. But the law, far from acknowledging and being indifferent to this bond made independently of it, not only positively acknowledges it, but disapproves and punishes it and, in certain cases determined by law, claims to separate the spouses by external coercion.

1301. For example, in the case of a marriage between a woman and a young man who has not completed his 18th birthday, or between a man and a young girl who has not completed her 15th birthday, the *Code* allows[143] the spouses, interested parties and the ministry of public affairs to bring an action for dissolution.[144]

Marriage itself is in fact dissolved by the use of public authority and force. The law is not passive and indifferent, restricting itself solely to the civil effects of marriage. Under the pretext of civil effects, the law recognises and tolerates only civil marriage and thus has the conjugal union itself as its object. Hence, to

---

[143] *Cod.*, art. 144.

[144] *Cod.*, art. 184.

pretend that the Napoleonic law concerns only the civil effects of marriage and not marriage itself is a poor deception.[145]

Let us therefore examine this system that divides marriage into *ecclesiastical* and *civil*. The law pretends a total ignorance of *ecclesiastical marriage*, and intends to sanction only *civil marriage*, even when civil marriage tends to destroy the former or is separated from it. On what legal principles is this unprecedented system founded? Can such principles be the foundation of an equable and reasonable civil legislation?

1302. These questions should have been thoroughly discussed and settled by the French law-makers. But they did nothing of the kind. Instead, secure in their prejudices, they disdained these questions; without any investigation or mature consideration, they gratuitously based the principles of their legislation on the popular philosophical opinions of the time. They would have been ashamed to doubt these opinions, which they consecrated by acclamation without any examination.

Let us see how the Counsellor of State, Portalis, in a few, confident words, expounds these wonderful principles as the basis of the law on marriage:

> Under the *ancien régime* civil and religious institutions were closely united. Learned magistrates acknowledged that they could be separated, and had requested the

---

[145] What I have said is confirmed by the initial principle of Portalis, Counsellor of State, in *Esposizione de' motivi della legge del matrimonio*: 'If the ministers of the Church can and must watch over the sanctity of the sacrament, the civil power alone has the right of WATCHING OVER the validity of the contract.' Here, 'watch over' by the civil power means that it alone determines all the conditions for the validity of the contract. This softer phrase is used to conceal more effectively the introduction of a deadly error. But 1. Portalis' words demonstrate a great ignorance of what Catholics believe about marriage. Catholics believe that there cannot be a valid conjugal contract without a sacrament. Portalis' principle is therefore contrary to Catholic dogma. 2. It seems derisory to affirm that the ministers of the Church must watch over the sanctity of the sacrament when a law is being made which renders such vigilance impossible, a law which establishes certain unions as marriages that the Church does not in any way recognise as sacramental or holy; on the contrary, the Church sees them as wicked unions, as reprehensible concubinage, which cannot in any way be marriages whose sanctity, according to our legislator, the ministers of the Church CAN AND MUST WATCH OVER.

[1302]

independence of the civil state from the cult professed by human beings. This change encountered great obstacles. Later, freedom of cults was proclaimed, and it now became possible to secularise legislation. The grand idea was conceived that we must tolerate all that Providence tolerates, and that the law, which cannot force the religious opinions of citizens, must refer only to French people as such, in the way that nature refers only to human beings as such.

(Session of the Senate, 16 ventôse, year 11 (7th March 1803))

This short passage contains all that has been said by these legislators in order to justify their system of *civil marriage* with its absolute neglect of ecclesiastical marriage. But should a philosophico-legal theory, intended as the foundation of the complete *marriage right* of a nation, be treated so briefly and superficially? If a building's foundations are unsafe, the whole structure is in danger. There is nothing in fact in the passage that bears serious philosophical examination. The following few observations should convince any reasonable person of this.

1303. 1. First, we have the authority of *learned magistrates* who recognised the possibility of separating civil from ecclesiastical institutions. If the question can be dealt with in this way the authorities alluded to should have been more precisely indicated; a general reference is not sufficient. Authorities should have been compared and evaluated. And *magistrates* should not be the only authority referred to; philosophers and theologians should have been mentioned, particularly in view of the stated wish not to harm anyone's religion. Portalis had confessed, shortly before the quoted passage:

All nations involved heaven in a contract that had so much influence on the future of spouses. Because the contract united present and future, it seemed to make their happiness depend on a series of uncertain events which, if verified, were understood as a special blessing. In contingencies such as these, our hopes and fears always invoke the aid of religion which, lying between heaven and earth, fills the immense space in between.

Portalis should have added that Catholic Christians (the great majority of French people) regard marriage as a sacrament

[1303]

instituted by the Saviour whom they adore. Granted all this, the only people who could have enlightened the legislators in their attempt to make civil laws without harm to religion were theologians, who alone know religion fully.

But the competent authority was not heard; the relevant doctrine was referred to but not discussed. Simply saying that, under the *ancient régime*, some learned magistrates requested the separation of civil and ecclesiastical institutions is really little more than words. The magistrates should have at least been named. It should also have been shown that throughout the ages learned magistrates, who have always existed, held the same opinion. What kind of authority in fact could magistrates offer who were imbued with a philosophy of wickedness that advised the separation of religion simply because it took no account of religion and the authority of the Church which indeed it eagerly sought and planned to destroy?

1304. 2. According to Portalis, these nameless magistrates had acknowledged the *possibility* of the *separation* of civil from ecclesiastical institutions. But we need to discover and seriously discuss whether what is possible is also helpful and fitting. A law-maker must prescribe what is shown to be opportune, not what is merely possible.

1305. Moreover, the phrase, 'the separation of civil and religious institutions' is not clear enough. 'Separation' means that two things can be separated and yet continue in beautiful harmony, or be separated according to a prearranged and predetermined mutual opposition. They can also be separated in such a way that one acts independently of the other, as if the other did not exist. When this happens, they act in random agreement or disagreement; in other words, their agreement or disagreement is purely accidental, without any deliberation or foresight. If a *separation* were desired between civil and ecclesiastical institutions relative to marriage, the principal, substantial question to be discussed is: 'Which of the three systems of separation must be chosen?' But we see no mention at all of such an essential, real question. It does not even enter the minds of the legislators! They do not discuss it in any way; guided by the instinct of the times, they go straight to the third of the three systems with such promptness and certainty that it seems the only one possible. Their own marriage legislation is indeed separated from the ecclesiastical, but in such a way that it very often contradicts and openly challenges the latter. The law-makers evidently did not see that their legislation was inconsistent with the principle they used to justify it, namely, that 'there was no question of making a law hostile to religion, but simply of separating civil from ecclesiastical institutions.' Because of this negligence and forgetfulness they did much more than they intended. Certainly, the principle of *separation* in itself does not entail the opposition which the civil Code introduced between the State and the Catholic Christian Church. Hence this principle was not sufficient to justify the law promulgated on marriage.

1306. 3. A similar observation must be made about Portalis' next words, where he says that magistrates under the Bourbons

> had requested that the civil status of human beings be independent of the cult they profess.

These words are equivocal, and in no way suitable for justifying the Napoleonic law on marriage. The civil status of human beings can certainly be independent of the cult they profess, and when determined by law need not in the slightest offend that cult. The question that should be discussed (and they should have discussed) is: 'What kind of independence is involved, and how can it be brought about?' If it is independence pure and simple, the civil status of human beings is independent of the cult they profess whenever the law grants the followers of a cult the status of citizenship. But it is one thing for the law to grant civil status to human beings which avoids any clash between that status and the different cults they profess, and another to grant them a civil status incompatible with and offensive to their cult. The Napoleonic law, however, as it stands, claims to be not only independent of a person's cult but able to force human beings to violate it; in fact it positively seeks *to protect* all those who wish to violate their cult against those who wish to uphold it. Let us suppose that a Catholic Frenchwoman, after making a solemn vow of chastity, has married civilly. The law forcibly defends this sacrilegious marriage; it sanctions it, claims to sanctify it and founds a happy, moral family upon it! The marriage, which in the eyes of the Church is null and non-existent, is not only tolerated by the civil law in the way civil law tolerates

[1306]

disorders, but is protected by the authority of the law and upheld by its force in the way that good actions are protected and supported. Now let us suppose that the woman, repenting of her fault, wants to separate from the man in order to observe the prescriptions of religion or, as the French legislators improperly say, of HER CULT . Despite being torn by remorse, she cannot do this; she is not free to profess the duties attached to her religious belief. On the appeal of the man with whom she is living, and whom the law declares to be her true husband despite her Catholic cult, she is FORCED to live with him AGAINST HER OWN CONSCIENCE, which clearly tells her she is in a state of grave sin.

This law therefore lies when it claims to be liberal and tolerant to all cults. It is not liberal or tolerant in any way; on the contrary it cruelly forces consciences. In the above example, it uses brute force to abolish Catholic cult and violently constrains a Catholic person to violate her cult. It is not a law *separated* from cult but *inimical* to it. It does not give human beings a civil status independent of the cult they profess, but a status that is offensive and destructive of their cult. It is therefore false that the law wishes to prescind from cult; instead, it wishes to enslave and tyrannise it.

Consequently, if Counsellor Portalis' words are reduced to a formula coherent with the law they defend, and are contained in the tenor of the law, they are as follows: Civil law is *mixed* with everyone's religion when the law takes care not to offend it, and is *separate* from their religion when the law does not care about offending and destroying it. We want civil law to be separate, that is, for religion to depend on and give way to the law. We want civil law to be able to modify and destroy religion, in the way it wants.

This is the *separation* of civil from ecclesiastical institutions which the French empire speaks about, the *civil status*, *independent* of everyone's religion, which was used as a basis for law on marriage. It is truly *secularised* legislation, as the legislators were so pleased to call it.

1307. 4. From all this we see very clearly that Counsellor Portalis introduces without any need whatsoever the *freedom of cults* into his exposition of the reasons for the law. As I said, there is no intention whatsoever of allowing this freedom. In fact, the Napoleonic law on marriage does not allow *freedom of cults*. On the contrary it destroys this freedom because in many cases, as we have seen, it forces consciences. The principle of the freedom of cults is valid, but a law that despotically clamps its iron hand on all cults is invalid; by restricting them, it enslaves and tends to annihilate the Catholic cult in people's consciences.

1308. 5. The same applies to the words that follow. Evidently, Counsellor Portalis wants to explain the nature of freedom of cults:

> A great idea was conceived that we must tolerate everything Providence tolerates, and that the law, which cannot force the religious opinions of citizens, must refer only to French people as such, just as nature refers only to human beings as such.

These few words, typical of our times, are evidence of hasty thought; they are empty rhetoric and totally lack solid legislative knowledge. Is it really true that 'a great idea has been conceived that we must tolerate everything Providence tolerates'? Does Providence tolerate evil? If Portalis means that Providence tolerates evil in the sense that Providence lets evil go unpunished, he is mistaken. In this sense Providence does not permit any evil at all; on the contrary, Providence prohibits evil by rational and positive laws and in due time punishes it in the other life. Even in this life, Providence works through scourges and remedial chastisements and has charged the Church to apply such remedies. Either we grant the first part of this thesis or we renounce natural religion; the second part is admitted at least by Catholics. The human legislator certainly cannot take Providence as his model; Providence punishes all evil and tolerates none. Civil law cannot do this — what a disaster it would be if civil law ever presumed to emulate Providence!

1309. If however Portalis means that Providence tolerates evil because it allows human beings the *physical freedom* to produce evil, civil law can only imitate Providence. It has no power to do otherwise, even if it wished. Civil law cannot despoil human beings of the freedom to do good as well as evil; no human being has this power.

1310. Finally, if Portalis is talking about the *external execution* of evil, the evils tolerated by Providence are those which are factually committed. Thus in peoples unrestrained by civil law, Providence tolerates the factual commission of many evils which could have been prevented by civil laws. But Providence certainly does not tolerate all these evils among peoples whose civil laws suppress certain evils, and prevent others. Indeed, Providence uses these civil laws as second cause to prevent evils and does in fact prevent them. In this sense it cannot be said that 'civil law must tolerate all the evils tolerated by Providence.' On the contrary, good sense tells us that 'Providence tolerates the evils that civil law tolerates' by allowing the law not to repress them for causes far more noble than those possible to a human legislator.

1311. 6. But even further away from correct reasoning and legislative wisdom is the statement that

> the law must refer only to French people as such — just as nature refers only to human beings as such — because the law cannot force religious opinions.

I grant and readily accept the last principle that 'the civil law cannot force religious opinions.' However, this proposition has no logical relationship with that which it follows and from which it is deduced. The law cannot and must not force religious opinions. But there is no forcing of religious opinions when Catholics are recognized as Catholics and Protestants as Protestants; in fact the very opposite applies. The law can and must refer both to French people as such and to Catholics and Protestants. The law, if it deliberately ignores them, risks offending them. Law, which must never be blind but examine carefully all that exists, has to acknowledge Catholics and Protestants to protect them, but without ever forcing the religious opinions of either party. If religious opinions were forced, Protestants could be constrained to become Catholics, and viceversa; this cannot and must not happen. Again, forcing religious opinions would mean forcibly making Catholics or Protestants act contrary to their religious persuasions and opinions; they would be forced to neglect what they consider their sacred duties, and to commit what, according to their religion, is sin.

In keeping with contemporary practice, the Napoleonic law on marriage has been proclaimed as a consequence of the principle that 'the law cannot force religious opinions.' But the law is so far from fulfilling this principle that it forcibly prevents Catholics (not to mention others) from fulfilling their most sacred duties, which it actually constrains them to infringe. Two Catholics who have married without their parents' consent are, according to their religious opinions, validly married and have satisfied all the obligations of a true marriage. This is certified by the teaching of the Catholic religion they profess. Religious faith is a fact that cannot be invented by law-makers, who must accept it as it is. If civil legislators claimed to determine the nature of the Catholic religion without reference to the common faith and decision of the Church (the reference point of the common faith), they would no longer be dealing with actual, existing Catholic religion but with a new religion which they themselves had invented to suit their needs. In our example, this is not the religion professed by the couple married without paternal consent. Their religion teaches as an undeniable fact that they must live together, help each other and perform all other conjugal duties, and cannot enter another marriage. This is what their cult and the dictate of their conscience commands. Catholic parents who press their own case fail in the duties of their faith; because of their irreligious stand, the law[146] forcibly separates the couple, prevents them from fulfilling their duties and robs them of their happiness. The civil law punishes the couple's fault against the law by *violating their religious opinions*, and forcibly tries to make them believe they are not married — a belief which they cannot hold without renouncing their faith!

Viceversa, if children of cousins german marry, their marriage, according to the decrees of the Catholic religion, is invalid; it is incestuous concubinage. Let us suppose that the more irreligious partner wishes to continue in the crime, while the other repents and wishes to end the cohabitation reproved by a dictate of conscience. The civil law immediately comes to the aid of the irreligious partner and brutally forces the other to cohabit. All this is done in the name of freedom of cults and sensitive observation of the principle that the civil law does not force

---

[146] *N. Cod.*, art. 182.

religious beliefs. Is it possible that responsible legislators were unaware of the contradictions involved?

1312. 7. Is it wise to try to separate the believer, the Frenchman and the human being, as Portalis claims can and must be done? Is this not one of those abstractions as harmful in practice as they are false in theory?

If you claim that the civil law applies solely to the French as such and not to human beings, the French will be merely abstract beings in the eyes of the law. In this case the law, in keeping with this principle, will sanction dispositions contrary to the Right of nature. If the law fails to consider the French as human beings first, and then as citizens, it will be unable to respect natural Right. The same must be said about the attribute of believer: if the law ignores this attribute, it is liable to offend religious beliefs, and thus inevitably harm *the French* in what they in fact hold most precious and dear, their faith. Certainly French law must consider the French as such, but not as abstract beings. They must be considered as they are, with all their particularities and real attributes, which become titles of law (cf. *RI*, 288, 576–577), and without which the French do not exist.

8. The legislator errs therefore when he makes the citizen an abstraction. He cannot in fact do this, even if he wishes. He can only posit the nebulous theory as a principle, and then forget the theory entirely when he expounds the laws; common sense, not empty speculation, must be his guide. As soon as the French legislator begins to declaim, the philosopher disappears; but once he begins to draw up laws, human common sense fortunately returns. French legislators have done little indeed to uphold Monsieur Portalis' principle that the law must deal only with *the French* as such. If the law had done this, the first title of the *Code*: 'The enjoyment and deprivation of civil rights' would have sufficed. But it did not take kindly to the poor philosophy imposed upon it at the start; it gently shook itself free from the limitation imposed by sole consideration of the *common attribute*, French, and necessarily took into account a great number of *special attributes*, for example, those of parent and child, of spouse, of elder and minor, of owner and of a person bound by an agreement. In the eyes of this and all other laws, each of these special attributes determines a distinct class of French people, not French people as such. For each of these classes many

dispositions were laid down which determined the obligations and rights of the class, as well as the form of entry into or exit from it. All this is undeniable. These kinds of special attributes and conditions were acknowledged without any possible alternative; the laws made for each of the classes would have been useless if enacted only for French people as such.

However, the legislators, when dealing with the special *religious* attribute and status of the French, and the classification of the people according to their cults (as they had been classified according to all the other particularities), declared that the law 'must deal only with the French as such'! The one special attribute of the French on which legislation bestowed the odious privilege of exemption, was the religious attribute; the sole reason adduced to justify this omission was the lie that the law dealt only with the French as such. This shows the partiality and weakness of logic in minds prejudiced from birth by religious antipathies.

1313. 9. Granted, then, for the moment that civil law recognises in citizens special attributes that can be distinguished into different classes, and determines the jural duties pertaining to each of these classes and protects their rights; granted also that civil law considers it necessary to exclude the classification founded on religious beliefs and not to protect the rights proper to these beliefs; the justification for this cannot be founded on 1. freedom of cults, or 2. the independent civil state of religious opinions, or 3. the separation desired between religious and civil institutions, or finally 4. the principle that the law deals only with the French as such, just as nature deals only with human beings as such. All these so-called reasons are simply phrases inapplicable to the French law on marriage.

The law considers the French as classified in many ways but not according to the cults they profess. The French, however, do profess these cults, and the right to profess them is expressly granted by the political law which proclaims and upholds in principle the freedom of cults. It is clear, therefore, that the civil law, if it wishes to prescind from the cults professed by the French, must not disturb the people by violating religious opinion and its consequences. On the contrary, it must leave everyone's conscience free to act in conformity with everything prescribed by his cult — something the law itself promises to do, and prides itself on doing.

The French legislators have only one way, consistent with their principles, to fulfil this duty and remain coherent: they must determine nothing about marriage which is prescribed by special cults. They must either leave the ordering of marriage to these cults or limit themselves to determining only that part of marriage in which all cults professed by the French agree, now or in the future. This is the only way open to the legislators based on their principles. If individual cults professed by the French impose obligations that are special and proper to their followers but not common to the followers of other cults and religions, either 1. the civil laws will recognize what is obligatory regarding marriage for the followers of individual cults (in this case, the laws contradict their principle of not wishing to consider the attribute of believer in the French as such and of not classifying them according to their professed beliefs), or 2. they start forcing those who profess different cults to follow the same norms in matters which, in the different cults, have different norms (in this case, civil laws now contradict their other principle of freedom of conscience, because the people must choose between renouncing their cult or violating the civil law). We see therefore that, if the law is to uphold the two principles it has proposed to follow, it must refrain from determining anything in all those matters and cases in which the individual cults determine and impose obligations on their followers relative to marriage, and every other object. But the *Napoleonic Code* does nothing of the sort: in many cases it forces Catholic couples to separate when their cult obliges them to stay together; in many other cases, it obliges them to live together when their cult obliges them to separate. It is not a liberal, but a despotic, tyrannical law; it shows contempt for people when it tells them to do all this in the name of freedom of cults and out of delicacy, and not to force religious opinions or consciences.

1314. 10. However, no wise legislator would in my opinion exempt the civil law from determining the constitutive elements of marriage and mutual rights of spouses in certain parts concerning religious opinions. Real legislative wisdom must carefully consider the two facets of the problem it has to solve: 1. it must not harm the religious belief of the citizens (freedom of cults);[147] and 2. it must determine the constitutive elements of marriage and the mutual duties and rights of spouses, and sanction them by its authority for the good of families and the State. The problem is solved when the laws enacted uphold these two conditions. It is clear that legislative wisdom is obliged to classify subjects according to their cults, as it is in many other ways. It must also apply to each cult dispositions coherent both with the cult and with rational Right which contribute to the greater good of both family and civil society. If civil law concerning marriage truly professes freedom of cults, it never forces a Catholic man and woman to live together as husband and wife when the Catholic religion does not recognise them as such and obliges them in conscience to separate; in this case even the civil law itself will decide for their separation. If the civil law were to remain silent on the matter, justice and the private sanction of rights would become necessary, and human beings would return to the state of nature. Similarly, civil law will never force two spouses to separate whom the Catholic religion declares to be married and obliges to live together; on the contrary, it will sanction the union. I repeat, any silence on the part of civil law in the matter would be dangerously defective. The faithful could only compensate for this defect by an association of their own, by a Code written by themselves or based on experience, by an external force of their own. Indeed, every community of the faithful has a full right to provide for the order and safety of their mutual rights when these are not safeguarded by public law. Consequently, when the wise legislator has to draw up dispositions on marriage, the sole, equable and wise thing for him to do, from the point of view of legal, religious and cult aspects, is to sanction what the State-recognised religions prescribe. This has been done recently by His Majesty Charles Albert, King of Sardinia, in his new Code.

[147] The reader should recall what I said about the obligation of civil society to respect individual rights (cf. *RI*, 1649–1688), and particularly rights relative to the religion professed by individuals, rights that are innate and truly imprescriptible (cf. *RI*, 167–238) if the religion is essentially moral and true, as the Catholic religion is. To use the law as justification for violations of a human being's most sacred rights is bombastic nonsense. *Civil law* has no more authority than the *society* that enacts it. *Civil law* therefore can never be a means for violating the supreme rights of individual human beings.

[1314]

1315. 11. I will add a last observation which to me seems important. The mental process by which the French legislators established a law so much at variance with the Catholicism of the great majority of the nation can easily be identified in the long passage of Portalis' *Exposizione de' motivi* where he tries to show that

> the Catholic Church does not have *per se* the faculty to apply diriment impediments; this faculty belongs solely to the civil State.

The logical error here lies in Portalis' failure to understand that the *Catholic religion*, like every other religion professed by human beings, is A FACT. As we know, a fact is verified not by reasoning but solely by trustworthy witnesses. In other words, we need to ask the followers of the religion in question what they profess to believe. It is absurd to try to show that they believe other than what they say, and even more absurd to prescribe what they must believe. This would be tantamount to imposing a new religion on them without recognising the old religion, particularly if the latter had existed for many centuries. *The fact* therefore to be verified in Portalis' case is this: 'Do Catholic Christians believe that the faculty to apply diriment impediments to marriage pertains to the State (as Portalis claims) or solely to the Church, or is it common to both State and Church?'

Catholics (and it is Catholic faith we are discussing) reply that they believe what the universal Church believes, that is, what the Church and the Sovereign Pontiff (the visible head of the Church) declare must be believed. Portalis has certainly not acted in this logical manner; he has made no effort to consult either the Councils or the perennial authority in the Church, the Sovereign Pontiff, who has complete right to declare what Catholics must truly believe. He is content to argue totally on his own account, to refer to a few decrees of Roman emperors and other princes and to divide the question up as he pleases. He is fully aware that he is addressing an audience which has no desire to contradict him and is probably incapable of doing so. Instead of acting as a historian, he makes the great mistake of playing a role as theologian, laying down what, according to him, Catholics are to believe instead of investigating what they really believe. In place of the existing Catholic cult, he has simply substituted another so-called Catholic cult, improvised on the spur of the moment. This is a danger to which unfortunately jurists are continually subject. They can of course easily avoid it by not undertaking a mission they have not been given; instead of determining the *fact* of faith, they should be content to verify it with fitting and logical modesty. I repeat, this fact can be verified only by listening to what the Church teaches. In order to discover, therefore, whether Catholicism entails belief that a particular union of man and woman is a true, ratified and sacramental marriage with the consequent obligations of the spouses to fulfil their conjugal duties, it is sufficient, in case of doubt, to ask the Pope, whom all Catholics believe themselves obliged to believe and obey. Thus the Council of Trent quite logically defined: 'If anyone should say that marriage cases do not pertain to ecclesiastical judges, let him be anathema.'[148] This is natural because, properly speaking, it would be contrary to good sense for any lawmaker to think that his own witness to what Catholics factually believe is more trustworthy than the witness of the Church or of the Pope who presides as teacher over the whole Church.

1316. Portalis will reply that this harms the imprescriptible rights of civil authority. I answer: do these rights contain the right to enslave the religious cults of the citizens to whom the laws are given? If such a right does not and cannot exist, particularly in the eyes of one who proclaims the freedom of cults, civil authority must clearly halt when any further movement would restrict the cults; religious cults obviously put a natural limit on civil authority whose rights cease where the rights of cults begin.

1317. To claim that civil authority can disregard cults means we desire the destruction, not the freedom of cults, under the despotism of the law.

1318. In the case of Catholic cult there is a further difficulty, because this cult, or rather, faith, does not change or undergo modification. The whole of the Catholic religion must be either accepted and respected, or abolished;[149] either Catholics must be

---

[148] Sess. 24, *De Sacram. Matrim.*, can. 12.

[149] Mons. Marchetti has made a very just observation on this matter in his extremely sound work, *Della Chiesa quanto allo Stato politico della città*: 'A

allowed to believe and always obey in every circumstance the Church, or the persecutions of Nero and Julian must be repeated. There is no other choice; only the greatest idiocy would think a *via media* possible.

B.
The unicity of the spouses

I.
Marriage must be between one man and one woman

a)
Demonstrated from the notion of marriage

1319. A consequence of the notion of marriage, which I have made to consist in 'a full union between man and woman befitting human nature' is that marriage entails only one man and one woman. The union would not be full 'if the woman did not give herself totally and exclusively to the man' or 'if the man did not give himself totally and exclusively to the woman', but each had many carnal affections.

1320. The union of the sexes is the specific part of conjugal union. If the woman is not entirely the man's, she cannot render the resulting debt according to his will; the man therefore is not owner of the woman's body. Similarly, if the man is not entirely the woman's, he cannot render the debt according to her will; she is no longer owner of her husband's body. This contradicts the concept of marriage.

1321. Moreover, there is a union of persons between spouses.

civil society can make innumerable sacrifices of temporal goods without destroying itself, even without ceasing to prosper in its order. True religion on the other hand (with the exception of some variable modification in economy, whose forced cessation or suspension is however contrary to the analogy of faith) destroys itself if it fails in the slightest way in just one of its principles, because truth is one and indivisible' (*Conferenza* 8, sec. 1). In this fine conference, the prelate shows that 'the first and greatest good to be established in the secular body is that of religion'. Religion is therefore a natural, inevitable limit to civil authority.

Although persons are unique and incommunicable, they do have a way of possessing each other. This, however, is so exclusive that a person cannot be possessed unless only one person is possessed by one person. This unicity produces the most exquisite feeling possible from the love of two persons of different sex.

b)
Demonstrated by the analysis of the phenomenon of jealousy

1322. If in addition we observe the feelings of human nature, we will be convinced that it is constituted and ordered in such a way that only an exclusive union between one male and female will satisfy it. One of these feelings is jealousy. I will analyse this extraordinary feeling because feelings are the *facts* in which, as I have said, rights are founded.[150]

1323. *Jealousy* is a feeling which is for the most part *subjective*. Thus it does not have the moral nobility of purely objective feelings.

1324. But what is its place among subjective feelings?

Jealousy arises from the *feeling of exclusive possession*. The spouses' reciprocal feeling of exclusive possession has two parts:

1. The natural *desire* of each to possess the other exclusively.

2. The *claimed right* of each so that offence is given if one withdraws from the other's exclusive possession. The consequence is *jural resentment* (cf. *RI*, 489).

1325. This feeling of jealousy is the fear in one spouse that the other may perhaps withdraw from full possession. It is a fear that the desire for exclusive possession of the other may be frustrated, with violation of the right they each feel they have to full possession.

Jealousy is therefore a feeling of fear which can change into grief, anger, etc., in which are mingled two other feelings: that of exclusive *possession* and of jural *ownership*.

---

[150] *ER*, 252–255 where I showed that the third constitutive element of right is feeling. Cf. also *ER*, 332–339 and *RI*, 387.

1326. Each of these two feelings can be analysed further. An analysis of the *right of ownership* is found in *individual Right* (cf. *RI*, 921–975), where we saw that this right is formed of two elements: *ownership as feeling* (fact of nature) and *ownership as right* (fact of nature, regulated and limited by law).[151]

The first and essential characteristic of *ownership as feeling* is *exclusivity* (cf. *RI*, 947). Consequently, the feeling of ownership of a spouse's body is itself truly exclusive. In other words, it is constituted by the feeling which naturally speaking accompanies and establishes every kind of ownership.

Ownership as right is *de facto* ownership to the extent permitted and protected by the moral law. The moral law neither forbids nor limits the mutual exclusive ownership of spouses; on the contrary, it protects this ownership and invests it with the dignity of right.

1327. Moreover, the *feeling of exclusive possession of one's spouse* has an exclusivity of its own, different from that which it derives from the aforementioned exclusivity of ownership. The exclusivity tied to such possession arises from the nature of the double object: 1. personal union, and 2. sexual union. These two objects are the extreme parts of the full union of man with woman; other parts may not require exclusivity, but, as we have seen, these two certainly require it.

1328. *Personal union*, in addition to being a most intimate union, is also the noblest of *subjective feelings*; it unites the subjects at the level of their higher and more excellent activities.

Sexual union is a less noble union and not the principal one; it is a spontaneous consequence of the union of persons clothed in flesh.

1329. These two exclusive unions produce the feeling of *exclusive possession in the spouses*, a feeling that has therefore both a noble and ignoble element. Thus, the fear that the feeling might be frustrated (jealousy) is a mixture of something noble

---

[151] Note, *ownership as right* produces *opinion of right* which arouses *feeling of right*. Feeling of right is thus a rational feeling, caused by some conception in the intellective principle. On the other hand, *feeling of de facto ownership* is an animal feeling arising from the unitive force or *unifying* faculty of the animal. Cf. *AMS*, 455–483.

and something material and ignoble. It is similar to human nature, one part of which touches heaven, the other, earth.

1330. We see therefore:

1. That the phenomenon of jealousy is not manifested when human beings seek carnal delight only.[152] As the feeling diminishes, behaviour gradually deteriorates and people find interchange amongst spouses less abhorrent.

2. On the other hand while upright morality makes *exclusive possession* of one's spouse more precious and therefore causes jealousy, it also diminishes the *fear* of losing exclusive possession because each spouse is sure of the other's fidelity. This causes the reduction and even the cessation of jealousy.

3. Again, jealousy is less apparent where the intellectual faculties are less developed, because intellectual development greatly increases the union *of persons*; it opens the way to many aroused and stimulated affections, stirring up jealous doubts in the imagination, that most evil of fabricators.

4. Jealousy increases as the strength of sexual love increases, provided this love is united with the noblest of loves. As we said, possession in the sexual union is, of its nature, exclusive.

5. Feeling and objective affection modify and limit subjective affections which are not as noble as objective affections.

---

[152] I said that the feeling of jealousy involves a *feeling of possession* and an *opinion of right*. Corruption of behaviour causes the *feeling of possession* to diminish but not the *opinion of right*. The phenomenon of jealousy therefore is modified according to the proportion of its two feelings of *possession* and *right*. Among the Malayan peoples of the archipelagos of the great ocean, the husbands often prostitute their wives. This shows the total absence of the *feeling of exclusive possession*. The infidelities of wives, however, committed without the husband's command, are punished by death (Bougainville, *deuxième partie*, c. 3, t. 2, p. 58). Here, the existence of the *feeling of exclusive right* is evident. The same is true about the jealousy shown by the North American savages, a bronze-coloured race (Mackenzie, *Premier voyage*, t. 1, p. 282–283; *Deuxième voyage*, t. 2, p. 199–200; Hearne, *Voyage à l'océan du Nord*, c. 9; S. Long, c. 10; La Pérouse, t. 2, bk. 7; Fleurien, *Voyage du capitaine Marchand*, t. 2, c. 4; Charlevoix, *N. Franc*, bks. 3 and 8; Hannepin, *Moeurs des sauvages de la Louisiane*, p.38). Some explorers have written that the feeling of jealousy is totally absent from the Indians of lower Canada, California and the tropics. If this is true, it would mean that these people have fallen to ultimate degradation. Cf. Lahontan, t. 2, p. 139; La Pérouse, t. 2, c. 11, t. 4, p. 61; Azara, t. 2, c. 10.

Thus, where there is great charity, jealousy does not exist or is suppressed and even totally prevented from expressing itself.

1331. We conclude. Jealousy is a *natural feeling*. This feeling shows that human nature is so constituted that, wherever it is not totally depraved, it requires unicity of the spouses. In this unicity, spouses find the most desirable and exquisite good of their union; without it marriage does not bring contentment.

c)
Demonstrated by the duty of fidelity

1332. In all nations, the conjugal union of man and woman has always been effected by an oath of mutual fidelity, with an appeal to the divinity as vindicator of the fidelity.

1333. The duty of *mutual fidelity*, therefore, acknowledged in all regions and throughout time, shows that, in keeping with the deepest and most upright feeling of the human race, marriage must be between one man and one woman.

II.
Reprehensible practices opposed to the unicity of the spouses: polyandry and polygamy

1334. The practices opposed to the rational, natural law of the unicity of the spouses are *polyandry* and *polygamy*.

1335. Those who maintained that polygamy was not forbidden by *natural law* began from a very imperfect concept of this law. I believe that *natural law* results from the fusion of all the feelings of human nature.[153] However, these feelings have a varying degree of exigency and, because of the defective actuation of nature, also have some exceptions when suppressed or weakened, or altered in a whole people,.

1336. In fact, a defect of the Hebrew people (and not only of the Hebrews), σκληροκαρδια [hardness of heart], made the plurality of wives tolerable. But Christ added charity to the human will and refined the heart. Thus, ever since his time, the

---

[153] By nature I do not mean defective nature (cf. 982); St. John Chrysostom states: 'You must not take opinions and judgments about things from those whose spirit is corrupt.'

defective condition which can justify and excuse the practice of polygamy no longer exists in baptised peoples [*App.*, no. 8].

1337. Hence, Benedict XIV quite rightly reproved the opinion of some theologians[154] and philosophers who maintained that polygamy was not alien to natural Right:

> It cannot be said that this extraordinary opinion was proscribed by the Council of Trent. The Council condemned the opinion only of those who denied that polygamy was condemned by divine Right. — Nevertheless this teaching cannot avoid being censured as improbable and alien to the common opinion of other theologians.[155] — On the other hand, there are those who, on solid grounds, after placing monogamy on the part of the man among natural precepts of the second class, maintain that monogamy on the part of the woman pertains to precepts of the first class. They argue that a woman joined to several husbands has great difficulty begetting offspring, and that her children are subject to many dangers in their education; furthermore, we read in the Old Testament that many holy men were joined to several wives simultaneously, but find no case of a holy woman having several husbands simultaneously.[156]

1338. The evils consequent upon polygamy are very great, as several writers indicate. Meli says:

> Polygamy shortens human life and makes the polygamist timid, base, pusillanimous and inept. We all know that normally polygamy is practised where there is a scandalous trade in women. A man who has bought one or more women for himself cannot become a husband when he has been a despotic master. Throughout the East, women, if unprocurable in the public markets, are bought from their parents by a husband who pays a dowry or *kalim* as it is called. These unfortunate women will never be the companions and equals of the man, and the men themselves, who share their heart or rather their pleasures with many women, are not compensated by true friendship and sincere love from any of the women. Thus, in polygamy,

---

[154] Durandus and the theologian of Avila.

[155] *S. T.*, *Suppl*, q. 65, 1; Bellarm., *De sacr. matr.*, bk. 1, c. 10 ss.; Estius, *In L. 4 Sent.*, Dist. 33, §q1 ss.; Sylvius, *in Suppl S. Th.*, q. 65, 1 ss.

[156] *De Synodo Dioec.*, bk. 13, c. 21.

women are not wives, companions or friends of the man; they are not the comfort of his life, intimate confidantes of his heart, and beneficent, sensitive helpers in his woes. Nor does their tenderness multiply his joys, reduce his troubles, and support him in declining age. Women, as the wretched instruments of his voluptuosity, are never sufficiently humiliated. This domestic despotism, exercised over woman by man, supports and maintains the despotism of the civil State. All historians and philosophers have noted the barbarism of those societies in which woman does not share everything with man. For this reason, Procopius and Ammianus Marcellinus describe polygamous nations as the most pitilessly ferocious in all their actions.[157]

Just as love is monogamous, so polygamy pertains to lust[158] or certainly to an affection different from love.

1339. Polyandry is even more contrary to nature because it is an impediment to the begetting of offspring, and involves the servitude of men to women, just as polygamy means the servitude of women.[159] This would be so monstrous that it could

---

[157] *Sulla Monogamia, sul Matrimonio*, Domenico Meli, in *Raccolta Medica*, Bologna, 1830, t. 10. An argument in favour of polygamy is that in some places the number of female births exceeds that of males. Meli replies that this excess is precisely the effect of polygamy, that is, of the lassitude produced by polygamy in the genitor. The observations of Cav. Dr. Bellingeri confirm this. The tragic effects of polygamy are also described in Euripides' *Andromachus*, v. 177 ss.; v. 464 ss.

[158] Hence, wherever polygamy has been introduced, vices contrary to nature hold sway. Montesquieu says: 'One cannot believe that the majority of women incline to this love which nature rejects; one vice is always accompanied by another. During the revolution at Constantinople which deposed the sultan Ahmed, it is reported that the people who pillaged the shah's home did not find a single woman. At Algiers the point was evidently reached where there were no women in the majority of harems' (*De l'Esprit des Lois*, 16: 6).

[159] The prevalence of women has a smaller role when polyandry is not chosen but necessary, as it was among the ancient Bretons. According to Caesar, several Bretons adapted to being content with only one woman, because women were so scarce. Some people, deceived by the superiority of the male, wrongly grant men the right to have several wives but refuse a woman several husbands. The fact that a man is superior in strength does not give him a right to be disordered. In the moral order, man and woman are two EQUAL beings. Even the pagans saw this truth. In *Mercator*, Plautus argues

never have any foundation, not even where disorder and corruption reign. Finally, polyandry deceives and frustrates the natural desire of the man to be certain of offspring to whom at his death he can commend his memory, ideas and feeling, all the goods he has. This feeling is the man's particular natural title to the chastity of the woman whom he has chosen as wife precisely for that purpose. But I will say more about this later.

III.
Delicate feelings concerning the unicity of the spouses

1340. Catholicism however is not content to keep inviolable the unicity of contemporaneous spouses. It adds some imputations and penalties to a second marriage contracted after the death of the first spouse.[160]

1341. This feeling, proper to good nature and clearly manifest even among pagan nations, is proof itself of the immortality of the soul through the immortality of affections.[161]

that there can be only one wife for precisely the same reason that the husband must be only one:

> A good wife is content to belong to one man.
> Which man would be less content to belong to one wife?
>
> (Act. 4, 6, 8)

[160] Bigamists are irregular, and the Church does not give its blessing to the second marriage.

[161] Roman laws attached certain penalties to those who married a second time. Some of the penalties exist in a few modern legislations, for example, Bavaria (*Cod. Civ. Bav.*, pt. 1, c. 6, §47, 48). In Virgil, Dido speaks as if marrying Aeneas (a thought that occupied her mind) would be a lack of fidelity to Sicheus, her first husband:

> Would that the earth open up its yawning depths to me
> Or the almighty Father, with lightning, drive me to the shades,
> the dreary shades of Erebus and deep night,
> before I violate you, O chaste one, or break your vows.
> He who first joined me to himself took my love;
> May he still hold it and preserve it in the grave.
>
> (Bk. 4, 24–29)

Dante expresses the same sentiment when he says of Dido:

> She broke faith with the mortal remains of Sicheus.
>
> (*Inf.*, V. 62).

C.
Cohabitation

1342. The third principal duty derived from the notion of marriage which I have defined as 'a full union between a man and a woman', is life together.

1343. This must be a ceaseless exercise and a perpetual exchange of beneficence that the spouses carry out between them. It must be the mutual, continual concern of each to lighten the other's hardships and increase the other's innocent satisfactions. The man must support the woman as the elm supports the vine, and the woman, whom the Creator calls 'helper given to man, like unto him', must bear delicious fruit for the one who supports her.

1344. 'A man shall leave father and mother, and shall cleave to his wife; and they shall be two in one flesh.'[162] The two spouses have vowed to each other that full, upright union which accords with nature. Whatever forcefully divides them after consummation of this union, unjustly despoils them of the rights they have through their contract of marriage, and moreover wrongly attempts to deprive their sexual union of its necessary dignity. Such a division also sins against them by preventing the fulfilment of their moral duty of cohabitation and reciprocal help; it violates the law of God, and, in the Catholic Church, is sacrilegious because harmful to the sacrament.

D.
Community of acquired goods

1345. Philosophers and jurists are divided regarding the community of external goods between spouses.

Philosophers favour perfect community. Kant deduces the community of goods from the necessary, undivided interest of the spouses.[163] Fichte says 'that if a wife did not allow her husband to dispose of her acquired goods, it would mean that in

---

162 Gen 2: 24 [Douai]; Ps. 44: 11.
163 *Jurisprud.*, §26, 157.

her eyes the dominion of the goods would have more value than her own personship which she unreservedly transfers to her husband by the marriage contract.'[164] C. S. Zaccaria also upholds the community of goods in marriage provided there are no agreements to the contrary.[165]

1346. Jurists however generally maintain 'that by virtue of the principal contract the spouses obtain reciprocal rights only over their persons, not their acquired goods', and that they 'equally have a proportional right to what they acquire in common during the marriage. The expenses of the shared house or family must be sustained by shared contribution. Other goods acquired by them individually before or during the marriage are objects of the distinct ownership of each.'[166]

1347. Consequently, positive legislations have distinguished the wife's goods into the following classes:

1. The *dowry* given to the husband for the support of his marriage responsibilities.

2. The *contra-dowry* made by the husband to the wife as security or recompense for her dowry.

3. *Donations between spouses.*

4. The gift, called 'Morgengab' by the Germans, given by the husband to the wife on the day after the wedding as a 'payment-in-kind' for her virginity.

5. *Nuptial gifts* made by parents and friends to the new spouses.

6. A*cquisitions* in common during the marriage.

7. *Paraphernalia*, or supra-dowry goods, which the wife brings in addition to the dowry and does not retain for herself.

8. *Reaccepted goods*[167] retained by the wife.

9. The *endowment* or *widowed state*, that is, the goods or their usufruct determined by the husband for the wife after his death.

---

[164] *Grundlage des Naturrechts*, pt. 2.

[165] *Principii di diritto privato filosofico* (Leipzig, 1804), §90.

[166] Zeiller, *Diritto privato*, §160.

[167] The Latin expression, *bona receptitia*, used in the precise meaning of the verb *recipere*, describes the goods retained by the wife after she has, as it were, given them to her husband and received them back. The expression shows how it was originally thought that all the wife's goods had to be consigned to the husband.

1348. What causes such a diversity of opinion between *philosophers* and *jurists* regarding the communion of goods between spouses?

Philosophers consider human nature in itself, and perfect marriage as it befits two perfect individuals of human nature. They have no doubt that marriage in such individuals is also *de facto* the fullest and most perfect union. This explains the communion of goods, which arises spontaneously and necessarily from this true concept of marriage. We have seen that external ownership is a psychological phenomenon; the soul by means of its unitive force joins external things to itself, that is, makes them part of itself.[168] Clearly, if these things are identified with person, two persons uniting in marriage and giving themselves to each other must unite what has become part of them, and out of these things make one single mass which belongs to the new collective person formed by their union.

1349. Jurists consider human nature with all its defects, and attempt to forestall the disorders of human malice and weakness by legal dispositions. Such understanding of the laws moves them to acknowledge an external ownership separate from the two spouses, a separation which only slightly harms the concept of the full union of the spouses. For them the principal part of the union is the personal, natural part; the goods joined to person are merely accessory, like clothing over the body.

1350. Note, moreover, that whenever legislations originate from the basics of philosophy, or the perspicacity of legislators arrives at the ultimate reasons derived from the essence of human nature, they seem to sense very clearly that the communion of all external goods is a spontaneous consequence of conjugal union.

We can see many indications of this in different legislations.[169]

---

[168] *ER*, 332–339.

[169] For example, in the *Code* (bk. 5, tit. 14), under the title of the emperors Theodosius and Valentinian, the 8th law combines both the *philosophical reason* and the *jural view*: 'It was good that the woman who COMMITS HERSELF TO HER HUSBAND together with her things be governed by the same will. Nevertheless, because IT IS FITTING that the founders of laws UPHOLD EQUITY, we want the husband to have no involvement whatsoever (as has been said) in the paraphernalia, if the woman forbids it.' The *equity* spoken of here is the *jural view* intended to defend the *freedom* of the woman against

Modestinus' definition of marriage quoted above leaves us in no doubt.[170] Even among jurists, those who studied Roman legislation more deeply for the sake of deriving from it a *Right of nature*, saw how fitting was the community of goods between spouses. Among them it is sufficient to name Samuel Cocceji, who in contrast to his father, Henry (a narrow-minded jurist who lacked high moral feeling, although his son was happy to refer to him always as 'blessed parent') maintained the community of goods of spouses. He says that the woman enters the husband's house for two ends: 1. 'to share her whole life with her husband' and be joined to him in a single manner of life, and 2. 'to procreate offspring for him and him alone'. From the first of these two ends, clearly indicated in Roman laws, he deduces the community of external goods.[171]

1351. If the principles laid down earlier concerning the nature

her husband's despotism.

[170] 'The union of male and female is THE SHARING OF ALL LIFE, THE COMMUNICATION OF DIVINE AND HUMAN RIGHT.'

[171] *Dissertat. Proem. in Grot.*, Diss. 12, bk. 3, c. 4, Sect. 3. It will be helpful to quote the consequences which, under the guidance of Roman law, this outstanding jurisconsult deduces from the first of the two ends:

'1. The wife becomes a member of the husband's family, and shares his divine and human rights (bk. 1 *ff. Rit. nupt*, bk. 22, §7 *Sol. matrim.*; *Goth.* ad Leg., 12 Tab. tit. 17, §3; *Foveat.* 10, c. 5. — this is found among all peoples, Just. 23, 2;. Tac., *De Mor. Germ.*, 18, and 12; *Ann.* 5, c. 3; Liv. 1, c. 19).

2. She shares in the husband's dignity even after his death, as long as she does not re-marry (bk. 8, bk. 10, C. *Rit. nupt*; bk. 13, C. *De dignit.*) and bears his name and insignia.

3. She follows the domicile (bk. 5, bk. *ff. Rit. nupt.*), civil standing and town of her husband (*l. p. ff. juris d. 1, f. §3 ad Municip.*; *l. f. c. de incol.*)

4. She is in a certain way mistress of her husband's goods (bk. 1, *ff. Rer. am.*; bk. 4 & 5, C. *Crim. expil. haer.*; bk. 52, *de re jud.*) of which, after her husband's death, she acquires half. This communion of goods is practised today in several regions. In ancient Roman Right the wife was considered as a daughter and succeeded to her husband as his necessary heir, like the other children (Dion. Halic., bk. 2, *Antiq. p.m.* 41).

5. The husband cannot repudiate or abandon his wife without just cause (*ff. de divortiis et repud.*)

6. When the wife's goods are acquired by the husband and she is left without anything of her own, the husband must maintain her, whether he has received a dowry or not (bk. 22, §8, *Sol. matr.*; bk. 2, *ff. injur.*). If she has no goods of her own (*d. l.* 16), he must bury her at his own expense (bk. 16, *ff. Relig.*).'

of the union of spouses are applied to the question of the communion of their temporal goods, they reconcile in a beautiful way the noble dictate of philosophy with the prudent circumspection of legislators.

The principles are:

1. That on the one hand the spouses have the greatest possible union befitting two individuals of human nature of different sex, and on the other, the union does not destroy their individuality in such a way that they are no longer *different subjects* of rights (cf. 1065).

2. That the *absolute owner* must be distinguished from the *relative owner*. Granted that the head of the house is the absolute owner and that the other members of the family, particularly the wife, are relative owners, the head of the house has a jural obligation not to prejudice the latter. I refer the reader to what I said on this matter (cf. *RI*, 1267–1293).

§2. *Duties and rights relative to the order befitting union*

1352. In conjugal union we must distinguish between an *habitual, continual* part which, properly speaking, forms the state of marriage[172] and an *actual*, transitory *part* which constitutes, as it were, its exercise.[173]

1353. The *habitual union* and the *actual union* of a man and a woman must 'befit human nature'. In the previous section I discussed what the habitual union must be if it is to befit human

---

[172] The habitual union is composed of *affections* (factual union) and *rights* (contractual union). We considered *affections* in two states: *natural spontaneity* and *stimulation* (cf. 1000). We said that first-level affections are sufficient for the fullness of the union which forms marriage. Second-level affections are not needed because the matter concerns a *fullness of species*, not a *fullness of level*. In other words, the union can be specifically full despite greater or lesser levels of intensity. Moreover, the distinction between inborn *affections* and *aroused affections* must be applied to both *habitual* and *actual union*. The distinction is a subclassification of both *habitual* and *actual affections*.

[173] Cf. *SP*, 545–573 where I explained how human beings are a potency in this life and cannot maintain themselves in a continuous, full act.

nature. In this section I will deal with what is needed by actual union if it is to befit nature.

A.
Duties of the spouses relative to the exercise of part
of the union common to all human beings

1354. Union between spouses, in so far as it can be common to all human beings even of the same sex, is *union of souls* and of *companionship of life*. Union of souls is exercised through acts of esteem and mutual affection. Undivided companionship of life, as we have said, furnishes a series of mutual benefits. Hence the following duties:

1. To avoid everything that might diminish mutual esteem and affection, and

2. To strive for the opposite things.

3. To avoid everything that might diminish the satisfying, harmonious life of the spouses, and

4. to pursue everything that can preserve concord, increase peace, attain unanimity of will and action, help each other to bear the burden of the day;[174] mutually reduce the evils and troubles of life; increase each other's goods and comfort one another in difficulties.

1355. The most elementary of these duties pertains to the husband: he must provide for his wife from the common owner-ship. The most sublime duty, pertaining to both spouses, is to further their *common moral perfection*.[175]

1356. Although these duties are common to both spouses, the difference in characteristics and gifts, which distinguishes the human male and female, makes the difference of sex impart a special character (a physiognomy of its own, as it were) to the *mode* of exercising them. Fichte is wrong when he says: 'Un-limited love on the part of the woman and unlimited generosity on the part of the man constitute the essence of marriage.'[176]

[174] Cf. Engelhard, *Saggi sulla vera idea del matrimonio*, Casal, 1776, c. 1.

[175] Cf. Tasinger, *Sistema del Diritto naturale*, §46.

[176] *Principj del Diritto di natura*.

These virtues constitute the perfect actuation, not the essence of marriage. We must however let ethics and anthropology determine in greater detail the modes and forms of this duty, when fulfilled by the gentle or the strong sex.

B.
Duties of spouses relative to the exercise of the union proper to them, that is, sexual union

I.
Principal duties

1357. The duties and rights of spouses relative to sexual union can be reduced to the following:

1. The right to request, and the obligation to render the conjugal debt.

2. The right and duty to carry out sexual union in a way befitting human nature and dignity.

3. The right and duty to respect the conceived foetus so that it experiences no harm from the behaviour of the woman or her husband.

4. These give rise to the duties and rights of raising and educating offspring born into the world.

These duties are so well dealt with by moralists and jurists that any further discussion seems to me unnecessary.

II.
Parents' influence on their offspring

1358. I will mention here a lesser known, more mysterious duty: the duty of the spouses, especially of the husband, to be virtuous in order to procreate children who are more perfect.

1359. As I have said, the work of procreation of children is principally an act of the soul (cf. 1055–1060). In the human being the soul not only feels, as in animals, but is also intellectual and moral.[177] The intellectual and moral part is most intimately connected with the feeling part, so that they identify in the common principle. Thus, these three faculties — animal feeling, intelligence and will — pertain to the human *subject* at its most simple.[178] The state of the intellective, moral part must therefore have an influence on the feeling, instinctive part. If the *moral* dispositions of the human being are good, they must communicate some *analogous* dispositions and modalities to the *feeling*. The feeling, therefore, as we can see, generates with dispositions completely analogous to the moral or immoral dispositions, and the term of generation, that is, the foetus generated by the animating principle possessing these dispositions, receives in its animal part dispositions and aptitudes similar to those of the generating principle. The depth of the impression made on the foetus is in proportion to the efficacy and fullness of the generating action.

1360. It will be helpful to confirm this important teaching with an opinion of Aristotle,[179] which Aquinas accepted and expounded as follows:[180]

> The univocal genitor[181] communicates *the nature* of its species to what it generates, and therefore to all the *accidents accompanying the species*. Just as a human being generates a human being, so someone who can laugh generates someone who has the aptitude to laugh. But if the power of the genitor is great, he imparts his own likeness to the generated even in regard to the *individual accidents*. This is true however only of accidents that in some way pertain to the body, not of accidents pertaining

---

[177] A very ancient opinion maintained that *intelligence* had a part in human generation. Creuzer, in his description of the ancient inhabitants of Samothrace, says: 'In this system, fire is the primitive force of nature, the generative principle of beings. Below him are Mars and Venus whose union, with the help of a fourth person, Hermes or INTELLIGENCE, produces the great work of generation' (t. 2, p. 1, p. 293 ss.).

[178] In *AMS*, the human being is defined as 'a volitive (moral), intellective, animal SUBJECT'. The human being is a *single principle*. Cf. the *Conclusion* [906] in *AMS*.

[179] Cf. *De Animalibus*.

[180] *De Malo*, 4, 8; *De Veritate*, 25, 5.

[181] 'Univocal' means that which generates beings of the same species.

to the soul alone, particularly the intellective soul — the soul is not a power existing in the corporeal entity.[182]

1361. The dispositions of which we spoke as suitable for communication to children by generation are those alone which the vice and virtue of the genitor leaves imprinted on the animality, as it were, of those generated. Properly speaking, these dispositions are not moral in themselves but ordered to the soul's moral nature; I call them 'analogous to the moral dispositions'. In other words, the body which has these dispositions disposes and inclines the soul to morality or immorality. In this way a father communicates a certain disposition to his son which influences the morality of all the generations.

1362. St. Thomas teaches that this is precisely the way original sin is communicated. Original justice, and its loss through the fall, affected the body also; it flowed as it were from the soul into the body. Thus if the first father had remained innocent and perfect, he would, in the act of generation, have communicated to the bodies of his children dispositions analogous to his original perfection and justice. But after sin and his own ruin, he communicated to his children dispositions analogous to injustice and disorder. These inclined the children's will to evil, which constitutes an immoral element.[183]

1363. Although the other sins of fathers do not pass into the offspring, it seems proven 1. that the parents' immoral state greatly influences the animality of the children, imprinting on them dispositions analogous to paternal defects, and 2. that certain vices affect generation more than others.

1364. Hence Scripture speaks about races cursed in a particular way. When Noah curses the son of Ham, he is simply declaring depraved the generation of a person who treated his father abominably by mocking his nakedness.[184] The expression

---

[182] This teaching alone, consistently professed by St. Thomas, that acts of intelligence are not done by means of some corporeal organ, is sufficient to show how mistaken people are who believe they can list the holy doctor among sensists.

[183] *De Malo*, 4, 8.

[184] Apparently Noah's curse was more a reflection on than a punishment of the insult he had received as a *sign* of Ham's depravation. It predicted evil for his offspring. Similarly the patriarchs foresaw perhaps the destinies of their

used in Scripture, taken literally, attributes depravity or goodness to the *seed*, to which it unites divine curses and blessings.[185]
Finally it says that God punishes the sins of the fathers till the
third and fourth generation, and rewards their virtue to a thou-
sand generations.[186]

1365. In fact, perusing the history of human opinions, we see
that always and everywhere people believed in varying degrees
that children were blamed or praised for the crimes or magnan-
imous actions of their fathers; it was a kind of presumption
either for or against them. Entire lineages have always been
considered marked and characterised by the generosity of their
ancestors or the ignobility of their base predecessors. Hence
outstanding children are expected from a line of outstanding
character according to the hidden law mentioned by Horace:

The strong are created by the strong AND GOOD.[187]

On the other hand, common sense considers offspring born
different from their father a rare exception to this constant law.
Everyone is amazed and calls the children 'degenerate' and
'depraved'

1366. That eloquent theologian, Bossuet, writes:[188]

> Scripture informs us of peoples who have been cursed in a
> particular way, in addition to the general curse. Why
> should some families and even individual people not bear
> in themselves a greater degree of the natural evil which
> comes from Adam and is aggravated by other causes?

descendants; with divine help they read these destinies partly in the character
of their leaders and founders at a time when generation was supremely
effective and had enough power to transmit even *individual accidents* to
children.

[185] Daniel calls the shameless elders: 'Seed of Chanaan and not of Juda'
(chap. 13, 56 [Douai]), and Ezekiel reproves the disorders of the people of
Jerusalem by telling them: 'Thy father was an Amorrhite and thy mother a
Cethite' (chap. 16, 3 [Douai]).

[186] Deut 5: 9; 7: 9. [*App.*, no. 9].

[187] The addition of the word 'good' could be seen simply as a makeweight,
but not if understood of moral good.

[188] *Défense de la tradition et des saint Pères.* Cf. also *De la Connaiss. de
Dieu*, etc., c. 4, §11; *Disc. sur l'hist. univ.*, pt. 2, c. 1; *Elévation sur les myst.*,
serm. 7.

Nothing prevents us from judging such people in a particular way as *alienati ab utero* [alienated from the womb]. The expression is not an exaggeration; rather it explains the real *throw-back* to original sin asserted by Augustine.[189]

1367. Moralists and doctors are therefore fully justified in recommending the practice of moral virtue to those who must generate lest they deprave and poison the line of human generations originating from them. An ancient precept required anyone immorally disposed to abstain from the conjugal act; only when the spirit was in a holy state, well disposed and practised in virtue was the act to be performed.[190]

1368. But we have another and new reason. The Redeemer of the world sanctified marriage and established a special grace for purifying and sanctifying spouses. This explains the happy marriage of Tobit (and the marriages of the ancient patriarchs) who remained faithful to the angel's directives.[191] Finally, it explains

---

[189] *Enchir*, 46, 47.

[190] Cf. the fine observations made by Conte de Maistre on this matter in *Veglie di Pietroburgo, veglia* 1 and 2. People commonly believe that the disposition of the male has a much greater influence on the *character* of the progeny than that of the female. Columella notes that 'a wild ass mated with a mare generates an untamed mule which, in keeping with savage behaviour, is ferociously stubborn' (bk. 3, c. 37). However, I have always noted that the woman has more influence than the man over the *intellective faculties*. I have always seen children produced with great intelligence when the woman, but not the man, was highly intelligent. I suspect that the opposite happens relative to the *moral faculties,* and my suspicion coincides with the opinion of antiquity which must have had more decisive examples before it. In the Code of Manu we read: 'The person generated by an honourable man and a base woman can become honourable through his qualities. But the person generated by a noble woman and a despised man must be considered base. This is the decision' (bk. 10: 67). Nevertheless, in antiquity we find different opinions about the greater influence of the father or mother on the child, possibly because no distinction had been made between the *intellective dispositions* due more to the mother and the *moral dispositions* due to the father. The Code of Manu says: 'Some wise men value the seed more than the field; others value the field and seed equally. The decision is the following: seed sown on unreceptive ground is destroyed without producing anything; good earth over which no grain is sown remains bare. But because, through the excellent virtue of their fathers, even the children of wild animals became honourable, glorious and holy men, the male value prevails' (bk. 10: 70–72).

[191] Tob 6: 16–22.

why the new Church, following in the same spirit of the old, warmly recommends spouses to prepare themselves for conjugal intercourse by prayer and temperance,[192] to use it chastely, with noble thoughts and the intention of generating children for God rather than for themselves, and of providing believers for the Church of JESUS Christ rather than successors for their own family.

Article 5.
The distinctive rights and duties of spouses

1369. So far we have considered spouses in their union; we must now consider them in their individuality.

Considered in their union, spouses constitute a collective person, a third jural person (cf. *RI*, 1650) whose only rights and duties are those in which both share. But considered in their individuality, they become subjects of distinct duties. This distinction is simply *numerical* when they are considered as equal but numerically distinct subjects; it is *specific* when they are regarded in their unequal part.

Spouses are distinguished numerically by *personship* (cf. 1235); *nature* distinguishes them specifically by sex. I call 'distinctive' those duties and rights which pertain to spouses as specifically different subjects.

Before expounding the duties and *distinctive rights* of spouses, I will summarise the duties and rights common to each as numerically distinct. I say 'summarise' because these rights pertain to individual Right, where I have dealt with them.

---

[192] For the benefits to be expected by spouses from temperance and sobriety in the generation of children see Plutarch, *De liberis educandis*, Columella, bk. 3, c. 37. We also recommend the *Memoria* of Cav. Bellingeri, *Della influenza del cibo e della bevanda sulla fecondità e sulla proporzione dei sessi nelle nascite del genere umano*, Turin, for Alessandro Fontana, 1840.

§1. *Summary of the rights and duties of spouses*
as equal but numerically distinct persons

1370. Because spouses are equal but numerically distinct *persons*, it follows that:

1. Connatural rights relative to *freedom* pertain to both (cf. *RI*, 48–51, 87–127). Hence the obligation of each to leave the other entirely free in the means for acquiring truth, virtue and happiness. Indeed each must reciprocally promote *moral perfection* both in self and in the other.

2. The right of *innate ownership* pertains to both (cf. *RI*, 53–58, 128–133).

3. Both can be *subjects of rights* (cf. 1235), that is, they are able to acquire new rights (cf. *RI*, 284–285), except for the wife's deference to her husband as head of the family; he has the obligation to keep her rights of ownership distinct from his, minister them to her and use them reasonably (cf. *RI*, 1277–1293).

1371. From all this we can conclude that:

1. Each spouse is an end, not simply a means, and as such must be respected by the other.

2. The woman cannot be forced into marriage but must give and submit herself to her husband with her free consent (cf. 1181).

3. The woman is a *companion*,[193] not a *bond-servant* of the husband. Each spouse has equal right to require the other to observe the natural, obligatory laws of conjugal union. These laws are: their full union, conjugal fidelity, cohabitation, mutual aid and the other duties listed above.

---

[193] Although Roman authors greatly favoured the power of the husband, they constantly called the wife 'companion'. Titus Livy adds that marriage is 'A SOCIETY OF ALL FORTUNE (1: 9). Justinus defines it as 'entering into a SOCIETY of bad as well as good fortune' (23: 2). Tacitus says the wife is 'COMPANION in any fortune whatsoever' (*Ann.*, 3: 15 & 34); 'the wife is COMPANION in good and bad times' (*Ann.*, 12: 5); 'COMPANION in labours and dangers' (*De Germ. mor.*, 18).

§2. *Distinctive rights and duties*

1372. If in conjugal society spouses form a single *collective person* without destroying the *individual persons*, each spouse must be respected by the other as a *subject of rights*, and, in so far as *person*, respected as end (cf. *RI*, 52). But granted sex as an unequal element in nature, the *sphere* and *mode* of the rights of the spouses differ greatly:

1. relative to the *sphere* of their rights, because the extent of the *matter* and therefore the *titles* of the rights differ;

2. relative to the *mode* of their rights, because the rights of the wife are under the protection and authority of the husband.

1373. Authors offer different reasons for giving preference to the husband in the conjugal union and declaring him head of the house. Some are satisfied with the greater *strength* of the husband. Grotius is content to say that the husband is head of the family *ob sexus praestantiam* [because of the superiority of his sex].[194] Certainly the reason for his jural superiority lies in this quality. Nevertheless the quality must be explained in such a way that the real *jural titles* of conjugal power are found within it. This is what I propose to do.

1374. Every society results from the *consent* of its members, although the consent may be obligatory or free. In the case of a man and a woman who unite in conjugal society the consent is *free*. Thus, the first source of the *real rights* of a man over a woman who becomes his wife is mutual consent.

1375. However, the object of this consent, *ideal right*, is not arbitrary but determined by nature (cf. 1076–1089). Hence, granted consent in the first place, the rights and duties of the spouses no longer depend on their free will but on the object of their society defined by the laws of nature and reason, that is, they depend on the ideal right they intend to realise.[195] I repeat,

---

[194] *De J. B. et P.*, bk. 2, c. 5, §1, a. 8.

[195] In this way the opinion of those who maintain that the subjection of the wife depends on her consent is reconciled with the opinion of those who say she is subject without her consent. Baroli writes: 'It has been demonstrated that the subordination of the wife arises from an intrinsic, connatural fittingness for this society. Consequently this dependence must be classified among those natural duties for whose efficacy no consent or covenant of any kind,

therefore, that we need to know the distinctive rights and duties of the husband and wife in the natural diversity which conditions their full union (cf. 1039). In a word, we must search the nature of the individual human male and female for the titles of the mutual rights posited in being by their marriage.

1376. *Titles* of rights can result from *nature* or from *society*. Thus, we can call them *individual* and *social*.

The *fact* of society can produce two jural effects:

1. It can give nature the opportunity to posit certain *individual titles* of rights.

2. It can give rise to titles, *social titles*, proceeding not from the nature of the individual person but from the collective person (cf. *RI*, 1020–1021, 1023).

These two effects are more evident in conjugal society, which results from a *natural* and from a *conventional, social element*.

1377. The source and origin of *individual titles* is *natural feeling*; the source and origin of *social titles* is the *end of society*. The prevalence of the husband over the wife results from a double individual, social title; it is required simultaneously by a *natural feeling* and by the *end of conjugal society*. Let us see how.

A.
The first title of prevalence of the husband:
the feeling proper to man, but not woman, which urges him
to be head of a line

1378. Marriage is desired by human beings for the sake of two goods:

1. The good of conjugal society itself (conjugal society is indeed a good);

2. The good present in offspring, the natural effect of conjugal society (cf. 1063).

1379. Both these goods are legitimate ends of marriage. In the

expressed or understood, is required' (*Diritto naturale-privato*, §226). Consent to the subjection was given with the consent by which the woman freely entered the conjugal state.

history of humanity we see one prevailing over the other at different times. Consequently, marriage itself takes on a different characteristic, and changes take place in the customs of peoples and in their laws.

1380. Both ends were present in God's original institution of marriage. The first, the good to be found in conjugal society, was made the basis and foundation of the other when God himself pronounced the solemn words: 'It is not good for man to be alone; let us make him a help like unto himself.'[196] These words express man's need for society, and the good to be found in this society, but without any mention of children. It is true that the 'help like unto himself', which God gave Adam amongst other goods, helped him to have children but this benefit was wisely fused and mingled by the divine Lawgiver into the complex of goods which the woman (indicated by the words 'a help like unto himself') had to bring to the man.[197] The benefit from children was not, however, proposed as a distinct, immediate end. Hence the true, original end of marriage is simply the good which man finds in the full, stable and perfect union with someone like himself but of another sex.

1381. The exquisite good of an intimate society presupposes a most noble feeling, a most affectionate heart. The first man was given this, but he did wrong. After sin, the exquisite feeling, the intensity and breadth of affection in man's heart were diminished. Consequently, the first, immediate, natural end of marriage gave way to the second, the possession of children.

1382. The prevalence of the second, partial end of marriage soon became so dominant that it seemed the only one. Conjugal society declined to a state of means, as if its sole value were children procreated through it. Nearly all laws were drawn up to regulate this end. Soon human dignity in the use of sex was considered to be completely assured 'when conjugal society was ordered to generation for founding a house or lineage'.

1383. The consequences were extremely serious: the procreation of children as the sole end does not in itself exclude

---

[196] Gen 2: [18 (Douai)].

[197] In calling woman *like* unto man, God indicated the part in which she is equal to man, that is, rationality and morality; when he called her a *help*, he showed that she was unequal and a bearer of happiness to man.

polygamy, of which Lamech was the first example.[198] Nor, in an exceptional case, does it exclude limited polyandry, different from promiscuous concubinage and prostitution, which was never considered upright.[199] Only the first, full end of marriage subjects it to those noble laws which exclude all defects and bring about its natural perfection. Here, however, I want to limit the discussion to this second end and draw from it the jural superiority of the husband.

1384. A parent desires to generate children as his successors in whom a great part of himself may live on[200] and to whom he may leave some record of himself, with his own affections and external goods. He is head and origin of his successors. But this

---

[198] If it is true that the queen of the Amazons, Thalestris, invited Alexander the Great to give her a son by him, she evidently did not see it as shameful or wrong, granted the end of having a son by so great a hero. The same is said of queen Saba: she desired and obtained a child by Solomon. It was not lechery that induced Lot's two daughters to commit incest with their father, but the desire for offspring. After the massacre at Sodom they were afraid that no male would be left to perpetuate their line. Consequently, they wanted to go into their father 'that we may preserve offspring through our father' (Gen 19: 30–38). Leah, because of her upright desire for many offspring, found it even less unbecoming to buy from Rachel the company of her husband and invite him to lie with her when he returned from the fields (Gen 30). Cesare Cantù says of the Spartans: 'Divorce with a sterile woman was easy and legal, but the husband could also bring a stranger into his wife's bed for the sake of procuring descendants (Xenophon, *Lacon.*, 1: 7; Plutarch, c 15; Müller, p. 199). Marriage however was not considered any less holy, and adultery was very rare' (*Legislazione* No. 2, §16). Sometimes several brothers had a common wife. The Spartans' conscience was not disturbed by these disorders because, once the noble human feeling for perfect union had weakened, the end of having good descendants was, in their opinion, the only practical purpose left in marriage.

[199] No nation considered sexual pleasure alone as an upright end of marriage. When this most base end of the use of the two sexes is the sole end, it destroys marriage, removing the union of man and woman from all the holy laws which earned it the noble name of *marriage*. Indeed, the very name given to marriage recalls the second end, not the first, because it comes from the concept of mother.

[200] In the most ancient documents this concept is expressed with great sensitivity. We read in an ancient Indian book that the husband is reborn in the form of a foetus, and that the wife who has conceived is called Djaya because her husband is born (*djayate*) in her a second time (*Mânava-Dharmasâstra*, 9: 8).

desire does not develop in the same way in a man and a woman. In a man it is an *active* feeling, urging him to associate himself with a female companion who can help him in the task. In a woman it is *passive*; she lets herself be associated with a man and enjoys helping him in his intention. The man's desire for off-spring for himself is absolute; the woman's desire to give heirs to her husband is relative. Because the woman loves her husband in all simplicity, the *first and greatest end* of marriage (the fullness of union) is preserved more in the woman than in the man; in him the second end is prevalent. Hence adultery was always regarded as a sin opposed more to the nature of the woman and more serious in her than in the man. Although polygamy could at times be tolerated, polyandry could not, except perhaps on rare occasions and in a very limited way.

Again, although the woman loves her children simply, as the most precious portions of her body, her maternal love finishes in them. Strictly speaking, it does not have the entire line, the foundation of future, prosperous and glorious progeny, as its object. Her thoughts extend to future generations only as a result of sharing in the desire she sees in the man she loves, and to whom she gives offspring.[201]

1385. Woman therefore considered relative to man's *philogony* takes on the notion of *means*, of help ('a helper like unto him'), and man, the notion of *end*. In this sense St. Paul says that 'man was not created for woman but woman for man.'[202]

1386. We see then just how great was the desire of the first human beings to found a house, to start a line of descendants. The most longed-for glory was to become father of a great lineage. Such a desire was supreme in all those men in ancient times who did not go astray and debase themselves with lechery. The force of *philogony*, greater at that time than now, was indeed providential at the beginning of the world when all

---

[201] The cases are rare where we see the woman's *love for offspring* prevail over possession of the husband. Nevertheless, Sarah's act of bringing the bond-servant to Abraham because 'it may be that I shall obtain children by her' (Gen 16: 2) seems to indicate that even in the woman there can be a prevailing love for offspring (cf. Gen 17: 13–17). But it is more true to say that Sarah shared the feeling of her sorrowing husband because he had no child, and because of her love gave up what must have been most precious to her.

[202] 1 Cor 11: 7, 9.

nations had to issue from few men, and was quite natural in the circumstances in which they lived. The following are some of the principal reasons:

1. Now that generations have been multiplied, and civil societies founded, many of them still uncivilised, the objects of *glory* to which human beings can aspire have become innumerable. The means for handing on to descendants one's name, feelings, opinions, the best part of one's very self, are infinite. When nations began, however, all these means were reduced to natural succession alone. All glory lay in becoming the head of a numerous, glorious line of descendants. Populations had to be created therefore for the sake of a glorious name; a human being cannot have a name and fame in solitude.

2. When the earth was still empty, maintenance of children cost nothing. On the contrary, the more children, the more *wealth* for the family. Many offspring could take possession of the most extensive lands. *Power* also increased when limbs, that is, physical force, were the prevailing, dominant element.[203]

3. Children could not find beguiling distractions and pleasures where civil society was either not yet constituted or little developed. Consequently they necessarily grew up very much attached to their parents, their only teachers (hence the proverb: 'A wise son hears his father's instruction'),[204] from whom they received and expected every good. This explains the divinisation of ancestors introduced into all ancient nations. Ancestors were given far greater honour after their death than during their life. Their ashes, their memory (duly embellished by feeling), their solemn pronouncements, their practices were all religiously preserved. They were looked upon as supreme models for their whole lineage; their statements and desires were extremely holy and venerable laws. Such a great feeling of filial piety, much exaggerated at those times, could only make children dearer to their parents, who confidently expected longed-for renown from them. Conversely, children sought their own glory in paternal greatness, a feeling expressed in the book of Proverbs as 'Grandchildren are the crown of the aged, and the glory of

---

[203] Cf. *The Summary Cause for the Stability or Downfall of Human Societies*, 127–143.

[204] Prov 13: 1.

sons is their fathers'.[205] This intimate union of feeling between the common origin and all the descendants was necessarily supported by another reason:

4. A fuller and more perfect generative power in the first human beings. This greater generative power allowed the parent to put his stamp, as it were, much more vitally on his offspring. He left his imprint indelibly on all his descendants in accordance with the above-mentioned law that the genitor communicates himself more faithfully to the offspring in proportion to the energy of the generative act.

1387. At the beginning, these and other reasons must have rendered the instinct of *philogony* extraordinarily powerful in the human being. In particular, the last reason produced a profound feeling in the father who saw himself reproduced and increased in his children and his most distant descendants. This feeling is indicated by many expressions in Genesis, the oldest book of all. God says to Abraham: 'I will make of you a great nation, and I will bless you, and make your name great, so that you will be a blessing.'[206] This is the same Abraham who will become a great nation and acquire the desired glory not just of a *great father (Abram)* but much more, of a father of many nations *(Abraham)*.[207] Again: 'To your descendants I will give this land,'[208] indicating the paternal substance in the children. And again: 'All the land which you see I will give TO YOU AND TO YOUR DESCENDANTS for ever;'[209] God promises to give him the land because he promises it to his descendants. The holy patriarch expresses so effectively the greatness of his natural desire for descendants when he says to the Lord: 'Behold, you have given me no offspring; and a slave born in my house will be my heir.' The Lord replies: 'This man shall not be your heir; your own son shall be your heir.' God reveals that Abraham will possess the land after four hundred years because he was considered as living in his descendants.[210] Expressions such as this

---

205 *Ibid.*, 17: 6.
206 Gen 12: 1[–2].
207 *Ibid.*, 17: 5–6.
208 *Ibid.*, 12: 7.
209 *Ibid.*, 13: 15.
210 *Ibid.*, 15: 2–21.

are frequent in the sacred books. Descendants are always given the father's name, as if the father himself were diffused in them.[211] Furthermore, the practice is not exclusive to Abraham's descendants; on the contrary, all nations bore the name of their founder, which afterwards became the name of the countries where they settled.

1388. If, then, this feeling of philogony is PROPER to the male but not the female in marriage, it becomes a title of superiority for the man because, as we have shown, *right* is rooted in *that which is proper*. The universal principle of the derivation of rights lies 'in an activity PROPER to a person',[212] and is one of those *facts* of nature constituting *titles to rights* (cf. *RI*, 293–295).[213] Thus, if the wife wanted to take for herself, against nature, the quality of origin and head of the family, she *would injure* the husband by violating and usurping his natural ownership (cf. *RI*, 343).

1389. The right given in every age to the man to be origin, head and prince of the descendants is therefore strictly *natural* because founded on a natural feeling. On the other hand, the woman's feeling of subjection is natural — as natural as the feeling of surrender to her husband as a help and means for him to satisfy his upright, natural desire to procreate children. The woman's good lies in this subjection and assistance; it is a necessity for her, just as it is a necessity for the man to be superior. It has been said most appropriately that the natural condition of the wife is posited in her *selfless love* for her husband and in sacrifice. Anything contrary in the woman would be waywardness, not nature; it would not be the feeling of the species but individual, false feeling which does not in any way form right because every jural title is founded on the feelings of *common*, well ordered *nature* (cf. 982).

1390. The different character of spontaneous feelings in man

---

[211] Gen 17. 'And I will make my covenant between me and you, and WILL MULTIPLY YOU exceedingly — And I WILL MAKE YOU exceedingly FRUITFUL; and I WILL MAKE NATIONS OF YOU and kings shall come forth from you — And I will give TO YOU, and to your descendants after you, the land of your sojournings.' The same form can be found in Gen 18: 18; 21: 13; 22: 17.

[212] Cf. *ER*, 332–341.

[213] Cf. *ER*, 76.

and woman informs marriage, imparting to it a kind of mysterious, dignified quality. Because of this difference, a man enters conjugal society to find satisfaction for all his natural desires which can be fulfilled in marriage; among these desires is that of becoming the founder of a progeny. The woman herself enters it at the same level, that is, to find satisfaction for her desires, among which is that of subjecting herself to her husband and pleasing him, helping, honouring, loving and serving him, and receiving in exchange protection, honour, happiness. These are the inborn, legitimate desires of the two sexes and the different titles of their rights. The husband's task, according to the fittingness of nature, is to be head and master;[214] the wife's task, which suits her well, is to be a kind of accession to and complement of her husband, totally consecrated to him, and called by his name.[215]

B.
The second title of prevalence of the husband:
the proximate end of conjugal society, mutual satisfaction

1391. The feeling which urges a man to be founder of a line of descendants relates not to marriage itself, the *union*, but to the effect of marriage, the *offspring*.

Nevertheless even if we consider the union, we clearly see that it cannot be full and perfect unless the husband is the head and directs communal living, and the wife is protected and directed, and serves the husband and his house.

---

214 'The husband is the head of the wife' (Eph 5: 22–23; Col 3: 18).

215 God called the first man 'Adam' (Gen 2: 19). He then took the woman from Adam and wanted her to have the same name. 'So God created MAN (ADAM) in his own image, in the image of God he created him; male and female he created them' (Gen 1: 27). 'This is the book of the generation of ADAM. in the day that God created man (*HUMUS*, ADAM, earth)he made him to the likeness of God. He created them male and female; and blessed them; and called their name Adam, in the day when they were created' (Gen 5: 1–2). This foundational law was universally preserved in the nations. The woman enters the house of the husband and takes his name and dignity. The *Digest* says: 'The use of the masculine in the text applies mostly to both sexes' (*Dig.*, bk. 5, t. 16, l. 195). Cf. also the *Code of Justinian*, bk. 5, t. 4, l. 10.

1392. This is because full union means happy union. Furthermore, conjugal society is one of those universal societies which include everything (cf. 134–135, 141). Hence when the members enter it, they undertake to use all possible upright means of making their society prosperous and happy.

Nature however distributes the means differently to the two sexes: one sex is given certain aptitudes denied to the other, with the result that they need each other. The aptitudes are so wonderfully distributed that when they are united they form the most exquisite accord and produce a single result, a satisfying, happy communal life.

The man's natural gifts are precisely those which render him suitable for exercising authority: courage, strength, activity, firm mind (or certainly a more developed mind due to his kind of life), an instinct for action, for business, government and command. The woman has all the natural gifts which render her suitable for obeying and satisfying the proclivities of the man: demure sweetness, gracious weakness, attentive docility; she is delicate, calm, homely, patient and refined — precisely what is required for internal family duties. Moreover, she has a very special need to keep herself withdrawn to avoid dangers, to prevent illicit desires in others, and not to cause jealousy in her husband.[216] These very dutiful requirements often prevent her

---

[216] The Romans praised the wife and gave her the title of *domiseda* [one who stays at home], as can be seen in an ancient inscription (cf. Fabretti, c. 4, n. 35). The following passage from Samuel Cocceji illustrates this necessity in the woman of keeping to the home: 'When the master of the house wants to propagate his kind and produce beings like himself, he chooses a companion, a female who offers the use of her body for that end. This intention of the master indicates that he seeks a companion in order to procreate children from his seed. To his children, as true parts of his body, he can pass on all his rights; he can leave the children as successors of his family. Because the sole end of this transaction is that the master has sons from his seed, it necessarily follows that he wants to be the certain, undoubted father of those born. But this certainty can only be had *by just marriage*, that is, by that union of male and female which "contains a single manner of life". Consequently, when a woman promises the use of her body to her husband alone and enters his household for that end, she is by this very fact constituted under his supervision and guardianship. Hence the rule of nature is: "He is a son whom just marriage indicates" (bks. 19, 24, *De stat. hom.*, bk. 4, bk. 6, ff. *his, qui sui, etc.*). And Julian says: "It is intolerable that he who has lived continuously with his

from dealing freely with external affairs. Finally, nature has placed in her heart that selfless affection we have spoken of by which she takes pleasure in the husband's good and in being his glory.[217]

§3. *The nature of the husband's superiority and the wife's subjection*

1393. Marriage is a society. The common *contribution* is the human individuals themselves of different sex who place themselves in common together with all they can dispose of. Individuals of different sex have a different character, different faculties and aptitudes, different proclivities and needs, which are all part of the common *contribution*.

If the man has an aptitude, proclivity and need to be the founder and governor of a family, this cannot be destroyed; on the contrary it must have its place in conjugal society. This, however, is not *seigniory*; it is a right, and a *socio-natural office*.

1394. Likewise, if the woman has an inclination and need to cling to her husband, like the vine to the elm, or a limb to the head, and if she has a very fitting aptitude to help her husband become a father, to be his trusted minister in the home, his comfort in hardships, his companion in joys, and finally a sweet, noble and willing instrument of all his upright intentions, then all this must unfailingly be brought into act. Once more, this is not *servitude* but a right, a *socio-natural office*.

1395. We have seen how *servitude* differs from *social office*. The end of servitude is the master; the end of social office is not the good of one member only of the society but of the whole collective person, that is, the good proportionally divided among all the individuals composing the society. Hence the only end of both the superiority of the husband and the practice of

wife may not wish to acknowledge his son as though he were not his own" (*D.*, bk. 6)' (*Dissert. Proem. in Grot.*, 12, bk. 3, c. 4, 141). The same reason explains the duty imposed on women by the Apostle of being silent in church, and of questioning the husband at home about religious truths; in short, all the rules of modesty, reserve and submission.

[217] 'But woman is the glory of man,' says St. Paul (1 Cor 11: 7).

[1393–1395]

subjection of the wife is the full satisfaction of both people, the prosperity and success of the common family.

§4. *The limits of the husband's superiority and of the wife's subjection*

1396. Many authors limit the subjection of the wife 'to marriage and family concerns'.[218] They do so because they examine only the *external end* of marriage, the procreation of offspring, and give little attention to the immediate, *internal end*, which is the natural good sought and found by two beings made for each other in their full union.

I have explained that the whole theory of conjugal society must be deduced 'from the concept of the perfect union of two human beings of different sex'. From this I inferred that the spouses place themselves totally in their society with all their possessions in a manner befitting nature.

1397. A consequence of this teaching is that the husband's *superiority* and the wife's *subjection* extend as far as the fullness and happiness of the union require.

1398. In general, I have deduced the husband's right to superiority from 'the duty of the spouses to contribute, each on their own part, to the greatest possible happiness of both, which is the end of the society'. Because the happy perfection of the conjugal society and of the entire family requires that one mind and will govern reasonably, and the other be upright and responsive, each spouse must co-operate with good will to produce this effect. If one must govern, it must certainly be the one who knows how to govern, can and wishes to govern, and whose government causes no trouble for the family. These conditions are verified solely in the husband. The wife therefore must be subject, precisely because she must want the end of the union

---

[218] Cf. Grotius, bk. 2, c. 5. He grants the husband 'the right to choose the domicile' and adds, 'if some other right is granted the husband, such as that in the Hebrew law of annulling the wife's desires, and among some nations, the right of selling the wife's goods, such right does not come from nature but from positive institution.'

[1396–1398]

and of the family, that is, because of the duty she has in common with the husband.

What then are the limits of this respective superiority and subjection? Generally, nature has not determined them; I mean, human nature as it is at present has not determined them. Nature has not made all women and all men with the same stamp. Just as certain men have more of a masculine character than others, so certain women have more of a feminine character than others. Hence the husband and the wife must exercise their respective superiority and subjection with the temperament suggested and indicated by equity, a sense of reasonableness and an instinct free from obstinacy. Immutable boundaries cannot be assigned to this kind of opposing social offices; they cannot be measured precisely. But the aim of producing the greatest good of the family and the mutual love of the spouses can and must determine them.

If there is an obligation to come to an adjustment whenever the rights of two persons seem to collide (cf. *RI*, 462, 501, 1026), a much greater obligation exists when two persons must form only one person. The adjustment must not only seek to remove the occasion of the disagreement, but to obtain the closest concord and deepest agreement possible. Thus, whenever the husband is *per accidens* less suitable for government, he must proportionately limit the exercise of his superiority. And if the wife is very strong and has in fact some male characteristics, he must make use of her gift for the good of the home. She may also act spontaneously for this purpose, provided she does not exceed the limit laid down by *jural resentment* in her husband (cf. *RI*, 580–581), which she must not arouse in any situation or under any pretext.

Chapter 6

The two systems which alter the relationships of superiority and dutiful subjection between spouses

1399. These teachings enable us to evaluate the two systems which alter the dutiful relationships of superiority and subjection between spouses. One system changes the *social superiority* of the husband into a *seigniorial superiority*, and the *social subjection* of the wife into a kind of *servitude*. By over-emphasising the husband, devaluing the wife and thus introducing what can only be called *tyranny* into the family, it disavows the element of *equality* proper to conjugal society (cf. 1236).

1400. The other system neglects the element of *inequality* and claims that the wife should be equal to the husband in all things. This introduces into the family a kind of *democracy* or uniformity of franchise.

1401. The first system was the error and plague which beset and slowly destroyed pagan families; the second makes its influence felt and harms Christian families as soon as they deviate from Catholicism.

We shall make a few, brief comments on these systems, both of which are mistaken and overthrow nations. In order to go to the root of the first, we need to see how the principle of servitude perverts all the holy laws regulating the family. Indeed, it renders this society impossible.

Article 1.
The principle of SERVITUDE considered in its relationship with domestic society

1402. The principle of servitude, which declares the bond-servant to be a simple means for the satisfaction of the master, is profoundly wicked, as we have seen. It is incompatible with theocratic society, and generates the most foul, harmful and disastrous consequences for domestic and civil society. Here we consider it only in relationship with domestic society.

1403. Keeping before our eyes the notion of marriage as 'a full society between man and woman', we see immediately that such a society cannot be brought about between masters and slaves (cf. 1167–1175).

1404. We could also take as the foundation of our argument the imperfect notion of marriage used by those who declare it a 'perpetual union between man and woman for the sake of generating children' — a notion which expresses only an effect or at most a duty of marriage, but which shows that the conjugal bond lies horribly injured and perverted by domestic servitude. We shall confine ourselves to this second point.

1405. The effects of domestic servitude can be considered prior to (that is, outside) marriage and during marriage itself. We shall look briefly at both.

§1. *Immoral effects of servitude before or outside marriage*

1406. First, the origin of *concubinage* is found in servitude. It is clear that when female bond-servants are purely *means* or instruments, the master can force them, at will, to have intercourse with him.[219]

1407. Secondly, the true origin of *prostitution* and of *polyandry* is also found in servitude. Here, the master can at will oblige the female bond-servant, a mere instrument, to have intercourse with one or more men.[220]

1408. Thirdly, the origin of *pederasty* itself must be found in servitude. The master can abuse male as well as female bond-servants.[221]

---

[219] From the beginning, Christianity proscribed all these abuses. Gradually, this proscription penetrated the civil laws. A Lombard law decreed that if a master violated the wife of his slave, both wife and slave should be freed (bk. 1, tit. 32, §6). This law was good in itself, and highly praised by Montesquieu (bk. 15, c. 12), but opened the eyes of slaves to an unlawful way of acquiring freedom.

[220] Cf. the foul language used by Varro (*De Re Rustica*, bk. 2, c. 10) to describe intercourse amongst pastoral people to multiply the race. He speaks of them as though they were beasts.

[221] This horrendous vice is found wherever servitude and polygamy have taken root. For the infamous excesses at which such disorder arrived at Constantinople and Algiers, cf. Montesquieu, bk. 16, c. 6.

[1404–1408]

1409. There is nothing more disgusting and shameful if the end of such filth is carnal pleasure. If the intended end of these temporary unions with female bond-servants (forced or unforced), is the procreation of children, it is still totally unlawful because sought outside the perpetual union of the two sexes. Nor does such union constitute marriage. Even when we keep to the more imperfect definition, we see that marriage is not constituted by the sole end of procreation, but requires perpetual union.

1410. Another monstrosity against nature is this: in the case of a bond-servant who copulates with her master outside marriage, the lack of any right as wife leads to her being deprived of her right as mother. Wherever domestic servitude is found, all the most intimate, sacred bonds uniting humanity are broken, sullied and monstrously perverted.

1411. Nevertheless, frequent examples of this disgusting brutality are brought about, allowed and protected by civilised nations. One of innumerable, recent examples may be given here for the sake of arousing indignation amongst the upright, shaming its authors, promoters and protectors, and seeing that justice is done.

Cosnard, a former director of the botanical garden of Baduel and Cayenne, a French colony, had a child named Marie Euphémie by one of his black slave-women. In his will, made in 1833, he gave the daughter freedom, but without making mention of her mother. At his death in 1840, his assets were sold, and an attempt was made to include the mother who at the time was breast-feeding another baby. This was done in order to enrich the daughter and sister, Marie Euphémie, with the price the others would fetch. The Procurator-Royal, appealing to article 46 of the *Code for Blacks*,[222] succeeded in having the sale stopped. Far worse than the attempted sale, however, and far more scandalous, was the decision of the royal court of appeal of French Guyana which at its hearing on May 9th, 1842, ordered the auction of the mother and the baby so that the price could be used to increase the dowry of the half-caste, Marie

---

[222] This article declares that a child under the age of puberty cannot be separated from its mother.

Euphémie [*App.*, no. 10]. At the moment, the affair has been brought before the Supreme Court.[223]

Domestic servitude introduces immorality into families. Immorality in turn disavows all rights and duties between husband and wife, between mother and child. Either slavery ceases, or the domestic bonds, which alone constitute the family in its jural or moral and even natural entity, are swept away.[224]

§2. *Immoral and unjust effects of servitude in marriage*

1412. Even if a master forms a perpetual union with a female bond-servant, and calls this marriage, oppression of the woman will always be the effect of servitude, unless he frees the woman by marrying her as his only wife.[225]

1413. I say that there must be only one free wife because,

---

[223] 'A colonial, writes M. Comte in his work on legislation (bk. 5, c. 8), does not enfranchise the children born of him and his female slaves; he demands from them the work and submission he requires from others. He sells and exchanges them, or leaves them to his heirs, as he judges convenient. If one of his legitimate children receives them by title of succession, the heir makes no distinction between them and other slaves. A brother thus becomes the owner of his sisters and brothers. He exercises the same tyranny over them; he requires the same work; he flogs them as he flogs the others; he satisfies the same desires in their regard. This multitude of white slaves, who are such a surprise for the European, are almost always the fruit of adultery and incest. The traveller notices the lack of affection between the parents in this colony where one rarely sees two brothers talking together' (Barrow, *Nouveau voyage dans la partie méridionale de l'Afrique*, t. 1, c. 1, p. 130).

[224] Cf. M. Comte, *Traité de législation etc.* (bk. 5), where the reader will find an accumulation of constant, universal facts which testify to the most immoral, unnatural consequences springing from slavery in the colonies.

[225] Dionysius of Halicarnassus quotes a law of Numa which forbade a father to sell his son whom he had permitted to marry and made a sharer in the family's religion and goods (bk. 2). This law protecting the wife is an example of legislation vibrant with the religious, upright spirit of the most ancient laws, close to the origins of the human race. Samuel Cocceji maintains for good reasons that fathers never had the right to sell their children, and says that Dionysius, Greek as he was, easily fell into error about Roman affairs (*Dissert. Proem.*, 12, t. 3, c. 4, §2).

[1412–1413]

although it is true that servitude is one cause of polygamy, polygamy itself is a degree of servitude. Where polygamy is practised, the woman is deprived of the right to equality. She has to love exclusively someone who does not love her exclusively; she has to be faithful to someone who does not observe fidelity;[226] the husband cannot have full union with her, although she is required to have full union with him.

1414. To maintain such injustice, which the strong individual exercises over the weak, many other injustices are needed. Hence, the enclosure in seraglios and harems, feet-binding in China, and so on. Injustice not sustained by further injustices collapses of its own accord.

1415. The woman ceaselessly and irremediably injured in this fashion either has to desensitise herself or be prepared for a state of continual confrontation to recuperate her rights, or at least vindicate herself. Both states are immoral, unjust and destructive of domestic happiness.

1416. Polygamy, as we said, does not favour fertility.[227] 'Nor is it any more useful to the children. One of its great difficulties is that the father and mother cannot have the same affection for their children. The father cannot love his twenty children with the love the mother has for her two.'[228] Moreover, a man cannot love equally several wives; and his love for the children he generates will be tainted with the same inequality as he has for his wives.

---

[226] Equality in the use of sex and in the observance of continence was strongly proclaimed by the Gospel as soon as it appeared in the world. This helped to raise the condition of women. St. Gregory Nazienzen addresses the husband as follows: 'How can you demand that which you do not give?' (*Orat.* 31). Lactantius wants the husband to be an example of continence to the wife, just as he must teach her, according to Christian principles, all the other virtues: 'The wife is to be taught how to behave chastely by the example of continence. It is wicked to require that which you yourself are unable to give' (*Inst.*, bk. 6: 23). St. Jerome, after showing that the laws of the Gospel are more perfect than civil laws, says: 'With us, what is unlawful to women is equally unlawful to men; and the same servitude is placed on an equal level' (*Ad Oceanum*).

[227] Cf. Chardin, *Voyage en Perse* (*Description du gouvernement*, c. 12), where he shows that Persian families, which practise polygamy, are not more fertile than French families, where only one wife is allowed.

[228] *De l'Esprit des Lois*, bk. 16: 6.

[1414–1416]

1417. The oppression suffered by women most certainly has several causes. One of the principal is lack of education and ignorance. If human beings lack education, and especially moral education, they act according to the laws of their *spontaneity* which, damaged by original sin, tends to ever greater disintegration.

Freedom, which is opposed to the spontaneous operation of the will, depends for its vigour on the development and exercise of reason and on the acquisition of education, especially sound, moral education. This principle of deliberate choice, which increases in force as intelligence grows and acquires cognitions free from error, subjects human spontaneity to a moral rule, restrains its natural tendencies and directs it along an upright, useful path.

Only Christianity, however, can provide the superior, truly sufficient forces to dominate the spontaneous tendencies of the human will. Only Christianity strengthens human beings so obviously against evil that experience is able to show what faith teaches: the human will receives a secret, supernatural and extremely efficacious help.

Spontaneity is subject to external causes such as genetic hereditary, climate, the manner of procuring food and attending to needs, and so on. *Freedom* (which draws its strength from education, especially moral education, and grace) intervenes, hand in hand with the progress of civilisation, to dominate spontaneity and draw it away from the impulses which push human beings towards evil. Where freedom is poorly developed, people are almost wholly abandoned to spontaneity. This is the case with barbarian peoples who lack intellectual development, have few cognitions and possess limited free will; *natural spontaneity* is almost their sole guide, and the influence of climate, needs and the means of satisfying needs, and so on, is very strong. This fact does not prove that intellectual and moral causes can do little of themselves, but only that these causes are not yet sufficiently applied to the betterment of nations.

This is the reason why these external causes and the inborn corruption of the will, which seconds these causes with spontaneous, natural affection, constantly produce tyranny of man over woman, together with oppression and its accompanying polygamy.[229] Facts proving this assertion can be read in Comte's work which describes the oppression of woman in every one of the five races into which some physiologists divide humankind: the Caucasian, Mongolian, Ethiopian, American and Malayan.[230] This oppression certainly varies in degree, according to the influence of innumerable external circumstances, but it is more or less universal. The human spontaneity which produces it shows very clearly the mark of the primitive fault. Amongst hunter and warrior races, the male is everything. His skill, agility and strength enable him to catch the prey which feeds the family, and conquer the enemies who assail it. It is clear that in these conditions the woman is forgotten, is nothing, is less than a beast of burden.

Article 2.
The principle of absolute equality considered in domestic society

1418. Disgusted by such inhuman injustices, others go to the opposite extreme. They set out to rescue woman from her abasement and unfortunately concentrate their attention solely on the element of natural *equality* that she shares with man; they

---

[229] This effect and punishment of sin seems to be indicated by God in the words addressed to the woman: 'You shall be under your husband's power and he shall rule over you' (Gen 3: 16, [Douai]). The *intrinsic* end of marriage, *perfect union*, was weakened and lost through sin. The *external end*, the desire for children, remained. Hence God's word to the woman after sin: 'In sorrow you will bring forth children.' And because this extrinsic end of marriage does not involve the *love of friendship* (the woman is considered as an instrument), God continues: 'You shall be under your husband's power, and he shall have dominion over you.' The *perfect union* between man and woman is expressed by the single name 'Adam', given to both spouses (Gen 5: 1–2). After sin, however, the woman no longer has a common name with her husband; she receives her own name: *Eve* (Gen 3: 20), which means *the mother of the living* and expresses very suitably the extrinsic end, the generation of children, still remaining to marriage. Hence virginity in the heavenly paradise; fecundity outside it.

[230] Charles Comte, *Traité de législation, ou exposition des lois générales suivant lesquelles les peuples prospèrent, dépérissent ou restent stationnaires* (bk. 4).

[1418]

forget to consider the other, *unequal element*. Their error, like that of their predecessors, has its origin in their neglect and disavowal of a part of the truth. The first error neglects the *person* of the woman, which is equal to that of the man; the second, mindful of personal dignity, neglects the *nature* of the woman which, as a complement and help to that of the man, is subordinate.[231]

1419. Those who fall into the second error want the two sexes equal in the family. Against everything maintained by the human race, and against common sense, they claim to introduce democracy into family life, that is, the system of universal franchise.

1420. There is no doubt that families were equal to one another in the state of nature. Consequently, the heads representing families were equally independent in this state. It is also clear that when families met in the persons of their representatives for the sake of settling some disagreement or to unite in society, each head had an equal foundation for a vote.[232] This is a kind of democracy amongst families living together in a state of nature. What remains of it, after the formation of civil society, becomes civil democracy.

1421. But it would be an extraordinary mistake to counsel the transference of this democracy into the very heart of each family. Such an argument would be an abuse of analogy. Although

[231] This error, which establishes an absolute equality between spouses, is more widespread today than one would imagine. According to Zeiller: 'The majority of authors dealing with *natural Right* do not admit any superiority in marriage' (*Diritto naturale privato*, §161. He cites Schott, *Giornale settimanale di giurisprudenza*, t. 1, p. 757). The reason for this error is certainly dependent upon an oversight: people do not realise that the superiority of the husband and the subjection of the wife is simply *responsible and social*; it is in no way *seigniorial* on the one hand, and *servile* on the other.

[232] However, it should not be thought that even in such conditions one head of a family did not have greater influence than another in the decisions reached. The power of a family has an indirect influence and makes one vote more decisive than another. This influence is exercised on the *spontaneity* of the other families who find it to their advantage to go along with the more powerful; this can protect or even harm them. As long as the powerful family makes its influence felt through use of its own rights within their proper sphere, it exercises a *legitimate influence* which cannot be denied it without injury.

[1419–1421]

civil society can indeed be a union of independent families, the members of conjugal society are of their nature dependent, as we have shown.

1422. Nevertheless, we have to distinguish the system which seeks to democratise the family from that which attributes political representation to women. A few words on this matter also will not be out of place.

1423. The union between husband and wife is *full*, according to nature. In the same way, the submission of the wife to the husband is *full* and universal. The *full submission* of wife to husband means that he has absolute right to all that the wife can alienate, whether this applies to her as an individual or belongs to her as an individual through the bond of ownership. *Absolute right* does not, however, exclude *relative right*. Although, relative to her husband, the wife has only her inalienable rights, she has and can have every kind of right relative to all other jural persons;[233] she is a subject of *relative rights*.

1424. The nature of *relative rights* is such that they can be exercised against people to whom they are relative, provided the absolute owner has no objection, or cedes his own right (cf. *RI*, 1277–1293).

The wife, therefore, can represent the family in three cases:

1. Conjointly with the husband, granted his consent, or as his designated delegate. In other words, the husband can defend the family and deal with family affairs through his wife. In union with her husband, the wife acts as his assistant; with his consent, she acts as part of him; delegated by her husband, she acts as his representative.

2. In the absence of the husband, the functions and rights of head of the house devolve on the wife.[234]

3. On her husband's death, she becomes the natural head of the house, and has naturally the rights of the father of the family.

---

[233] *ER*, 326–327. I sometimes used the words *full, complete, absolute* about right to distinguish it from right *relative to certain persons*. It would have been better to have used constantly only one of these three adjectives, but it is difficult to choose. Perhaps the word *absolute* expresses the concept better than the other two.

[234] If the husband were to abandon the family morally, that is, by refusing to carry out his duty as head of the house, the wife could, and indeed would have to supply for his defect.

1425. If civil society is constituted as an aggregation of families which regulate their confederation according to the votes of their heads, the wife can have the following part in political affairs.

In the first case we have mentioned, she can be the *counsellor* of her husband, if he consults her. She thus operates conjointly with him.

1426. She can vote as proxy for her husband, and deal with family affairs on his behalf when he is unavoidably absent and has no one whom he can more conveniently use as his representative, or when he does not wish to be represented by others (cf. 255–258). This is especially the case in serious matters which, if neglected, could be the cause of grave damage to the family.

1427. Nevertheless, moral duty requires that the husband represent the family in person when there is no obstacle to this. A special reason for this, outside the case of necessity, is that acting as a public representative is repugnant to the natural reserve which is the duty of wives.

1428. In the second and third cases we have mentioned, a woman has the right to represent the family at any time or place, although such a right can be exercised more decently by her through delegation to some upright man, relative or friend of the house whom she chooses as her procurator.

1429. A woman has no right to representation in public meetings, therefore, if she is considered as an *individual*; but she has this right, jurally speaking, when she acquires the dignity or exercises the office of head of family.

1430. In the same way, a woman as *wife* has no right of representation in political meetings. This is repugnant to the unity of the head of the house, to the full submission due to her husband, and to the agreement of will that she should have with him. It would be untoward and intolerable if her political opinion were contrary to that of her husband, and husband and wife belonged to opposing political parties as, for instance, could happen if the wife were able to give a separate vote in public debate.

CHAPTER 7

Sanction of the wife's rights in the state of nature

1431. We have imposed on the wife the jural duty of *full submission* to her husband but have nevertheless maintained her rights: we have maintained her *absolute rights*, that is, all those which are summed up in the preservation of her *personal dignity*; we have also maintained her *rights relative* to jural persons different from her husband.

Moreover, we have imposed on the husband jural obligations towards his wife: the obligation of not offending her *personal dignity*; the obligation of exercising his *absolute rights* in such a way that the corresponding *relative rights* in the wife are not lost or injured, but guarded and well-administered by him (cf. *RI*, 1279–1283).

1432. But what sanction is there for the wife's rights in the state of nature? It is certain both in the state of nature and in the social state that the best guarantee of rights is a great love of justice present in both parties, and especially in the stronger party. *Moral education*, therefore, is always the best and most efficacious means, even politically speaking, for the maintenance of mutual rights.

1433. Moreover the woman can also defend her rights efficaciously by moral means. Her virtue, words, tenderness and modest graces can bring about a change for the better in her husband: 'For the unbelieving husband is consecrated through his wife.'[235] This is the first weapon of defence which she can securely employ.

1434. Another moral weapon available to the weak is recourse to God[236] who hears the prayers and tears of those who call upon him with faith and purity of heart.

1435. Besides these moral aids, certain defences and human,

---

[235] 1 Cor 7: 14.

[236] Even pagan political laws, which furnished no civil rights of any sort to slaves, recognised some remaining natural right in them, that is, the right to have recourse to heavenly protection. In Athens, slaves who were harshly treated could flee to the temple of Theseus, or to some other asylum provided for them by religion.

exterior guarantees are available to the woman in the state of domestic society.

1436. First, however, we have to point out that she must observe the rules of just, *natural procedure* both in the exercise of her right of defence (cf. *RI*, 1764–1819, 1942–1950) and in the exercise of her right of restitution[237] (cf. *RI*, 1977–1994).

1437. One of the headings of this procedure is the natural law in favour of the *competent judge*. The competent judge is the social superior — in conjugal society the *husband*. The wife cannot therefore use coercive means against the husband unless she has the kind of certainty about damage done to her rights which would be needed to proceed against a competent judge (cf. *RI*, 611–612).

1438. If then (granted the respect due to the competent judge) the wife has some possibility of action against the husband, she can normally use those means and aids that she has at hand. If this is not sufficient, she can appeal to external persons: first, to her father, brothers and relatives, and then to others. In the state of nature all have the right to come to her assistance (cf. *RI*, 144–156).

1439. Finally, we have to distinguish the *right of defence* of one's own rights, which pertains to the wife, from the *right to cause some harm to the husband* as a result of her defence. These are two rights (cf. *RI*, 1706) governed in their exercise by different norms.

1440. The *right of defence*, without positive harm to the husband, is granted to the wife in all its extension, as we have said, because it is not of itself opposed to full, conjugal union. Simple *truth* and *justice* are not opposed to true love and true charity.

1441. Positive *harm* to the husband,[238] however, is opposed to union. The wife must love the husband to the point of sacrifice;

---

[237] The case of restitution in favour of the wife is verified, for example, when the husband wrongly uses up the external goods to which the wife has a right of relative ownership (certified by the indication mentioned in *RI*, 1283–1284). The husband is obliged to indicate in this way a quantity of his own property equivalent to the quantity of his wife's wrongly used property.

[238] Harm to the husband is not understood as that which he has to suffer by way of satisfaction, or by returning his wife's rights to their pristine state. There is no harm in this.

she must love him even when she suffers. She is not permitted to harm him in the exercise of her right of defence and restitution against him except in the case where the husband attempts to violate her pure, formal rights, or her life, and she has no other way of saving them. In all other cases where her husband is habitually wicked she can at most *harm him negatively* by withdrawing from communal living. She must always be ready to come back to him if he rectifies his unloving, vicious way of life.

1442. The nature of marriage thus tempers the right of defence and restitution possessed by the wife.[239] But the same must be said about the right to defence and restitution that the husband

---

[239] Many errors arose through the over-general application to *rational Right* of certain rules with only a partial value. Positive legislation, incapable or uninstructed, was unable to descend to more special distinctions. It took these rules and gave them a general value. Writers on *natural Right*, but educated through study of positive laws and more intent on elucidating them than on anything else, took these rules as human legislators had made them, and restored them to rational Right, but with their presupposed over-general value. As a result, the science of rational Right was entangled with a great deal of the arbitrariness proper to positive laws.

One example of this can be seen in Wolf's rather odd words: 'Naturally speaking, a husband cannot abrogate to himself encroachment over an unwilling wife; if however the wife does not contradict the husband who abrogates encroachment, her LENGTHY PATIENCE finally passes into right' (part 7, §497). In this way, the heroic virtue of the wife would make her lose her rights, and constant arrogance on the part of the husband would make him acquire them. The *rule* abused by Wolf is valid only when the encroachment exercised by one human being over others 1. is not in itself culpable (the arrogance and pride of the husband in our case is such); 2. when silence is not the result of virtue, but a tacit expression of consent arising not from the impossibility of eliminating the yoke, but from finding it light, useful and lovable (cf. *RI*, 584–585). If these two conditions are absent, the encroachment is simply unjust, and unjust in proportion to its duration. The longer the injustice, the greater it is, and the greater the right in the offended person to defence and restitution.

New rules are needed to judge whether the two conditions we have mentioned are present. Sometimes they must be supposed, although they may not exist, when it cannot be proved that they are lacking; sometimes, even when there is proof of their absence, the exercise of the right of the offended person to throw off the yoke must be denied for reasons of public good, that is, through obligations proper to a higher order which sometimes require people to relinquish the use of their rights.

[1442]

can exercise against his wife towards whom, however, he also has another kind of right, that is, of *correcting* her and inflicting on her moderate corrective punishment.

1443. Rights originating from the *jural state of persons* modify all the other rights that have things as their object (*real rights*). We have seen this occur when speaking of the right of defence and restitution that children have against their parents (cf. *RI*, 841–843).

We go on now to expound the right of parental society.

SECTION TWO

PARENTAL SOCIETY

1444. *Conjugal* society generates within itself another society: *parental* society. The full union of two human individuals of different sex called conjugal society or matrimony was structured by the author of nature to have two levels: 1. *habitual* and continual *union* or 2. *actual union* (cf. 1095). The effect, when actual union fully unites the bodies of the spouses according to their natural fittingness, is to give life to new human beings (cf. 1063). Children, therefore, are a result of the full, actual union of their begetters, and are as it were an addition and extension of their parents. Through children, domestic society is increased in number and becomes two beautifully interwoven societies: that of the spouses, and that of the spouses with the children (*parental* society).

1445. New jural relationships now begin: 1. between parents themselves relative to the offspring; 2. between parents and their offspring; 3. between the children themselves. These relationships are the object of *Right governing parental society*, which we still have to explain. We shall do this briefly. A great deal of *parental Right* has been dealt with in *individual Right* to avoid undue separation of closely related matters (cf. *RI*, 528–863, 1294–1449).

CHAPTER 1

The principle determining the jural relationships between father, mother and children

Article 1.
The principle declared

1446. Generation is the title sustaining *patria potestas* (cf. *RI*, 781–790). What we have said already about generation would be sufficient, except that we still have to determine the rights of the mother relative to the father. We must deal, therefore, with the title of generation in such a way that we can state the respective rights of *patria potestas* of father and mother over the children. Our thought on this matter can be briefly indicated as follows: 'The principle determining the jural relationships between father, mother and children is the special collective person formed according to nature by these three jural persons.'

Article 2.
Application of the principle for determining the difference of *patria potestas* in the father and in the mother

1447. In order to apply this principle, it is necessary to state what is special to the collective person formed on the one hand by the father and mother, and on the other by the parents with the children. There is not in fact a single species of collective persons, nor can the jural relationships we are seeking be deduced from the concept of collective person in general. We have to go to the concept of the special person formed by the three members of the family together: father, mother and child.

1448. Collective persons can exist without the addition of natural bonds as the result of a willed decision on the part of more than one individual person. Such collective persons can be dissolved by the will which in fact formed them. This is not the case with those collective persons in whom, along with the willed decision that forms them, nature itself unites an element of its own which becomes the title of jural-moral obligations.

These obligations cannot be renounced because the title from which they spring was not the work of a willed decision. Such is the case with marriage.

1449. The element placed by *nature* in marriage gives this union four marks *specific* to the collective person of the spouses. These marks are:

1. *Perpetuity*. Marriage cannot be a *full union* between the two individuals who contract it if it is not perpetual.

2. The *equality* of the union from the first day of the marriage to the death of one of the spouses.

3. The union is such that it involves full, dutiful *subjection of the wife as wife* to the husband.

4. Finally, the union is prior to the existence of children and to the new collective person which begins with the birth of children.

1450. This final mark of priority possessed by the collective person of the parents — the fact that children on coming into the world find their parents already united indissolubly — allows us to conclude that the duties and all the jural relationships of children have first to be considered relative to the collective person of the parents. The offspring's first duties are towards this indivisible person, and the first rights of the parents are also those of a single person towards the children. The parents therefore first possess their rights over the children *in solido*, just as the children have jural-moral obligations towards the parents *in solido*.

1451. But how is this solidarity divided? To answer this question we have to return to the principle already posited about the *specific collective person* of the spouses, that is, to the third mark which determines this specification. According to this mark, the wife is fully subject to the husband with a subjection that assists and perfects the full union of the two spouses.

1452. We assigned two titles to this duty of subjection and to the corresponding right of government in the husband: 1. the dynamic feeling shown in the man which moves him to want to be head of a family; 2. the different forces and aptitudes of man and woman.

It follows from the subjection of the woman to her husband that although father and mother have rights and duties of the same *nature* relative to their children from the point of view of their union, they possess them in a different *mode* from the point of view of their inequality.

If the woman's subjection is considered in so far as it proceeds from the natural feeling proper to the man that makes him want to be head of the family, the rights of the man over the children are *formally* different from those of the woman; the father is the *absolute subject* of these rights and duties, the mother is the *relative subject*.

1453. We have already explained what is proper to the *absolute subject* and what is proper to the *relative subject of rights* (cf. *RI*, 1279–1290, 1332–1339). It follows from this teaching that:

1. After the father's death and in his absence, or with his express or tacit consent, the mother can jurally do everything in the children's regard that the father can do.

2. She cannot act in any way against the just and lawful will of the father. She must always esteem this will as just and lawful as long as she is not completely certain that it is unlawful and unjust. The absolute owner is also the competent judge.

1454. But if we consider the different aptitudes and faculties of the husband and wife, we find that by nature they divide their duties to their children. This division is not *according to form*, but rather *according to matter*. In other words, although both father and mother are the subject of the same duties, one is capable of exercising some of them to a higher degree than the other. Preferably, therefore, the exercise of these duties must be given to this person. The rights corresponding to this kind of duties are divided between father and mother according to the same principle.

Article 3.
Application of the principle to determine the nature of *patria potestas* in general

1455. Having determined the relationship of father and mother towards the children, we still have to determine the relationship of both collectively towards the children.

As the jural relationship of father and mother is derived from the *specific difference* of their collective person, so the jural relationship of the collective person of the parents towards the offspring is derived from the *specific difference* of the collective person formed between children and parents.

1456. To clarify the specific difference of the collective person formed between parents and children, it will help if we compare this person with that formed by the parents themselves. Above all, we need to look at the first two marks of the collective person of the spouses, *perpetuity* and *equality*.

1457. The union of parents with their children is *perpetual*, but not always *equal*. We have seen (cf. 1063) that the child is brought into being by a material, living element which is first a portion of his parents but then has its own life.[240] This element, constituted as existent *per se*, is the *nature*, not the *person* of the child (the person is given by God).[241]

1458. The rights of the parents as *specific authors* of the child are relative, therefore, to the *nature* of the child; the *person* of the child remains free. The parents have full *dominion* over the child with the exception of his personal dignity, which is essentially free and seen as an end coming not from the parents but from the Creator.

1459. The *person* of the child occupies its own *body* from the

[240] The act of separation does not prevent the continuation of life. It is the point where the extremities of the two individual lives touch and continue. In other words, it is simply life itself with two personal relationships, which then cease.

[241] *AMS*, 812–837. Samuel Cocceji derives the *patria potestas* principally from the *right over the seed* (*ex jure seminis*): 'The true origin of *patria potestas* is DERIVED NOT SO MUCH FROM GENERATION (where mother and father contribute equally), but FROM CONSENT and FROM THE RIGHT OVER THE SEED' (*Note on Grotius*, bk. 2, c. 5, §1). It is true that *consent* forms marriage, but it is not the principle determining the rights of the spouses. These rights are determined by the *nature of the conjugal union*. Nor does the woman on marrying intend to renounce any right which comes to her from the nature of the union into which she enters. The *right over the seed*, in turn, does not allow anyone to be owner of the plant growing from it unless his ownership of the ground in which it grows is presupposed. It is the ownership of the ground — in this case the dominion of the husband over the wife — which gives the husband priority even in the *patria potestas*. However, the ownership that the husband has over the body of his companion, does not prevent her from retaining some *ownership*, *relative* to all other men, over her own body and *over the seed she receives* from him. As we said, she retains a *relative patria potestas*.

first moment of existence. The physico-moral bond that constitutes this ownership could not be closer because the intellective soul and the body form a single *individual*. The child, therefore, retains naturally the ownership of his own body which cannot be alienated by the parents. It is true that the first elements of this body were once the parents', and consequently owned by them. Now, however, they have separated these threads from themselves and allowed, or rather wanted, the child's soul to inform and individuate them. But since ownership is the result of the physico-moral union of person with the object of ownership, it follows that the ownership the child has over its own body is greater than that retained by its parents. In other words, the child has an *absolute right* over its own body; the parents have a *right relative* to all other people (cf. *RI*, 383–401, 485–495, 529).

1460. Nevertheless, the child, having the right over its own body from the will of its parents, also has a never-ending *ethical duty of gratitude* which obliges it to *use* the body it has received to their advantage and according to their lawful and just will.[242]

1461. We must also note that the baby does not immediately make full use of its own faculties. There is a time during which the parents can make use of the child to their own and its advantage without doing it harm (cf. *RI*, 546–547). It is lawful to use what belongs to others provided this is done without harm to the owner.

But the baby grows and gradually comes to use its faculties to its own benefit. The person in the human being dominates ever more, and thus renders himself less apt to be used by his parents.

1462. The union between parents and offspring, although perpetual, is not therefore always equal, as it is in the case of spouses. It diminishes at various stages of life. Nor is it in any way such that the two become *one flesh*. It is a union of feeling, a moral, jural union, nothing more. And it will help if we expound more at length this union, the foundation of the right that parents have over their offspring.

---

[242] *PE*, 200–205.

CHAPTER 2

Limitations of *patria potestas*

1463. To clear the way we shall begin by indicating the terms beyond which *patria potestas* cannot extend even though certain nations abusively transgress them.

Article 1.
Patria potestas cannot harm the pure, formal rights of the child

1464. We have already indicated the first limitation: neither parents nor others can offend the personal dignity of anyone, be they child, wife or even self.

Article 2.
Patria potestas cannot take a child's life

1465. We have distinguished *ownership* from the *right of ownership* (cf. *RI*, 921–959); in the same way, we must distinguish instinctive and *de facto dominion* from *de jure dominion*. Ownership considered as an instinctive fact of nature is unlimited; similarly, we have to recognise in human beings an instinct tending to unlimited dominion. This natural instinct is easily seen in parents who have given their all to their child and have kept him in their physical power for so long. However, if this *instinctive dominion* is not tempered by *jural-moral reason*, and does not accept the limits which this imposes, it is not raised to the dignity of jural dominion, that is, to the right of dominion.

1466. Keeping in mind the dictate of *jural-moral* reason, we say that the child's connatural right to life (cf. *RI*, 53–58) is valid relative even to the father, who has no more power to kill the child than to kill anyone else.

1467. In fact, the death penalty in civil society is justified only by the necessity for some *exemplary punishment*. We do not think that the head of a family can ever be under such a necessity, which would seem to be present only in a case of a great multitude of people who cannot be ruled except by examples of terror. In a family, it would not seem possible for a recalcitrant child to communicate his indocility easily to siblings who are united through natural love with their parents, whom they normally defend against a wayward brother. Moreover, the head of a family has many other means, made available in nature, for ruling the family. The first is his very own paternal love and the good up-bringing he must provide for the children. The extreme remedy to be used against a child or any other wayward member of the household in the effort to save the domestic society from subversion is the separation and exclusion of the recalcitrant member from the body of the family.[243] Killing the child is directly opposed to the *generative* feeling which moved the father to give him life, and which alone has made him father. The father, by the very fact of renouncing this feeling and acting in a way directly contrary to it, divests himself of his paternity and becomes jurally *inferior* as a result of his wickedness (cf. *RI*, 1995–1996). It seems, therefore, according to the Right of nature, that it is less lawful for a father to kill his child than for him to kill anyone else. However, the father retains his common rights of pre-emption and self-defence which are reinforced by his dignity as father.

1468. Here I would like to make a comment. As long as people lived in domestic society, it seems that God did not allow them to inflict the death penalty. Cain, although guilty of fratricide, is defended by God against the instinct for revenge and for penal justice which would have been aroused in others.[244] It seems that Cain did not fear Adam, his father, but other people. The same can be said about Lamech.[245] The right to inflict the death penalty is not found in Scripture during the entire period preceding the flood. After the flood, the violence of Nimrod is

---

[243] An example of this kind of separation is found in Abraham's family. He sends away Agar, with her child, for the sake of peace with Sarah. Cf. Gen 21.

[244] Gen 4: 15.

[245] Gen 24: 24.

not a jural act, but hateful injustice on a par with that of Cain and Lamech.

The apparatus of legitimate killing is found for the first time in an express order of the divinity. Moreover, it is not an exemplary punishment, but a sacrifice made by a most tender father of his most beloved son in recognition of the supreme dominion of the Creator to whose absolute sovereignty pertain all human lives. Yet, while God requires human willingness to sacrifice life in order to teach people to acknowledge his supremacy, he also refuses these same lives. Isaac does not die under the knife of the father of believers.

Only later does God himself exercise the right to inflict an exemplary death penalty. Such is the case with the two wayward sons of Judah, Her and Onan,[246] as well as the preceding chastisements inflicted on the world or on entire cities. He also seems to have reserved to himself, immediately after the flood, the execution of the death penalty against murderers.[247]

This explains why the first record which has reached us of a jural process with a death penalty is that of Tamar in the twenty-third century of the world.[248] This trial however seems to pertain to a great extent to *civil society*. The people accuse Tamar before Judah, who was not her father. Tamar had been the wife of Judah's son, and on her husband's death had returned as a widow to her father's family. It was not her father, therefore, but her father-in-law who condemned her.[249]

This fact is subject to various explanations: 1. Judah could have condemned her to be burned alive moved by the feeling of revenge for his deceased first-born child, to whom Tamar had been unfaithful — she should have waited to give her hand to the younger sibling promised her for the purpose of raising up

[246] Gen 38.

[247] Gen 9. This can be inferred, it would seem, from the universal prohibition about shedding blood, and from the explicit mention of husband and brothers who could be more interested in inflicting bloody revenge for previous violent deaths and other offences.

[248] Gen 38.

[249] I cannot understand how Jahn is able to say: 'This *patria potestas* was absolute, and took the matter to its extreme of punishment.' He cites in proof of his assertion the passage about Tamar, and the other about the sending away of Agar (*Archeol*. P. 1, c. 11, §167).

children for his brother; 2. he could have condemned her as a result of that feeling of justice (cf. *RI*, 147–156) which is so vehement that it excludes the kind of reflection limiting exemplary punishment; finally, 3. he could have condemned her as a public example at a time when, through lack of fully organised civil society, the people or any individual, but especially the relatives who acted as judges, thought themselves authorised to impose such a punishment.[250]

1469. Although the first two reasons are not valid in the light of developed jural reason, there is nothing to prevent their having a *subjective value* in those times when the understanding was incapable of many distinctions and people were directed more by the faculty of thought than that of *abstraction*, which had scarcely been used.[251]

1470. The third reason enables us to explain other ancient laws which gave fathers the right to kill their children.[252] These were *civil* laws through which fathers were brought to act in some way as judges in civil society.[253]

1471. As a result, the following advantages accrued to the law of the city:

1. It seconded the instinct of dominion which, placed by nature in the bosom of parents, was spontaneous. Human beings were unable to submit immediately to wholly regular order without giving way to a great extent to their native tendencies.

[250] It would seem, from the fact that Judah releases Tamar from the punishment as soon as he discovers that he himself had had intercourse with her, that the first explanation is the correct one. As the representative of the dead husband to whom Tamar had been in some way unfaithful, he was the offended party. And according to the Mosaic laws, the guilty person was handed over for punishment to the person he had offended (Deut 17:[10]). This was in conformity with the natural Right of superiority and inferiority (cf. *RI*, 1995–1999), and is another reason for excluding *patria potestas* from this incident.

[251] Cf. *SP*.

[252] Cf. Dion, *Orat.* 15.

[253] Justinian mentions this explicitly in his *Institutions* where he derives the power of Roman fathers over their children not from *rational* but from *civil Right*. 'The right of power over our children is PROPER TO ROMAN CITIZENS. There are no other people who have the kind of power that we have over our children' (bk. 1, t. 9).

2. It strengthened domestic government, and provided a civil magistrate in every family.[254]

3. It lessened the punishment by entrusting its application to fatherly love, at least for crimes done within the household. At the time, there were no clearly established criminal laws or laws of procedure. This meant that judgments were to a great extent left to arbitrary decisions. In this state, it was better to commit them to paternal decisions than to those of strangers.[255]

Article 3.
Patria potestas cannot sell a child as a bond-servant

1472. The servitude which disavows the dignity of end in a human being is intrinsically unlawful (cf. *RI*, 128–133). The attempt to reduce any human being whatsoever to such servitude is always wrong; it is much worse if this human being is one's own child.

1473. What is the situation if the servitude in question consists only in the permanent placement of a human being in work? It cannot be said that this is intrinsically unjust, but it is very hard for the person subject to it and is opposed in the highest degree to paternal love. We can only judge whether a father can have such a jural-moral faculty if, in an extreme case, we find a combination of circumstances which provides sufficient reason for his taking so cruel a step.

These reasons are not sufficient to give the father a reasonable stimulus to such action unless they also indicate simultaneously in the child a *jural obligation* to put himself or allow himself to be put in this position, in this way.

As far as I can see, there is only one case which provides these reasons. It concerns the well-being of the child and is often

---

[254] Livy says that amongst the Romans the house was governed as the city was. He calls the father 'the domestic magistrate'. Seneca says the same: 'Because it is useful for youth to be ruled, we impose domestic magistrates, as it were, on them' (*De Beneficiis*, bk. 3, c. 11).

[255] 'The law, knowing that a father would judge rightly, granted him this section of right,' says Sopater. The Mosaic laws allowed parents only to accuse children before the tribunal and have them punished by themselves (Deut 21: 18).

found in our poor human history.[256] If the child is offered the choice of death or servitude, his father can command him to accept servitude and the child would have to obey. The father has the right to safeguard the life of the child he has generated even against the child's will. The case for the father is further strengthened if the child is only a baby.

1474. He cannot place the child in work perpetually to punish or chastise him. Punishments inflicted by the father must be

1. *Corrective*, that is, aimed at the child's amendment. Punishments cannot be perpetual if they are to cease when amendment has come about.

2. *Necessary* for the good order of the family. The punishment of perpetual placement is not necessary because in an extreme case it would be sufficient to exclude the incorrigible child from a share in the family goods.

1475. We still have to see if such perpetual placement could be carried out for the father's good. I have no doubt that this is the case if there is a question of saving the father's life. The child must forever place his work, or let it be placed, if there is no other way of saving the life of his parent. This is a *jural obligation* because 1. the child is by nature a thing of his father in everything that does not harm his personal dignity and 2. placement contributes to the ordained good of the family.

Article 4.
Patria potestas cannot inflict any punishment nor cause any harm to the child unless this is necessary for the ordained good of the family

1476. Finally, *patria potestas* cannot capriciously inflict any punishment nor cause any harm to the child.

1477. In the first place, parents have the rights and duties given

---

[256] In order to save the lives of the children they could not feed, Mexicans sold their offspring. Jornandes narrates that the Goths sold their children to save them from death: 'Parents do the same thing as they try to care for the safety of their beloved children. They decide that it is better for them to lose every natural quality rather than life; better to be sold and mercifully fed than to be kept and die' (c. 26).

by the concept of individual Right to all human beings. These rights and duties are somewhat modified by the parental condition.

1478. Parents also have the right to inflict corrective punishment on their children even after they have left home. The exercise of this right must be carried out prudently and with the probable hope of attaining its end, that is, amendment. This is a governmental right, which cannot be called *social* because the punishment and correction of an *individual* does not pertain properly speaking to social reason.[257]

1479. If, however, the child remains in parental society, the right of correction and of inflicting punishment is a right pertaining to social government, which must be exercised only for the ORDAINED GOOD OF THE FAMILY, the principle determining at one and the same time both the *extension* of governmental right of domestic society and the *limits* of this right. This will become clearer in the following chapter.

CHAPTER 3

Patria postestas can do all that is required
for the ordained good of the family

Article 1.
Unlawfulness of a power, and unlawfulness
in the way it is exercised

1480. In fact, the *patria potestas* which presides over domestic society is aimed solely at the *good of the family*. This good, therefore, determines the extension of the *patria potestas*.

1481. To proceed with clarity, we first have to distinguish

---

[257] We noted that the person who governs or administers a society need not belong to the society he governs or administrates (cf. *USR*, 313, 188). His office, however, is no less social because of this. On the other hand, government which does not concern a society, but mere *individuals*, is not a social office or right. For example, the right of a teacher over his disciples is not social, etc.

power from the *way* in which power is exercised. It is possible to conceive mentally of a power which is *per se* harmful to the family. This kind of power does not enter into the sphere of *patria potestas* from which indeed it is excluded. Examples of this would be the killing or mutilation of the child, or his moral perversion.

1482. But harm can also arise from a wayward manner of exercising lawful power. In this case, the parent possess the power, but not the right to abuse it.

1483. The child can use those means of defence against the abuse which we have assigned to the wife against her husband.

Article 2.
The ordained good of the family

1484. If we want to determine precisely what is consistent and what inconsistent with the ordained good of the family, we first have to know the nature of this ordained good. This in turn leads to another question: 'What is the value of each member of the family in the total sum of the good of the body?'

1485. We have to consider that 'family' is not understood as the simple social aggregation of father, mother and children, but above of all the specific nature of the bonds uniting these three elements of domestic society. The preservation, the respect for these bonds is the principal, essential part of family good. We have to consider these bonds, therefore, in determining the nature of the *ordained good* of the family.

1486. For the sake of brevity, we shall reduce the bonds to two. The first, binding children with their parents, is a *blood-bond*. Hence the rights, common to father and mother, which the jurists call *jura sanguinis*. These never cease, even when the child leaves the parental society to found a new family.

1487. The second bond normally follows on the first, although it is not as insoluble as the first. It is a *bond of society*. Hence the rights which jurists call *jura familiae*, and which we shall call *rights of domestic society*. In the word 'family' we include both kinds of rights, rights of blood and social rights. These rights are not common to the parents, but pertain properly only to the head of the house as his very own.

1488. We said that the *social bond* in the family normally arises from the *blood-bond*. The reason is that although the blood-bond immediately produces of its nature a right of seigniory, it is nevertheless the occasion and also the jural-moral cause of the society. I say that it is also the cause because, although a *master can* form a society with his bond-servants (cf. *USR*, 185–190), father and mother are *obliged* to form a society with their children as soon as the latter are capable of society. Hence, there is a jural, moral necessity for such a society.

1489. The blood-bond therefore occasions the social bond because it produces the following rights for the parents: the right

1. To *occupy* the child born to them (cf. *RI*, 816–819).

2. To *use* the child for their own advantage, but without harm to the child.

3. To *rear* the child physically.

4. To *educate* the child in the way they think best for the child.[258]

---

[258] This right is truly the most precious that a father can have. At present, it is being vindicated in France by the complaints and remonstrations of all decent, religious people against its violation by the monopoly exercised over the universities. It will be helpful, therefore, if we add some comments here.

1. Fathers have the duty to give their children the best education and soundest instruction. It follows that they also have the right, and an inalienable right, to do this: 'Every human being has an inalienable right to fulfil his own moral duties' (cf. *SP*, 219–220).

2. Fathers are the *competent judges* about the best education and soundest instruction to be given to their own children. Each person is the competent judge of the use of his own right (cf. *RI*, 195) — as he is of his own good and evil (cf. *RI*, 610) — which fathers see in their children.

3. The importance of such a right and of the moral obligation of exercising it with conviction is obvious in the case where fathers see their children exposed to irreligious and impious instruction at the hands of teachers established by law. It cannot be wondered that the whole of the French episcopate has risen, as one man, against the instruction, often contrary to Catholic doctrine, forced upon French youth by the government.

4. Because the right of fathers is inalienable, it cannot be impeded or violated in any way by civil authority, which must protect and help it, as we shall see later.

5. Finally, Catholic fathers have the duty, imposed on them by the perfect

5. To *keep the child in their society* until he marries and forms a new family, or certainly until something intervenes which makes it helpful to the child and his descendants to permit him to leave the domestic society of his parents (cf. *RI*, 820–822).

These five rights characterise *parental society* and distinguish it from other societies in so far as these rights are considered as the jural effect of the *blood-bond* that exists between children and their parents.

1490. The maintenance of these bonds and the rights which result from them is therefore an essential part of the *ordained good* of the family; *patria potestas* can do everything which leads to this end, with the exception of intrinsically evil actions.

Article 3.
Continuation: the value of each member of a family in the sum total of the good of the body

1491. We have to analyse the fifth of the rights we have listed, that is, the right 'to keep children in the society of their parents'. Our question, 'What is the value of each member of the family in the sum total of the good of the body?' will to a great extent depend for its answer on the analysis of this right.

1492. Usefulness is a constitutive of every right.[259] What utility is present therefore in the right that parents have to keep their children in their society?

The utility is twofold: first, relative to the parents, then relative to the children. The entire ordained good of the family is reduced to this double utility, the elements of which we need to compare for the sake of understanding their relative values.

1493. Nature has inserted two feelings in the heart of parents which sometimes develop in opposition to one another. These are:

1. The feeling for generating children for one's own good.

theocratic society to which they belong, not to recognise any religious instruction other than that which comes from their pastors, to whom Christ has said: 'Go therefore and MAKE DISCIPLES OF ALL NATIONS' (Mt 28: 20).

[259] *ER*, 252–255.

2. The feeling for generating children for their good and the good of their descendants.

1494. The first of these *natural feelings* gives rise to the right of parents to draw profit for themselves from the children. This right finds its response in the obligation of children to second this effect.

1495. The second feeling gives rise to the right of parents to provide for the good of their children and their descendants.

1496. The first is a *right of dominion*, the second *of beneficence*.

1497. If these two feelings are considered in their perfection, we find that the first, which is easily contented, is willingly sacrificed to the second, prevalent right. In other words, if we consider human nature in its perfection, parents find it sufficient to live. For the rest, their greater good lies in that of the children themselves and their line. Granted a tolerably comfortable life for the parents, the line of their children has greater value in the total sum of the ordained good of the family.

1498. In this light, it is easy to determine the character of *patria potestas* in its exercise according to nature. It has

1. A small element of *dominion* (useful to the parents).

2. A large element of *beneficent government* (useful for the children).

1499. Our conclusion is that *patria potestas* can do everything needed to obtain the utility of parents and children according to these natural proportions, but that it cannot alter these proportions which constitute the *ordained good* of the family.

Article 4.
The relative proportions of seigniorial and governmental right found in *patria potestas*

1500. We can say, therefore, that *patria potestas* is a governmental right, but in a society whose members do not all have the same value.

1501. The ruler has to lead his society in such a way that the available utilities are divided amongst the members according to the degree of value of each member. In domestic society, where the father possesses the dignity proper to author, master and head, it is right that he should take account also of himself in exercising his government. His very office as ruler of the society authorises and obliges him to maintain his own *right of seigniory*. This right of the father is therefore an element indivisible from governmental right in parental and domestic society, and indeed gives rise to governmental right.

1502. On the other hand, *seigniorial right* is led to its end by *governmental right* which tends to ensure that all the members of a society retain and enjoy in their entirety the rights they possess. Seigniorial right is, in this respect, subordinated to governmental right in the way that rights are said to be subordinate to the faculty that has to regulate their modality.

1503. If we wish, we can synthesise the principal lines in the father's seigniorial right and reduce them to the following:

1. The father possesses the *right of government* over what is his own, and as father. This right cannot be taken from him by anyone.

2. The feeling that has moved the father to found a family was without doubt *his own satisfaction*. Under this original title the father, head of the family, is also its *end*, and must be considered so by all the members of the family who, as such, draw their existence from him. Under this aspect, the father is master and the others *bond-servants*. The seigniory and the bond-service are, however, altogether special, and are determined by the quality of the *paternal feeling* and by the *natural satisfaction* sought by the father through his paternity.

3. The natural *satisfaction* sought by the father in paternity (in other words, the end of paternity and of the family itself) is that of leaving on earth after himself children who, endowed with all external and internal worth, perpetuate a flourishing line. This particular characteristic of *paternal satisfaction* tempers, as it were, seigniorial selfishness.

If we consider paternity in its psychological origin, there is no doubt that it manifests itself with a character of selfishness inseparable from seigniory. Considered in the object to which it tends, however, and in which such selfishness seeks satisfaction, the selfish connotation is diminished. The selfishness is transformed into a tendency to love, into a propensity to diffusion, into a beneficent instinct, all of which belong to the very reality of things. Paternity, therefore, is a human feeling that seeks and posits its own good in the good of others — not of any others, but of the beings generated by it. It seeks its own good which, however, is found in the good of the offspring. The interest and the love proper to parents leads them to maximum disinterestedness and generosity. According to nature, parents feel they possess such a qualitative and quantitative *good of their own* in the *good of the offspring* that they place this good before all their other good, and even before the good of their own life. It is true that this intensity is characteristic rather of parental love in its perfection (in stimulated affection) than of the degree to which it normally attains as a result of spontaneous affection. Only perfection, however, is the basis for determining, according to nature, the rights of parents and the duties of children.

Article 5.
Comment on Roman legislation about *patria potestas*

1504. This last observation shows why the most ancient Roman legislation grants to fathers the fullest power over their children, and why this power was gradually restricted. Opinion about paternal rights, as well as customs and legislation recognised and sanctioned by the city, take their norm from the *average love* shown by a nation in its fathers. If common *paternal love*, that is, the *average* level of love, is in fact greater, fathers necessarily have more rights. Opinion accords them more rights, and legislative instinct transcribes as public laws all those things which opinion grants to fathers. If such love decreases, the citizens immediately become restless and see as necessary some limitation to *patria potestas*.

1505. The reason for this is profound, and flows from the theory of rights that we have expounded. The principle determining rights is that of *ownership*,[260] *a feeling* (a love) which binds things to persons (cf. *RI*, 936). The greater this *feeling* the more pronounced the ownership, the more painful its violation, and the more lively the jural resentment. In our case, if a father

[260] *ER*, 329–359.

feels he has a greater good in his child, *patria potestas* is, according to nature, more absolute.

In addition, if paternal *love* is more intense, *patria potestas* can extend itself without fear of abuse.

These are the two motives according to which civil law normally grants greater breadth to *patria potestas* wherever paternal love is more vigorous. It is at this point that *patria potestas* is 1. effectively greater, according to nature; 2. less likely to danger of abuse.

1506. On the other hand, a comparison between civil legislations enables us to indicate peoples and periods in which parental love has been greater. There is no doubt that normal, average parental love is more restricted where limits placed to *patria potestas* are more restricted.

1507. The use of this criterion enables us to conclude that paternal love was generally greater at the beginning of the Roman republic than in later, degenerate times.

1508. Ancient Roman legislation left *patria potestas* untouched, just as it would have been in the pure state of domestic society. Moreover, it constituted fathers as magistrates and civil judges within their own families where they could even condemn their children to death.

1509. The child was considered by these laws as the father's *bond-servant*.[261] This servitude of the child, inherent to paternity, was however *relative to the father*, and united to *freedom of the child relative to all other human beings*, before whom the child enjoyed the same freedom as the father with whom he formed a single person,[262] and whose accessory and increment[263] he was. The father's *relative seigniory* is therefore one of those inalienable rights that certain authors have admirably named *jura personalissima*. As a result, fathers could not sell their children as bond-servants, according to the explicit statement of

---

[261] *Res mancipi, Just.*, bk. 1, t. 9. When the first human being was born, his mother expressed the law of dominion of parents over their children with the words: 'I HAVE POSSESSED A MAN through God,' the very meaning given to the name of Cain, the first-born (Gen 4: 1 [Vulgate]).

[262] Samuel Cocceji, *Dissert., Proem.* 12, bk. 3, c. 4, sect. 2, §159.

[263] In Num 32: 14, children are called *patrum incrementa*, just as Virgil spoke of *magnum ovis incrementum* (*Ecl.* 4).

a rescript of Constantine inserted into the Code: 'Freedom was so highly considered by the ancients that fathers, who (once) had the right of life and death over children, were not permitted TO DEPRIVE THEM OF FREEDOM.'[264] The reason for this is found in the very nature of paternal seigniory which is certainly higher than any other and indeed directed to the good of the father. But this good, if determined by upright, natural feeling, as we said, can only be the good of the child. It is, therefore, a *seigniory* of an altogether special nature which above all seeks the *good of the bond-servant*. If the child were to be sold by the father, he would enter a servitude of an altogether different nature from that of *filial servitude*; he would no longer share in paternal freedom. On the other hand, the father cannot sell his own seigniory, which is inalienable, precisely because he cannot sell either his love or his paternity. According to natural Right, therefore, it is unjust that the father should at will sell his child as a bond-servant. For the same reason, the power of life and death was entrusted by the city to the father alone, and could not be alienated; it pertained to the very nature of paternity: it was a *jus personalissimum*.[265]

1510. Many rights, useful to the children themselves, derived to the father from *paternal dominion* and from *filial servitude*. For example: parents could take action if the child had sold himself, or others had sold him;[266] they could prevent the trial of their children;[267] they could bring action for theft against those

---

[264] *C.*, bk. 8, t. 47: 10; *ibid.*, bk. 7, t. 16: 1.

[265] Later, this right to inflict the death penalty was restricted in such a way that the father could establish it, but only the judge could pronounce it: 'You will not forbid this person (the son) from being chastised by the right of *patria potestas* if he does not acknowledge due piety towards his father, and you will employ more severe remedies if he is contumacious. You will bring him before the Procurator of the province so that he may PRONOUNCE THE SENTENCE THAT YOU ALSO WISH TO BE INFLICTED.' Thus a rescript of the Emperor Alexander (228 AD) inserted into the *Justinian Code* (bk. 8, t. 47: 3). Fabro (*Cod. de patr. potest.*, bk. 8, t. 33, def. 1 *et n. ult. in allegat.*) says that there were examples in the senate of Savoy where children were condemned to the galleys on the sentence pronounced by their fathers, who could remit the penalty granted slight damage inflicted on them by the children.

[266] *Dig.*, bk. 6, t. 1: 2; and bk. 43, t. 30: 1.

[267] *Dig.*, bk. 43, t. 1: 2.

[1510]

who tried to take the children away;[268] they could use the Aquilian law against those who harmed their children.[269]

1511. Other rights, as useful to the whole family as to the child, were those of correcting and chastising the child himself.[270]

1512. The right of absolute ownership by the father over all the goods of the child was also recognised. Consequently, what the child acquired, he acquired for the father [*App.* no. 11].

1513. Finally, the right to locate the child's work was always left to the father, as we said, when there was a question of sustenance for the child.[271]

CHAPTER 4

The jural rights and purely moral rights of parents

1514. The things impossible to *patria potestas* (which we have enumerated) constitute the *jural rights* of the father relative to the children. Because they *harm* the children, these things detract from the children's *activity*.[272] Moreover, they are not required, but excluded by the end of domestic society. On the other hand, the duty of parents to give their children a good physical, intellectual, technical, moral and religious education,

---

[268] *Just.*, bk. 4, t. 1: 9; *Dig.*, bk. 47, t. 2: 37.

[269] *Dig.*, bk. 9, t. 2: 5, 7.

[270] 'It is not true that a father was able to hand his children over for punishment. It is rumoured that Tribonianus did once obtain this, but there is no trace of this custom extant in the *Digests*' (Samuel Cocceji, *Dissert. Proem.* 12, bk. 3, c. 4, sect. 2, 160. Cf. Heinnecius, *Antiq. Rom.*, bk. 3, t. 8, §3. The faculty of chastising children recognised by the laws was gradually restricted amongst the Romans by means of the interpretations given by the *prudent*, and by the *edicts of the rulers*, as we can see from the *Code of Justinian*, bk. 9, t. 15. This shows on the one hand that the faculty was abused by fathers as corruption increased, and on the other that public authority (the legislative instinct) and the children themselves gradually became less tolerant of abuses. The laws of a nation become more vigilant as *jural resentment* increases because 'the *average degree* of jural resentment influences the legislative instinct, which allows itself to be directed by jural resentment.

[271] *Cod.*, bk. 4, t. 43, and bk. 7 and 16.

[272] *ER*, 274–292.

while extremely serious, is only of a *moral* character (cf. *RI*, 795–803).

1515. It follows that children abandoned by their parents, and accepted and educated by other people, cannot, according to rational Right, take any jural action against the parents. These children are simply free not to recognise *patria potestas* in the parents, or in the one who abandoned them, although there is still a duty of never offending persons who have given them life, and of giving the bare honour which is always part of *blood-right*. The father or the parents who, having what is necessary to nourish their children, do not acknowledge them and leave them exposed, deprive them by that action of the life they have given and, by showing their unworthiness and incapacity, deprive themselves of the sacred rights springing from paternity.

1516. But why is it that authors are normally inclined to attribute a jural character to the parents' duty of rearing and educating their children? If we leave aside their reasons, explained elsewhere (cf. *RI*, 797–802), we still have to indicate the feeling that secretly moves them to embrace this opinion. I think we can find its origin in the special character of the previously mentioned duty of parents.

1517. Purely moral, human duties are divided into two classes. Both have as their object the respect due to human feeling. The first includes those duties intended to produce something pleasing to human feeling, that is, to increase this feeling in a satisfying manner, and perfect it. The second includes duties which require that nothing should be done to injure or harm this feeling in any way.

1518. *Jural duties* also have the object of not injuring or harming human feeling. How are they distinguished from purely *moral* duties? To uncover this distinction, it is sufficient to recall the definition already given of jural duty: we defined it as 'that which obliges a person to leave intact and free any activity proper TO ANOTHER PERSON'.[273]

'To leave an activity intact and free' is exactly the same as not injuring or harming 'human feeling'. Every human activity is in

[273] *ER*, 294.

[1515–1518]

the feeling, and is a feeling. The specific difference is found only in the words: TO ANOTHER PERSON.

1519. Therefore, *purely moral duties* of the second class (that is, negative duties), as well as *jural duties*, oblige human beings not to harm *human feeling*. This feeling, however, can be in the person who has the duty or in a different person. In the first case, it is not a jural, but simply a moral duty; in the second case, it is also jural. It is characteristic of jural duty to regard other persons, not the person who has the obligation.[274]

1520. Let us apply this teaching to the parents' duty of rearing and educating their children. There is no doubt that rearing and educating them is pleasing to the natural feeling of the children. If, however, parents do not rear their children, they are not actually doing anything to harm the natural feeling of the children; they are simply leaving this as it is, as nature has made it (cf. *RI*, 802). If therefore we consider this duty of parents towards the feeling and activity proper to their children, we see that it is simply a moral duty pertaining to the first class.

1521. We must also consider the parents' duty relative to the feeling of the parents themselves. This feeling is active, and requires that the parents perfect through education the work they have begun with generation.[275] If they do the opposite, they oppose their paternal and maternal feeling and thus, by their inactivity, harm human nature, of which the feeling is such a noble part.[276] But the prohibition on harming or opposing a human feeling is precisely what the duty of educating one's children has in common with jural duties. What separates one from the other is the seat of the contradicted, opposed feeling. In jural duties, as we have said, feelings are involved that have

[274] *ER*, 299.

[275] The obligation of education can also be deduced from the principle that 'every rational being must, according to his capacity, produce perfect works'. This is *logical*. But operating logically is a duty that people have towards the impersonal truth and towards themselves. It is also a moral duty towards others if the action regards intelligent beings, but it is never a jural duty.

[276] Parents who refuse to satisfy the natural feeling urging them to rear their children do not leave the feeling in the state it has according to nature, but actually oppose it. They have to make an effort to resist their natural love, if indeed they have not already extinguished it in their own souls through prolonged wickedness, which is always contrary to what is naturally good.

[1519–1521]

their seat in a person different from the one who is the subject of duty; in paternal and maternal love, the feeling has its seat in the parents who themselves are the subjects of the duty of which we are speaking. The duty of education is, therefore, a moral duty pertaining to the second class.

The equality between the element indicated in both jural and purely moral duties pertaining to the second class may have led authors to attribute a *jural* quality to the duty of rearing and educating one's children.[277]

CHAPTER 5

Jural blood-relationships, social domestic relationships and civil-domestic relationships between parents and children

1522. We have already distinguished in the family *blood-rights* and *social rights*. Both become *civil rights*, without ceasing to be natural rights, when civil laws consent to them, recognise and sanction them.

1523. But because civil laws go further and attribute or deny to parents and children certain relationships for the sake of public good, we have to say something about each of these three founts of jural relationships between parents and children, that is, about *blood*, the *social bond of the family* and the *social bond of the city*.

Article 1.
Jural blood-relationships between parents and their children

1524. Jural blood-relationships, because founded on a *fact* that cannot be undone, never cease. Consequently, the law which places an impediment to marriage between blood-relations, is equally efficacious in forbidding and rendering more blameworthy all illegitimate unions.

1525. In the same way, parents preserve the same natural

---

[277] Cf. on this duty, *PE*, 215–217.

duties towards children they have generated outside marriage, even though such duties are not safeguarded by the civil law.[278]

1526. When the *social bond* ceases through the departure of the child (for any reason) from the paternal family, *simple honour* is always due to the parents. It is for this reason also that the diriment impediment forbidding marriage to such children remains.[279]

1527. Finally, the father retains perpetual and inviolable rights to teach, correct and punish his children not according to a *social title*, but through a title of *seigniorial, individual* right which has as its aim the good of the child, founded in blood-relationship. The father also has the right to live off the goods of his children if he is otherwise unprovided for.

Article 2.
Socio-domestic relationships between parents and children

1528. The father of the family, or the mother in his place, has *full power to govern* his children. This is the result of nature, not of the children's will. Nature also determines the exercise of this government by placing in the hearts of parents *paternal* and *maternal feeling* which, kept upright and sincere,[280] must direct their government.

---

[278] According to Roman law, the right to provisions relative to parents was not given for children born of incestuous marriages. The parents' fault was thus punished in the children (*Cod.*, bk. 5, t. 5; and *Nov.*, 12, 139, 154). The Church, however, always wise and beneficent, did not take account of such laws. She introduced a contrary custom and gradually succeeded in amending civil law on this point too by bringing it in line with the requirements of humanity and rational-Christian Right.

[279] Adoptive children do not have these *jural blood-relationships* with *those who adopt* them, but *social relationships* only. We shall speak of these in the next two articles.

[280] We have noted that *fatherly feeling* can be destroyed or perverted by malice. The feeling, constituting the rule of which we are speaking, is therefore the feeling that *conforms to nature*. Note, however, that it varies in degree. Consequently, *paternal government* also is subject to *lawful variations. Patria potestas* cannot therefore be identical (relative to its degree and accidents) in all families if we consider humanity in the state of nature and of family.

1529. Because a great part of this government is the good of the children, it extends as they grow up (cf. *RI*, 637–771). The adult children gradually become the father's counsellors in the government of the family, and the older children must have some natural preponderance over their younger siblings [*App.*, no. 12].

1530. According to Aristotle, followed by Grotius,[281] three stages can be distinguished in children: that which precedes the use of *moral freedom* (προαιρεσις),[282] which Aristotle calls the time *of imperfect judgment;*[283] that in which *moral choice* is shown although the child continues to remain in the paternal family; that in which the child has left the paternal family and has formed his own.

1531. In this final stage, relationships of merely domestic society ease between parents and children. Only blood-relationships remain.

1532. Parents have the right to propose spouses for their children, but not the right to force consent if the spouses are not acceptable. Parents do have the right, however, to insist that the children choose partners whom the parents judge suitable — descendants of the children are their descendants and they have the right, therefore, to provide for sound offspring. The children have a corresponding jural duty to choose spouses thought suitable by the parents. The parents' right here is co-extensive with that of competent judges, and they can punish children who spurn their right judgment. Blind passion does not excuse the children. On the other hand, it is highly advantageous to the children to be directed in a matter of such importance by the mature, affectionate, good sense of their parents.

1533. In the second stage, the children are subject to the natural head of the family for the sake of the family good itself. But with the good of the family dutifully assured by the head, the children are then free.

If children, therefore, have some public dignity or office, they would not depend upon paternal authority in exercising it. This

---

[281] *De J. B. et P.*, bk. 2, c. 5: 2.

[282] For the period when *moral freedom* begins in the human being, cf. *AMS*, 564–566.

[283] του βουλεττικου ατελδυς, *Pol.*, 1, c. 8; *Nicom.*, bk. 3, c. 4.

freedom does not of its nature prejudice the good of the family (provided there is no abuse). It is useful for the children and for the family itself, whose principal good is that of the children.

1534. At the first and second stages, both parents have full, governmental dominion over the children which, however, in the first stage, extends almost accidentally to a greater sphere: 1. because they have to take total care of the children who, with their faculties still undeveloped, cannot provide for themselves; 2. because they can more easily turn the children to their own advantage and comfort (without doing them harm), just as they can with things that are occupied (cf. *RI*, 539–553). Nevertheless, children are suitable subjects of rights, ownership and relative dominion even at this first stage. According to Plutarch,[284] infants have these rights as a matter of *possession* (εν κτησει), not as a matter of use (εν κρησει). I would say that they are not even a matter of possession, but of mere ownership and, still less, of mere relative-jural freedom (cf. RI, 254–256).

1535. Finally, we should note that even when the children leave their parents, or the latter die, the social bond never ceases entirely. This explains why in Roman laws the word 'family' sometimes means the domestic society properly so-called, and sometimes the more ample grouping made up by agnates as well: 'The name "family" signifies a certain body which is limited either BY ITS OWN RIGHT or by the right COMMON TO ALL COGNATES.'[285]

1536. In fact, natural and hereditary successions, which we have defended and expounded (cf. *RI*, 1294–1449) presuppose that jural relationships between ascendants and descendants do not cease when families divide or at the death of certain ascendants or descendants. The principle that the ancestor, although dead, unifies the relatives, is often extremely helpful according to natural law for solving certain intricate questions relative to succession which threatened to disturb public tranquillity.

---

[284] *De Fortit. Alex.*, c. 11.

[285] 'In common right, we speak of the family composed of all the agnates. Although the father of the family may be deceased and all the individuals have their own families, all those who were under a single power are rightly said to be of the same family because they issue from the same house and people' (*Digest.*, bk. 50, t. 16, l. 195).

When Lothair II died, should he have been succeeded by his brothers, or by his uncles Louis of Germany and Charles the Bald?[286] If the question had to be decided on the basis of simple, rational Right, the succession would obviously have gone to the brothers as the nearest relatives. They belonged to the same domestic society as Lothair because they were the offspring of the same predecessor, who provided unity for his descendants. The uncles were not part of these descendants.

1537. It would seem that the advantage of the first-born in respect of his siblings should be recognised: 1. in his right to the choice of shares in the division of goods and also 2. in his right of preference to that which is of its nature indivisible (the other children should receive in recompense what is possible and equable). Indian laws, which determine successions minutely — because they are laws aimed principally at regulating domestic rather than civil society — are mindful to maintain this and other rights for the first-born. They say about the right to what is indivisible: 'A single male goat, a single sheep or any single animal with uncloven foot cannot be divided. . . any male goat or sheep that remains over after things have been shared out belongs to the eldest brother.'[287]

[286] Cf. G. Miiller, bk. 14, c. 14.

[287] *Mânava-Dharmasâstra*, bk. 9: 119. The principle which attributes to the eldest brother what is of its nature indivisible in the paternal heritage determines the succession of empires in favour of the first-born. In fact, every civil society is of its nature indivisible and exceeds the attributes of the person with the supreme right to govern or divide it. It is not the *right of government* which can divide a State, but the *right of seigniory* which is sometimes mixed with the right of government. When Constantine, Charlemagne and Vladimir (1000 AD), all princes called 'Great', divided their empires amongst their children, they considered themselves as *lords*, not as *civil rulers*. Whether this was right or wrong cannot be discussed here. What is certain is that such divisions caused wretched quarrels in the ruling families with unlimited damage to the people.

Article 3.
The jural civil-domestic relationships
between parents and children

1538. The positive laws of the city have two aims: 1. to guarantee the natural rights of individual jural persons; 2. public good. Normally, the majority of laws with the first aim are called *civil* just as the majority of laws with the second aim are called *political* (cf. 417–424).

In the present state of legislation, both kinds of laws, whether they have the rights of *individuals* or *domestic societies* as their object, are found mingled together in what is called the *Civil Code*.

1539. Consideration of the *civil, political* laws determining jural relationships between parents and children shows that these laws differ from *natural Right* (in so far as it is opposed to positive Right) in two ways: either

1. by *not acknowledging certain jural-natural relationships*, which are thus left undefended (abandoned in this fashion they pertain to what we have called *extra-social* Right); or

2. by *adding certain jural-positive relationships to natural relationships*.

1540. *Status familiae*[288] is the name given by Roman laws to the condition by which a person was constituted member of a family in the eyes of civil society. This condition results from the complex of natural jural relationships recognised by the city and added to those which the city itself creates positively.

1541. The natural relationships of *illegitimate children* are amongst those not acknowledged by certain legislations. The Romans, for example, did not acknowledge such people as children because the law began with the principle: 'A child is one shown to be such by rightful marriage'.[289]

---

[288] The *family condition* is therefore a complex right which can be impugned or defended before the law of the city. Legal actions taken amongst the Romans to defend a *person's condition* as citizen were called *pre-judicial*, not *real* or *personal* because the question under discussion concerned a more general right which was, as it were, preliminary to the defence of other rights. Only after verifying the jural *condition* of a citizen as such was it possible to pass judgment on the real, personal rights pertaining to that *condition*.

[289] *Dig.*, bk. 1, t. 6: 3, 6.

1542. The basic reason of this law was: 'If the marriage is not legitimate, only maternity, not paternity, can be verified.' This gives rise to the other rule: 'In the case of legitimate marriage, the father is followed; the populace FOLLOWS THE MOTHER in its enquiries.'[290]

1543. Often, however, paternity can be established in the absence of legitimate marriage. Why exclude the father if sure proof is available of his identity?

1544. These imperfections of the law, often caused by poor development of the faculty of abstraction, need to be noted.[291] Initially, legislators were content to reason on the basis of principles which were sometimes, but not always, true. In these last cases, when the principles were insufficient, *natural Right* suffered from their dispositions. It was either devoid of recognition and defence or even violated by its dispositions on the part of the city. Bringing laws to perfection consists, at this point, in descending from the few general principles which govern frequent, jural cases to more special rules and principles which come to light in cases where the general principles cannot be applied. Such additional rules and principles take more extensive account of natural and rational Right.

1545. Another point of view demonstrates a further imperfection in the rule, 'A child is one shown to be such by rightful marriage.'

Not only is rightful marriage not the sole proof of paternity (there could be many other proofs); sometimes, it is not even an efficacious proof. A woman's child is not necessarily generated by her lawful husband. In a word, rightful marriage is a *legal presumption*, not a *logical proof*. Consequently, later Roman jurisconsults would acknowledge different cases in which the *presumption* of lawful marriage had to give way to the truth when actual illegitimacy was proved in some other way.[292]

[290] *Dig.*, bk. 1, t. 6: 3, 3.

[291] Cf. *SP*, bk. 4.

[292] 'We define a child as one born from husband and wife' (Ulpian); this is the rule. The exception is: 'But if we imagine that the husband has been absent for ten years and comes home to find a baby there, WE ARE HAPPY to accept Julian's decision that this is not the husband's child.' Note how Ulpian speaks of something so evident as if it were the mere opinion of a jurisconsult. Equal timidity and reserve, which show him to be unduly attached to the letter of

But granted that paternity is unknown, or that conception outside marriage is proved, is it according to justice that an innocent person should suffer the penalty due to the fault of his parents, a fault which gave him life? Notoriety and the privation of certain rights, decreed by civil laws in the case of illegitimate children, pertain to an age of the world in which the individual principle was still entangled with common nature, and operated within it. The time when offspring was punished for the fault of the individuals has passed. Under the Gospel it has vanished altogether; human personality has revived. Public opinion is changing on this matter, although held back in its progress by the inflexibility of legislations.

Our civil laws, while punishing with appropriate severity the fault of parents[293] and parents alone, should now protect innocent illegitimate children and declare them free of any notoriety, and of any harm consequent on this notoriety.

1546. However, it is not easy, according to rational Right, to determine succession in the case of a child born out of matrimony. Nourishment and education are certainly due to him from the father and, in his absence, from the mother. This is a *blood-right*. But the mother, if she is already married, is not

the positive law, is apparent when he goes on: 'IT SEEMS TO ME, AND SCAEVOLA ALSO APPROVES OF THIS, that if a husband has not slept with his wife because of sickness or for some other reason or, while father of the family, was prevented by illness from generating, the child born in the house, although born there with the knowledge of the neighbours, is not his son' (*Dig.*, bk. 1, t. 6, l. 6). Finally, childship came to be proved in six ways: 1. cohabitation of husband and wife; 2. treaty; 3. nomination or institution; 4. public knowledge; 5. judicial decision; 6. confession and assertion on the part of the parents.

293 All crimes against common mores should rightly be punished by public opinion with some note of dishonour. It is sufficient that governmental wisdom should work to form this severe, holy opinion, and take care not to weaken it by adopting an attitude which shows that it wants no part in it, or even looks upon moral disorder without disgust, or opens the gates to immorality. Government has many ways in which to indicate its moral or immoral stance; indeed, almost every step it takes shows how it feels on this matter. Adultery then must be punished as an attempt to violate a prized possession. The same should be said about seduction, violence, rape, and so on. The legislator must never neglect to unite the *punishment* with *satisfaction* for the damage done.

obliged to this because all that she has belongs to the family of her husband. Even food and drink must be given in such a way that it does not disadvantage the family to which she belongs.

If the mother is single, or the only surviving member of the family of her husband, the blood-bond determines the natural succession of the child to the goods she possesses. If she marries her accomplice, she takes her place as mother of the family relative to her children. The man, however, has the same obligations and the same society with his natural child as he has with his legitimate child. The condition of woman and man are not equal, therefore, in these jural relationships. It follows from what we have said that, according to natural Right, the adulterous mother who introduces an illegitimate child into the house of her husband harms the legitimate children. This is not the case with the adulterous father. Indeed, according to natural Right, he must look upon his illegitimate child as he does upon the legitimate children and admit him to the same society, although the illegitimate child cannot share in the goods of the wife offended by the adultery.

1547. Roman laws had begun to return to the dictates of natural Right concerning illegitimate children when they introduced *legitimisation* which was brought about in three ways: *through subsequent marriage, through an offering to the curia,* and *through the rescript of the ruler.*

1548. *Legitimisation* is a return to natural Right from the deviation of positive Right; *adoption* is an addition to natural Right itself.

Adoption is only a legal *fiction*. In the state of nature a *contract* could be formed between two people, one of whom assumed (in part) the rights and duties of father, the other the rights and duties of child. The contract would be genuine, although its vocabulary would be fictitious and the pretended child could never prejudice the true children in their succession to the father.[294]

---

[294] Hume found it very difficult to decide adequately whether the true, but younger son, should give way to the older, adopted son in the case of succession to Augustus. This shows how legal fiction could confuse even philosophical minds! I believe that no legal fiction can break natural rights; the child must succeed; the non-child must be excluded.

1549. Moreover, the laws of the city, in so far as they tend to guarantee the rights of the person of father and child and impede abuse of these rights by the parties concerned, actually restrict the natural sphere of *patria potestas* in many cases. They provide the child, whom they protect more assiduously for the sake of the new line which he will found, with many rights not given by nature. This is especially the case in matters relative to temporal substances and other real rights.

1550. Civil legislations have also considered and determined through positive law those broad bonds of domestic society preserved amongst agnates, despite the agnates' division into various families.

Roman laws made common and guaranteed to agnates 1. family privileges; 2. the right to vindicate injuries; 3. the right to defend cognate relatives, and so on.

1551. For the rest, I have noted many times that it is an extremely dangerous matter to invent and imagine rights which are not present in nature. Our civil legislators have done this up to now with altogether too much self-assurance, especially by inventing arbitrary rights which cut across the natural course of ownership. Here, I consider it a principle both of justice and political wisdom 'not to impede the accumulation of riches nor to prevent their division and dispersal by presuming to disavow the natural titles of just acquisition.' I believe that each individual and each society must be able to acquire without limit provided this is done under some just, natural title (cf. *USR*, 446–449). Each individual, each society must equally be able to alienate its goods without limit, provided once more that this is done in ways which conform to natural justice. Civil laws cannot prejudice titles of acquisition or ways of alienation which are truly just according to natural and rational Right. If this does occur in one of these two cases (for example in the case of accumulation of what seems excessive wealth), civil legislation by that very fact forces itself to damage the other case (the feared, excessive division of patrimonies). Such injustices bring about a forced, inconvenient, unjust state of human society which suffers like a body with dislocated bones. In a word, the legislator must never wish to be wiser than nature by contradicting its laws.

1552. The right of attorney (cf. *USR*, 255–258) pertains to fathers of families.[295] Consequently, no one, not even the civil government can impede them from 1. choosing arbitrators or judges to pacify their disagreement (when quarrelling families agree about the choice); 2. choosing at will procurators and defenders to argue their case before the civil tribunals.[296]

1553. Civil society, therefore, must maintain and protect, not alter, pervert, impede or destroy the rights which, according to natural and rational Right, belong to the single individuals composing domestic society. Civil society has been instituted precisely for this purpose. It does not have the power to dispose of rights, but only of regulating their modality in order that the rights themselves may co-exist and be exercised in the most free, convenient and advantageous way possible. This explains why incorrupt peoples are often heard to complain bitterly when civil society attempts to dispose of and interfere with these domestic rights at its own pleasure. But we shall have more to say about this when we deal with the Right of civil society.

CONCLUSION

1554. The nature of domestic society is therefore very deep; it has its roots in the very heart of humanity. Is anything more profound than the way in which humanity views itself? Simple and one, humanity touches heaven on the one hand and earth on

[295] Ecclesiastics who have their own households are also fathers of families according to civil law because 'the father of the family is considered the person who has dominion in the home. He is rightly called paterfamilias even if he has no children. We shall speak not only about his person, but also about his right' (*Dig.*, bk. 50, t. 16).

[296] Civil government can very usefully: 1. provide lawyers with a certificate of competence which will serve as a recommendation and guide to fathers of families in their choice of procurators; 2. grant decrees of merit and other distinctions to lawyers in proportion to their ability. This ability must not depend solely on their knowledge, but also on their uprightness and other matters.

[1553–1554]

the other. It is a mixture of a heavenly and an earthly element. The same is true of domestic society: it, too, is simple and one, a mixture of a heavenly and an earthly element. There is nothing more profound, nothing more wonderful in the sight of self-contemplating humanity than this single, extremely simple species, the human-as-idea, which never exhausts itself and yet never realises itself completely despite the number of individuals in whom it takes on subsistence. There is nothing more wonderful than the sight of these innumerable individuals who with inborn eagerness go on renewing the unity of the species through the reality of their union — this species which exists not in space and time, but in the regions of eternity.

The entire human race, scattered over land and sea, divided by mountain ranges, oceans and deserts aspires (without always being conscious of this loving preoccupation in its nature) to come together in the same centre, the same truth, the same virtue, the same good whose proper and hidden source is the supreme Being.

This affectionate tendency of the real, the finite and the multiple to emulate the unity of the idea is explained by the heavenly element of human nature which, informed by *ideal being*, — unique in all human beings — simply seeks the completion of its own form when it desires to feel the *real being* actuating and completing what it sees, but does not feel, in the idea.

This is the depth to which thought must penetrate when a person seeks a sufficient reason to explain why the human heart loves everything, loves every reality, and especially its fellows, the most noble and excellent of all the feelable, perceptible realities open to that person. Every human affection, therefore, has its sublime source in that light, that ideal being, that common good which, embraced by the principle of human nature, constitutes the human being, binds together universal society and is the vestige and beginning of theocracy (cf. *RGC*, 633–670).

1555. This is also the point from which thought has first to move if it wishes to explain the possibility of conjugal society. Marriage, by conjoining the human individual subsisting in two forms, in two halves as it were, presupposes affections already common to human individuals of the same form, and the fount and explanation of affections that we have already illustrated (cf. 997–1028). The indissolubility, the full union between the spouses, can only come from the principle that one human being wishes, through nature, to be united with every other human being. This desire is stronger the more each human being feels and perceives the other with whom he wants to unite in every way permitted by character, conformity, proximity and fittingness. Amongst all these ways, one is offered by the animal condition of humanity where we find the difference of the sexes, the law of communication and of the exaltation of common life, together with the multiplication of the species. This mode of union differentiates conjugal union from all others (cf. 1029–1068).

This mode, however, would not of itself constitute marriage, which is something dignified and human, not merely animal. If intercourse, which concerns the lowest parts of two rational beings, proceeds according to nature, a strand of uninterrupted love rises and makes its way to the most sublime heights where it attaches itself to what is eternal and divine (cf. 1041–1055). Natural affection, which invites man and woman to an undivided communion of life, is itself a tributary of that great fount of all affections worthy to be called 'human'. It is a branch of the natural inclination shown in every real, finite being when he receives, as every human being does, the capacity to intuit, in the idea, unlimited *being*. He is moved to seek everywhere the reality of this unlimited being, and wants to feel it however he can and as much as he can, without ever being fully satisfied, until he finds it and tastes it, infinite and one, just as he sees and desires it in the idea.

1556. Thus domestic society has a religious nature. Its dignity and beauty are given by the union taking place at the apex of the souls of the spouses where they lap against the divine, sublimely simple element which by nature enlightens them and where, lifted by Christ above the created universe, they unite in God himself. Two *persons*, who live their lives in an identical *nature* from which emerges a third person, are already a symbol of the divinity; two principles, one passive, the other active, who become fertile in their mutual embrace, were acknowledged even by the pagans as symbols of the Creator who lifts and unites to himself the intelligent creature, whom he then fills with himself.[297]

It was altogether fitting, therefore, for the Christ of God, in whom the divine and human natures consummated their marriage, to make matrimony one of his sacraments (cf. 1102–1103, 1245, 1251–1254). It was also most fitting, granted that marriage of its nature was already a sign of divine things (cf. 1262), that Christ's most powerful love should also render it an *efficacious sign* bestowing on spouses virtue, constancy and supernatural charity.

Domestic society is religious for yet another reason: it stimulates and nourishes at an ever more vital and deep level the feeling denoting humanity's incessant need for a loving Providence. God's intervention immediately makes itself felt in that mysterious activity, of which the spouses are ministers and through which a third, intelligent individual begins from them.

What will become of this precious fruit that God moulds in their loins?[298] Will it have a base or generous character, mind and heart? How will it have been made by the One who models human beings as a potter moulds the clay? Everything is uncertain; the child lives, yet he could have been still-born; people are happy, as though some great adventure were over. But will the child go on living? His thread of life could be cut any day; every day his suppliant, thankful mother asks again and receives that child from God's almighty power. She knows perfectly well that it is God alone who daily gives back the child to the embrace which binds him to her breast. About the future of the newborn she knows nothing, despite her longing for an inkling of light which God alone can give. All is darkness, and she can only hope and pray that the divinity will lead the child through the uncertain and dangerous journey of life, protected from woe

---

[297] The Indian monuments, in which we see how the whole of the ancient Orient regarded the conjugal union as a symbol of the union between God and man, have been collected and illustrated by Kistemacher in his admirable booklet on the Song of Songs.

[298] The feeling expressed by the mother of the Maccabees is natural and common to all mothers. Encouraging her sons to die courageously, she said to them: 'I do not know how you came into being in my womb. It was not I that gave you life and breath, nor I who set in order the elements within each of you' (2 Mac 7: 22).

and blessed with happiness, until he in turn can leave behind blessed and happy offspring.

These and other natural affections, present in domestic society, continually turn the parents' thoughts to the power and providence of God. They give rise to humble prayer, domestic worship, and sacrifices to the eternal God on whom rests, as parents clearly acknowledge, the uncertain lot of their own life together, the preservation of what is most dear to them, and, in a word, the prosperity of the whole family. Christ, in succouring this pious, human feeling, gave spouses sacramental grace, that is, a power which comforts the hopes and trust they naturally place in protection from on high. This power nourishes their religious affections, is a pledge of blessings to come and a solid shield and sure guide against adversity in human life and the uncertainty of events.

1557. The Right that we have expounded has sprung from our efforts at a thorough and intimate investigation of the nature proper to domestic society. I have divided the treatise into two distinct sections because domestic society results from two lesser, interwoven societies, *conjugal* and *parental*. Domestic society begins with the former and ends with the latter. The conjugal society produces and nourishes the parental society without losing its own first unity. The children who extend and perfect conjugal society (its new members, members of a new nature adhering to it with new bonds) remain within it. Conjugal society blessed with children is indeed conjugal society, but enlarged; it is like a tree which endures as a tree even when heavy with fruit.

1558. The deduction of the Right proper to both societies was simple enough when considered as a consequence of two very simple principles. One, the principle of *conjugal Right*, states: 'Conjugal society is the full union of two human beings of different sex.' As far as we can see, there is neither duty nor right of the spouses which is not logically, clearly and justifiably derived from this simple definition (cf. 987 ss.) The other, the principle of *parental Right*, was concerned with the specific relationship of the collective person of the parents amongst themselves, and the specific relationship of the collective person of the parents with the children. From the analysis of these specific differences flowed the equally spontaneous, ordained duties and rights of each of the parents, and of the children.

1559. I examined each of these Rights, conjugal and parental, founded in nature and consecrated by religion. We saw that the primitive, most noble end of conjugal society, obscured by the great shadow of sin, had been placed once more in the light, and elevated even higher by JESUS Christ, the great restorer of humanity (cf. 1231–1296). We saw that paternity, established in the primitive design as the great principle of unity in the human race, had remained, after the introduction of death in the world through the ancient fault, as the sole principle of unity for each of the divided families (cf. 994). Later these families were re-called and gathered from their separation and dispersal into a new and much happier unity within a sublime theocracy, the family of the divine Father from whom proceeds all paternity in heaven and on earth. The Father rules this family through his great first-born, the Word incarnate.

The direct connection between theocratic and domestic society is the greatest honour of the latter, the most solid foundation of its development and final happiness. Every right and every duty is fulfilled in preserving this precious connection. Yes, let families, which are religious through natural feeling, be so of their own free will; let them be so in their way of life and in their Christian faith. Then they will be happy. Religion sanctions the Right of domestic society, promotes its observance and is itself its greatest honour; Right in civil society collapses with the collapse of family Right:

> Centuries fertile with evil
> First polluted marriage, the race, the home;
> Disaster sprang from this fount
> To flow over fatherland and people.[299]

---

[299] Horace, bk. 3, ode 6.

Appendix

1. (1131).

According to Xenophon (*Memor.*, 4: 4, §22), Socrates appeals to the difference in age when he reproves marriages [between spouses of vastly different age] for infertility and perniciousness. It would seem that he saw no other intrinsic reason for excluding them. Nevertheless he says that they are 'forbidden by a law given to mankind BY THE GODS.' Plato also seems to allude to an unwritten law in book 8 of the *Laws* where he reasons to great effect about the intimate opposition between parental and sexual love. According to him, this law comes from ancient traditions and forbids such unions, which he calls θεο–μιση, that is, 'things detested by God'. Note in reference to such places that: 1. the Greeks often hint at a very ancient, traditional law, in harmony however with nature and even written in the human heart, as Plato explicitly mentions here; 2. the fact that no other intrinsic reason could be found for rejecting such unions, according to Xenophon, shows that the son of Sophroniscus also considered human beings more from the spiritual than the animal aspect. Plato could, therefore, have taken from him his tendency to dictate such strange laws about marriage for his Republic. Nevertheless, anyone reading bk. 8 of Plato's *Laws* will see how the great man mentally embraced the whole complex of human nature. He was quite aware of the moral and jural rules needed to refrain sensuality.

Finally, we should note that impediments in the direct and transversal lines are considered obligatory by Scripture not only for the Hebrews but also for all the peoples. This is clear from Leviticus 18 where we find the following preface to these impediments: 'You shall not do as they do in the land of Egypt, and you shall not do as they do in the land of Canaan, to which I am bringing you. You shall not walk in their statutes.' The writer immediately adds to the prohibition of marriages between relatives a veto on other indecent things. He considers them together and concludes: 'Do not defile yourselves by any of these things, for by all these the nations I am casting out before you defiled themselves; and the land became defiled, so that I punished its iniquity, and the land vomited out its inhabitants.' He goes on: 'But you shall keep my statutes and ordinances, and do none of these abominations. — (for all these abominations the men of the land did, who were before you, so that the land became defiled); lest the land vomit you out, when you defile it, as it vomited out the nation that was before you.' These words certainly and clearly show that rational law forbade marriage amongst relatives, but they indicate equally clearly the probability of a divine, positive law which determined the limits within which such unions could be made, according to circumstances. Hence, the Hebrew teachers place the law about impediments amongst the precepts given to Adam by God (cf. Selden, *De jur. nat.*, bk. 5, c. 11); Grotius also, after quoting several places from the Gentiles concludes: 'These all show the knowledge the ancients had of the divine law against such marriages; we see that the word WICKED was used to describe them' (*De jure B. et P.*, bk. 2, c. 5, §13; 7).

2. (1139).

We must recall what was said about the state of domestic society in the East, especially amongst the Indians (cf. *SP*, 337–344). Note here:

1. This law of the sixth degree applied only to the three most noble castes, that is, to the Brahmins, the Kshatriyas and the Vaisyas, not to the ignoble Sûdra class. This shows that the need to prohibit marriage amongst blood-relations was felt in so far as some noble race preserved the memories of their ancestors. The text of the *Mânava-Dharmasâstra*, according to the translation of A. Loiseleur Deslongchamps, says: 'A woman who does not descend to the sixth degree from one of the maternal or paternal ancestors of the future husband, and does not belong to the family of his father or mother through a common origin indicated by the name of her family, is wholly

fitting in marriage and carnal union for a man of the first three classes' (bk. 3: 5. Cf. also the *Digest of Hindu Law*, bk. 3, p. 531).

2. That such long-lasting traditions about the ancestors was preserved by means of religious ceremonies which commemorated the elders for seven generations (these sacred relationships were called *Sapindas* or *Samonadakas*). 'According to the laws of Manu which we have quoted, the relationship called Sapinda (that is, the relationship of people bound together by the offering of rice cakes — *pindas*) ceases with the seventh person or with the sixth ascending or descending degree. The relationship called *samonadaka*, proper to those who are bound by means of the same offering of water, ceases WHEN THEIR ORIGIN AND FAMILY NAME ARE NO LONGER KNOWN' (bk. 5: 60).

3. These last words, and the definition that Indian commentators give of the relationship called *samonadaka* ('that which ceases only when parental relationships leave no trace in human memory'), contain the true philosophical reason for the impediment of relationship in the transversal line. It is curious that this reason, which is totally lacking in modern legislations, should be so clearly expressed in the very ancient monuments of India. This proves that the reason for laws and institutions is known better by those closer to their origins, as I noted in *The Summary Cause for the Stability or Downfall of Human Societies*, 43–49.

3. (1140).

This intrinsic reason [for impeding marriage between close relatives] does great honour to the Church which extended the impediment of consanguinity to cousins of the fourth degree. Roman laws did no more than forbid marriage to first cousins. This means that amongst the Romans civil society prevailed over domestic society. The situation was reversed by the Church when she undertook to safeguard the family against the tyranny of the State. Moreover, the increased holiness of Christian marriage brought in its wake greater reserve and caution about contracting marriage. Dumoulin is fantasising when he wants us to believe that such an extension of degrees arose from an error of interpretation of Roman law which understood the fourth degree as cousins-german, while the Church understood it as nephews of cousins-german. Nevertheless, despite the nebulous quality of any consideration that would erroneously suppose such ignorance in the entire religious and political world (which was never without persons who cultivated the study of Roman law), we shall add a factual observation intended to free the Church from such an inept calumny.

It was political authority, inspired by religion, which first prohibited marriage between cousins towards the end of the fourth century. St. Ambrose (*Ep.* 60, *ad Paternam*), speaking of this law of Theodosius writes: 'The Emperor Theodosius forbade siblings, and cousins on the part of the father and the mother, to come together in marriage. He established very severe penalties for anyone who dared to contaminate the holy bonds amongst siblings.' St. Augustine, praising the same law, says: 'Who can doubt that it is more decent at this time to forbid even the marriage of cousins on the mother's side?' (*The City of God*, 15: 16). It is clear that both political authority and the Fathers knew perfectly well the limits of the ancient law, which they did not extend through the error supposed by Dumoulin. Nevertheless (and this is scarcely credible) this malicious fantasy was eagerly embraced by the sophists of the last century who were prepared to believe even the most idiotic things provided they were harmful to the Church. As a result, the *Napoleonic Code* did away with the third and fourth degrees of relationship (art. 163) despite the ecclesiastical laws.

4. (1141).

In dealing with consanguinity, we went no further than examining the intrinsic, *moral* reason that persuaded us to see it as an impediment. But its effects also show its *usefulness*. Such utility, a consequence of this and all other impediments established by the Church, could give rise to a treatise on the subject. Our argument, however, is confined to seeking *right* and *uprightness*, not what is *useful*, although utility does indeed follow of its nature in the wake of what is upright and just. Even so, we shall glance briefly at the physical advantages accruing from the prohibition of marriage between siblings and blood-relations.

Doctors show how such unions cause the human species to deteriorate.

> The truth of this is proved by the marriages permitted in ancient Egypt between brothers and sisters, which brought so much harm to the physical prosperity of that nation; by the incestuous marriages permitted by Zoroaster amongst Persians and Parthians, which produced weak, infirm offspring, and above all increased sterility; finally, by the experiments done some time ago in Bohemia when the best breeds of horse, joined always in the direct line, gradually degenerated. Love between siblings must necessarily decrease or temper physical love, which is more ardent in so far as individuals are new to one another. — There is no more efficacious means of destroying the germs of family illness, especially tuberculosis, gout and glandular trouble than uniting different families or even different races in marriage where the weakness on one side is compensated by vigour on the other. — It was already known that the mixture of Mongolian Tartars with Russians produced fine, robust individuals. The mulattos coming from unions between Blacks and Europeans are much more vigorous and active than the offspring of Whites with Americans (cf. Vandermonde, *Essai sur le perfectionnement de l'espèce humaine*, Paris, 1757; Humboldt, *Essai politique sur la nouvelle Espagne*; Virey, *Histoire nat. du genre humain*, etc.) On the other hand, the Hebrews, who have consistently refused to mix with other populations at all times, have become or are becoming ever weaker and smaller as they degenerate from the physical well-being of their ancestors. Moreover, they have transmitted or are transmitting with their typical Jewish features, the initial stages of and the disposition to many skin diseases. They have not been able to change their custom even when benefiting, in the latest revolutions, from the enjoyment of all rights in society.
>
> (Domenico Meli, *Sulla Monogamia*, etc., a little work inserted in the 10th volume of the *Raccolta Medica*, Bologna, Tipografia Marsigli, 1830).

5. (1161).

Incorporation into a religious order is finalised either by *religious profession in the strict sense* or with *profession in the less strict sense.* The former is a perpetual personal self-surrender to the religious order with full and absolute acceptance on the part of the order; the latter is a perpetual personal self-surrender, united to the three substantial vows, accompanied by a conditioned acceptance on the part of the order. When the self-surrender and the acceptance are absolute on both sides, the vow is *solemn.* Prior to the institution of the Society of JESUS, this was the only kind of vow that served as a diriment impediment to marriage because it was the only kind of religious profession recognised. The decree of Boniface VIII (*In Sexto*, bk. 3, tit. 15) was understood in this sense:

> By this present decree we declare and sanction that the only vow to be called 'solemn', relative to annulling any marriage contracted after it, is that which was solemnised through the reception of holy orders or through expressed or merely tacit profession in one of the religious orders approved by the Apostolic See.

However, in the Society of JESUS, before *religious profession in the strict sense* in which the acceptance of the oblation and the self-surrender to God is absolute on the part of the religious order as well as on the part of the person making the profession, a lower grade of 'scholastics' was instituted which was accompanied by another kind of profession. This, as we said, comes about by means of the three substantive vows and the oblation and self-surrender on the part of the person making the vows who intends it as absolute and perpetual. It is accepted by the religious order, however, only for a time, that is, until the order either admits the person to profession in the strict sense or dismisses him. In this case, dismissal frees him from his vows.

In these circumstances, the vow of chastity is not called 'solemn', because this title had come to be applied properly speaking only to the vow solemnised by the first kind of religious profession (even though it was pronounced without any external rite or even tacitly) or by sacred ordination. Nevertheless, it is a diriment impediment because it is united to an offering and self-surrender that renders the person making it a true religious and because it includes a kind of *profession*.

The Institute of Charity also has this way of uniting substantial vows to the perpetual offering and self-surrender which renders the person making it a true religious, even though it is accepted with certain conditions by the Institute and by the Church which has approved the Institute.

Authors pose the question: 'Does the vow render marriage null of its nature or through a positive law of the Church?' Steyaert (§9, n. 3 *ss.*) gives the arguments in favour of the former answer; Wigger (*De Relig.*, Tract. 8, c. 4), the arguments in favour of the latter. The two opinions can be reconciled as follows:

1. If the vow of chastity under discussion is not accepted by the Church, it does not render the marriage null because it is a simple promise, not a full contract handed over and accepted.

2. The Church accepts this vow when the person makes it in the act with which he becomes a *religious*.

3. By divine institution *the religious state* requires for its constitution the three substantial vows, which must either be expressed or included in the vow of obedience. To these must be added that recognition and approbation of the Church which brings about an *ecclesial state*. All this was true even of the religious of antiquity who were not united in societies. Such religious, however, are no longer recognised; their state, therefore, is not an ecclesial state.

With this in mind, we can see: 1. that the recognition and approval of the religious state pertains to *positive Right*; 2. that after recognition by the Church, the religious state can be joined to a given vow of chastity. This vow of its nature and according to *rational Right* must render marriage null because it includes, of its nature, the alienation of the right to marry and corresponding acceptance on the part of God by means of the Church. This completes the contract and passes over the ownership itself (which happens in all *determined promissory contracts* (Cf. *RI*, 1072–1080).

Hence Gregory XIII, in the Apostolic Letters *Ascendente Domino* (25th May 1584) says, against those who denied diriment force to the simple vows of scholastics in the Society of JESUS:

They forget that the solemnity of the vow is dependent upon the constitution of the Church alone, nor do they realise that the three vows of this Society, although simple, were accepted as substantial religious vows by this See and truly placed those making them in the religious state. Those making such vows dedicate and actually surrender themselves through the vows to the Society, binding themselves by their vows to the divine service. No one besides the Roman Pontiff can intervene in such vows.

We see from these words that:

1. The *solemnity* of the vows was introduced by Church law in so far as *solemnity* is understood as every formality or external rite required as a condition of acceptance by the Church.

2. This solemnity is distinguished from the substance of the vows (*vota substantialia*).

3. The vows are 'substantial' as soon as they constitute a religious state. They do this as soon as the Church accepts and recognises them as such, even if the external solemnity indicating this acceptance, and the conditions laid down by the Church for these external solemnities, are changed.

4. Before the introduction of the Society of JESUS, the Church required as a condition for such acceptance religious profession in the strict sense. In confirming the Society, however, the Church was content that persons making the vows 'dedicate themselves through the vows, handing themselves over in act to the Society, binding themselves by their vows to divine service.' The Society, however, accepted this perpetual self-offering only for a time.

6. (1286).

If we compare Roman and Oriental legislation on marriage, we see that the civil element in the former is more developed and powerful than in the latter, which is always encumbered and entangled in invincible customs, prejudices and arbitrary, family decisions. Even in the Orient, people contracted marriage in various ways depending on the degree of their moral decadence.

Eight ways of contracting marriage are listed in the laws of Manu: the way of Brahma, of the gods (Devas), of the holy men (Richis), of the creatures (Pradjapatis), of the evil spirits (Asouras), of the heavenly musicians (Grandharbas), of the giants (Rakchaseas), and of the Vampires (Pasatchas) (bk. 3: 21). The first four are religious and pertain to theocratic and domestic society; the others to the state of decadence, that is, to nature in opposition to the state of society. There is no evidence of a *civil contract*, and civil society plays no part at all. The following is a description of the first four ways:

> In a legitimate 'Brahma' marriage, a father first presents his daughter with a dress and some ornaments, and then gives her away to a virtuous man learned in holy Scripture who has been expressly invited and honourably received by the father. In the 'divine' way, the name given by the Mounis (holy people), a sacrifice is begun, the father attires his daughter, and then grants her to the officiating priest. In the way 'of the Holy Men', the father is first given a cow and a bull by the bridegroom, or an equivalent pair of mates, to perform a sacrifice or to give them to his daughter (but not for gratification), and then grants the hand of his daughter. In the way named 'of the creatures', a father gives his daughter in marriage with the relevant honours by saying: 'Practise together the prescribed duties.'
>
> (Bk. 3: 27–30)

In all these ways the father is present and gives his daughter in marriage. It is an authoritative act of the head of the family. Religion plays a role particularly in the first three. For the priestly class it is recommended that the marriage be preceded by libations of water (*ibid.*, 35). Other rites prescribe the nuptial fire to be carried out by the one who presents the wife and has become head of the house (*ibid.*, 67–286). In the other four ways of contracting marriage, the father plays no part as author of the bond. They are described as follows:

> In a marriage 'of the evil spirits', the bridegroom is fully content to receive the hand of a girl and, according to his ability, offers gifts to the relatives and to the girl. A marriage called 'of the heavenly musicians' is the union of a young woman and young man founded on a mutual vow; it originates from desire and its purpose is the pleasures of

love. In a marriage 'of the giants', the paternal house forcibly carries off a young woman weeping and shouting for help. Anyone who opposes this violence is killed or wounded, and the walls of the enclosure are breached. In the detestable marriage 'of the Vampires', a lover secretly approaches a sleeping, drunk or mad woman. This is the eighth and basest kind of marriage.

(Ibid., 31–44)

It is not clear that any punishment or sanction forbids this last kind, or the other three. They are simply reproved, and recognised as ways of contracting true marriages. All the other laws of Manu demonstrate that civil law concerning marriage did not exist; the despotism of the family stifled all such legislation. This was the great cause which prevented the progress of the Oriental nations and kept them stationary.

7. (1293).

Among the Hebrews only men were allowed to divorce, but this was not unjust to women because:

1. Divorce was a *remedy* granted to avoid greater disorders in domestic society. Hence it was not a *right*. The *remedy* had to be applied in so far as necessary to counter evil and no further. If it had been applied to the woman, it would have had the contrary effect of increasing, not reducing evil in the family.

2. Granted that it was sufficient to allow divorce to one of the parties for the good of domestic society, it fully accorded with reason to grant it to the man rather than the woman because: a) a man's passions are more active, and he is able to satisfy them more freely; b) a woman's passions are of a passive nature and find a corrective in her subjection to a man; c) divorce granted to a woman makes her mistress of herself and of the man. This is contrary to the order of nature and opens the way to infinite evils in the family; d) feminine levity and mutability would more easily abuse such an indulgence; e) in love the woman is more tender than the man, but her love more easily becomes depraved and changes its object. For these and other reasons divorce was permitted only to the man by both the

Mosaic law and the ancient legislations of Greece and Rome. However, the divine legislation of Moses maintained unchangingly this limitation of divorce until Christ abolished it entirely. The permission given by Herod to women to divorce was not properly speaking a law of the Hebrew people. The human legislations of Greece and Rome gave in to the impetus of depraved morals, and later granted divorce also to the woman. The effect was immensely harmful. Bonald notes:

> Among the Romans divorce was rare in the first years, so that in five centuries we have no example of it. In the later years it became so habitual that, according to Seneca, the women counted their age by the number of their husbands rather than according to the consular annals. Augustus was forced to command citizens to marry (the only example in history!). In the early years of the Greeks, and of all other peoples, divorce must have been very rare, but in the time of peace, customary contempt for women and deviation from all natural laws reached such an excess that a single sentence of Plutarch, in his moral works, is sufficient to give us an idea of it: 'We know that as far as true love is concerned, women have no part in it'.
>
> (*Du Divorce considéré au 19 siècle, etc. Résumé*, §8)

8. (1336).

We should note carefully that *as awareness of our moral strength* changes, moral teaching changes — moral teaching and awareness always correspond. One social period, nation or class of persons may maintain and declare obligatory a high level of morality; another dare not obligate itself or others at such a level. The former evidently possesses greater awareness of its own moral strength than the latter, who tend to reduce the obligation because, to their mind, it seems an excessively heavy burden on humanity. This consideration, an undeniable fact, reveals an intrinsic worth in Catholicism which alone is sufficient to demonstrate its divinity and truth. This intrinsic worth is shown by Catholics' awareness of a much greater moral strength than that of non-Catholics. This is shown by the fact that Catholics constantly accept as obligatory 'a much higher and more perfect moral teaching than non-Catholics, who see it as impossible to practise'. A more perfect, obligatory moral teaching is understood and admitted solely in virtue of human awareness of a greater moral strength, an awareness that would be impossible if moral strength were in fact not greater. Catholics attribute this strength to a special divine influence they call 'grace'. Let us apply these considerations to the moral teaching on marriage.

The Catholic Church alone recognises absolute indissolubility of the marriage bond and prescribes absolute unicity of the spouses. As people gradually distance themselves from the Church, they are fearful of such perfect teaching and, because they cannot bear the sight of perfection superior to their strength, introduce arbitrary modifications and relaxations. I could give many examples, but will take the single example of Henry Cocceji in his Commentaries on Grotius' well-known book. In *Diritto di natura* this learned Protestant jurist lacks the courage to admit the indissolubility of marriage and the unicity of spouses. He himself objects that Christ established indissolubility and unicity (Mt 5: 32; 19: 9), but then has recourse to those vain distinctions which are so useful to anyone wishing to make light of the clearest and most decisive authorities:

> We must distinguish between a *corrupt* and an *integral* *state*. If human beings had persevered in an integral state, there would not have been divorces; lust, discord and inconstancy of heart, which are causes of divorce, would not have been known. In the present corrupt state it is impossible to know what must have been of right in the perfect state, because today the heart craves for adultery with a married woman and hates her husband to the point of murder.

He then compares Moses and Christ. Moses gave the law of divorce to provide for human beings as they are. Christ spoke of the perfect human state of long ago, and inculcated

> not what is required by law and necessity, but that which pertains to virtue and was commanded only in the beginning, before the fall.
>
> (*In Grot. De J. B. et P.*, bk. 2, c. 5, §9)

This extraordinary interpretation clearly presupposes that the *moral strength* of human beings has not increased in any way since the coming of the Saviour; on the contrary, it is still the same as that of the Hebrews with their 'heart of stone', as the Bible describes them. The consequence is obvious. These teachers, separated from the Catholic Church, show they have not the slightest knowledge about the grace of JESUS Christ which, in the words of Scripture, gives human beings a 'heart of flesh'. Their separation from the Church has, by their own admission, returned them to the state, feelings, needs and morality of the ancient Hebrews. The permission given by Luther and his associates for polygamy on the part of the landgrave of Hesse (1539) is a demonstration of this.

We can say in conclusion: the Catholic Church ALONE preserves uncontaminated the sublime and perfect moral teaching about marriage; she alone constantly proclaims and practises it. This shows that she ALONE is *holy*; she ALONE possesses *grace*; she ALONE is dignifiedly aware that her moral strength is greater than any possible to human beings in the corrupt state in which they are born; she ALONE possesses this strength in reality, and with it a dazzling attribute of truth.

I have shown elsewhere that *law* and the *obligation* it produces are not the same. Law cannot produce true obligation in those who lack strength to execute it, because it cannot oblige to the impossible. Hence, varying degree of moral strength is one of those *humanitarian differences* that change (*ER*, 80–83) the *modes* of duties and rights. St. John Chrysostom says:

> There was a time when we were not commanded such great virtue. We could take revenge on the one who had injured us, repay one outrage with another, strive for wealth, swear honestly, claim an eye for an eye and hate our enemy. We were not even forbidden to enjoy pleasures, express our anger, repudiate a wife and take another. Indeed, the law even allowed two wives simultaneously. At that time there was truly great indulgence in these and other matters. But the way has been made much narrower after the coming of Christ.
>
> (*On Virginity*, c. 44)

In the initial ages of humanity generative power must have been stronger and paternal elements more deeply ingrained both because bodies were constituted more robustly and because the free, individual element was undeveloped. Nature and the species played a much greater part than the individual. This must explain the very ancient origin of nobility, the prevalent superiority of some lineages, the power of the oriental family and the division of the castes. In this connection it is well worth reading book 10 of the *Mânava-Dharmasâstra*, or *Laws of Manu*, which speaks about the mingling of the four Indian castes. Every possible combination of birth is considered the beginning of a different lineage with different moral characteristics and a name of its own. Each line had different tasks assigned to it according to the aptitudes which were generally supposed to be found there. The moral indications of the despised line are given as follows:

> Anyone born of a despicable mother into a base class, but not well known and apparently honourable (even if not so in fact), will undoubtedly be recognised by his actions. In this low world, absence of noble feelings, vulgarity of speech, cruelty and negligence of duties denote a person who owes his life to a despicable mother. A person of abject birth has the natural wickedness of his father or mother, or of both, an origin he can never conceal. No matter how distinguished a person's family, if he is born into a despised class, he shares more or less visibly in the natural perverseness of his parents.
>
> (Bk. 10: 57–60)

Again:

> A being called Ougra is born from the union between a Kshatriyas and a Sûdra girl. Such a being is ferocious in his actions, desirous of cruelty, and shares in the nature of the warrior and the servile class... A son born from an excommunicated Brahmin is naturally perverse and called, according to the country, Avantya, Vatadhana, Ponchpadha and Saikha.
>
> (Bk. 10: 9, 21)

We see here how the behaviour of a new lineage resulting from the different possible unions between the four castes is determined. The descendants improve or are determined according to their union with descendants at different levels of generosity. The descendants of a Sûdra can climb through seven generations to the nobility of Brahmin lineage by contracting marriage seven times successively with a Brahmin (bk. 10: 64, 65). Now and then, however, in Indian traditions we find mention of the efficacy of the *individual* element. For example:

> By virtue of their austerities and the merit of their fathers, all can, in every age, attain a higher birth here below among human beings, just as they can fall to a lower condition.
>
> (Bk. 10: 64)

Here we see that some power is granted to individual virtue, but the merit of the parents is still associated with it.

Prevalent opinions are for the most part a mirror of the civil-moral state of the human race. If the *History of Humanity* were to be written by a more broad-minded author than we have seen so far, the writer would have to investigate the strength of the influence of these two elements, *species* and *individual*, at every age of the world (cf. *SP*, 406–418). The relative degree of influence and development of these two elements can sometimes be measured with greater accuracy than people believe. Opinions, at least, express it with total precision. Here are some examples.

In the following passage of the above-mentioned *Mânava-Dharmasâstra* we see that the two elements, the individual and the family or species, counterbalance each other:

> After comparing a Sûdra who fulfils the duties of the honourable classes with someone of the distinguished classes who behaves like a Sûdra, Brahma himself said: 'They are neither equal nor unequal because their evil conduct establishes a relationship between them.'
>
> (Bk. 10: 73)

Here, Brahma dare not place a Brahmin of evil behaviour above a Sûdra of good behaviour out of respect for the individual virtue of the latter. Neither dare he place him below the

Sûdra because of the honour in which he holds the generous lineage of the Brahmin. Hence, at that time the two concepts conflicted with each other. M. Chézy maintains that the *Mânava-Dharmasâstra* can be attributed to the 13th century BC (*Journal des Savants*, 1831). If this were true (his date is probably too ancient) and if documents relative to the dominant opinion at the time about the degree of prevalence of the *individual* and *family* elements were brought together, we would perhaps discover that the individuality of the human being began to develop and assert itself about the 10th century BC in such a way that it countered the prevalent influence of the family element, procreation.

In divine Scripture, from the 15th century BC, God commanded the Hebrews, of whose need he was aware, not to kill fathers for the crimes of their sons, nor sons for the crimes of their fathers (Deut 24: 16). The precept, although limited to killing, was found very difficult to observe and was not always observed. Nor was it always possible to observe it in the 11th century: David himself believed that he had to give in to the demands of the Gibeonites and hand over to them seven sons of Saul to be crucified for the sins of their father (2 Sam 21) whose depraved descendants they wished to eradicate. In the 9th century, it was considered extraordinary that Amaziah, king of Juda, did not kill sons for the crimes of their fathers (2 Kings 14; 2 Chron 25).

Only at the beginning of the 6th century BC (a century well known for a new movement throughout humanity) did the concept of individual justice shine in the minds of the people to whom punishment for the crime of one's father now seemed strange and unjust. So they complained, and God solemnly promised the Hebrews that the practice would no longer be carried out. His promise is in Ezechiel 18, beginning:

> The word of the Lord came to me again: 'What do you mean by repeating this proverb concerning the land of Israel, "The fathers have eaten sour grapes, and the children's teeth are set on edge"? As I live, says the Lord GOD, this proverb shall no more be used by you in Israel.

The Lord goes on to promise them that only the person who has sinned will die, not the father, nor the son for him, provided the son does not imitate his father in evil, or the father is not guilty of the same evil as his son, or the guilty person repents.

But individual justice shining brightly in the minds of people is totally different from real progress among descendants by force of individual free will. The individual did indeed progress continually in awareness of his free power to resist tendencies he had received at birth from his perverse predecessors, but he certainly did not succeed in conquering his evil inclinations. This was to be the great task of the grace of the future Redeemer; God himself promised it to the Hebrews through another prophet, Jeremiah, saying in so many words: You now understand that only the individual who sins must be punished, not the entire family. You are right, provided the whole family is not depraved or individuals in it resist iniquity, or repent of their evil. But humanity is too weak in itself to resist the depraved inclinations of corrupt nature. My mercy therefore will come to aid your weakness. I promise you that great power will be given you, and that I will then be able to make a new covenant with you, such as has never existed before.

> In those days they shall no longer say: 'The fathers have eaten sour grapes, and the children's teeth are set on edge.' But every one shall die for his own sin; each man who eats sour grapes, his teeth shall be set on edge.
> Behold, the days are coming, says the Lord, when I will make a new covenant with the house of Israel and the house of Judah, not like the covenant when I took them by the hand to bring them out of the land of Egypt, my covenant which they broke, though I was their husband, says the Lord. But this is the covenant which I will make with the house of Israel after those days, says the Lord; I will put my law within them, and I will write it upon their hearts; and I will be their God, and they shall be my people.
> (Jer 21: 29–33)

The Saviour, therefore, the only Saviour with healing grace, rendered the individual, free element powerful and superior to all the evil instincts inherent in lineage. Since the time of Christ, anyone who makes use of his Sacraments can conquer every obstacle that blocks his way to virtue. The individual, regenerated by Christ, improves the lineage itself. Consequently, individual justice in Christianity is fully restored (cf. *SP*, 476–486).

An observation will not be out of place, although it does not directly concern *domestic Right*. The natural foundation of any wise, political constitution must include total separation between the *administration* and the *judiciary*. This principle has been religiously observed in the Austrian dominions.

The administration is normally composed of *interested parties*; here the power must be divided according to ownership (the social contribution). The judiciary is normally composed of the most *disinterested* and just men available; here the most impartial and virtuous judges must be chosen, whatever class they belong to, rich or poor. This is the notion that we shall endeavour to put in its fullest light in *Della naturale costruzione della società civile*, which will form the second volume of the *Philosophy of Politics* [*Society and its Purpose*].

As far as I can see, these two principles have not been followed rigorously in any of the many *political Constitutions* that have been made, or rather improvised, in our days. The distinction, however, should be thought through carefully by indiscriminate supporters of a *universal vote*. It is, in fact, strange that where the theory of universal franchise is more loudly mooted, less care is taken to form tribunals composed of persons without any private interest in the matters they judge. The trial provoked by Cosnard's will is one of the many proofs of this, at least as far as France is concerned. The appeal court had no shame in pronouncing the inhuman, immoral and unnatural decision that we have indicated: it ordered the sale of a mother for the sake of enriching her daughter, and the sale of a sister for the same purpose. This tribunal was composed of six judges, five of whom were Creoles, owners of slaves and consequently judges and interested parties in the litigation (cf. *l'Univers*, 16th October 1842).

Let us look for a moment at another, greater trial which concerns the abolition of slavery in the French colonies. If we look closely at this matter, which is concerned not with vindicating but finally bringing to an end millions of cruel, impious injustices against millions of people, we shall learn how, generally speaking, a person with vested interests is a wicked judge, to be eliminated from tribunals and committees destined to decide matters of right. This is especially the case when self-interest is bound up with immorality.

In our case, the colonial Councils have always decided against emancipation in their representations to the metropolitan government. These opinions, relative to the French colonies, can be found in the *Report* (already quoted) of the Duke de Broglie to the Minister, the Secretary of State for Marine and Colonial Affairs. The document is extremely significant and instructive.

> In July, 1840, it (the government) appealed ONCE MORE to the colonial councils, asking again for the help of their light and experience, while insisting that this appeal would be the last. The colonial Councils may have thought that until the present they have been consulted for the sole purpose of allowing their difficulties to bring to a halt any plan for emancipation. If so, they should recognise that their systematic opposition will be useless today against a government which declares that the moment has come to occupy itself with the abolition of slavery in our colonies. It is regretted that this language has not been better understood.
>
> The colonial Council of Martinique replied, in its sitting of 2nd March 1841, with a formal protest, stating their opposition in principle against any emancipation whatsoever at any time and asserting that the metropolitan authority had no right in the matter.
>
> The colonial Council of Guadeloupe, without going so far on the last point, and without expressly contesting the rights of the metropolitan legislature, nevertheless was bold enough to proclaim, in its sittings of 23rd and 24th December 1840, the necessity of maintaining indefinitely the benefaction of slavery (this is the term used in their report) and simply to await the transformation of the colony from the fusion of the races, voluntary enfranchisement and the progressive increase of the population.
>
> The colonial Council of Guyana decided, in its sitting of 19th January 1841 which it adjourned *sine die*, that in its opinion emancipation could only be the work of time and patience.
>
> As far as the colonial Council of Bourbon was concerned, it not only thought that slavery was a relative benefit in a state of transition; it also thought it was an

absolute benefit in a perpetual state of things. In its eyes, the condition of the slave is morally superior and materially preferable to that of the free worker. It would be absurd and hateful to deprive him of it. Slavery is the great tool, the providential and permanent tool of civilisation. Moreover, it would be impossible to suppress slavery without trampling underfoot the rights of the colonies, even if the colonists were indemnified and effectively guaranteed the maintenance of work.

The Commission makes the following observations on the decisions of the colonial Councils.

These declarations cause no surprise. There was no difficulty in foreseeing them. As far as we are concerned, we did not turn to the colonial Councils composed exclusively of colonists, but, through the intermediary of the department for the Marine, to the governors and magistrates who make up the special Councils of the colonies. We did this to obtain the documents and clarifications necessary for progress in our work. While we recognise the justice of the motives which appear to have determined your predecessor to give formal notice for the last time to the interested parties, we had not placed any great hope on their co-operation.

The arguments brought forward as a support of these declarations have not caused us any concern; they contain nothing new. They have been maintained over and over again during the past 50 years, sometimes in order to combat abolition of the black slave trade, sometimes to oppose the admission of coloured people into the ranks of civil and political society. In both cases, they have already been appraised.

(*Report to the Secretary of State for Marine and Colonial Affairs*, p. 2 ss.).

11. (1512).

It [the acquisition by the father of what the child acquired] was a consequence of the principle that the child formed a single person with the father. Samuel Cocceji sums up the Roman laws derived from this principle in the following way:

Father and son are considered as one person. Hence, there is no possibility of obligation between father and son. The son solemnly contracted out by his father acquires no right, nor can he even be held as a promisee. No one can be obliged for and to the same thing (*Dig.*, bk. 46, t. 1: 36). Nevertheless, the father's heir is held responsible for affairs relating to the father's property (*Dig.*, bk. 12, t. 6: 38). Equally, if the father is solemnly contracted out by the son, no action is possible against the son; but the promisee given by the son is held (*Dig.*, bk. 46, t. 1: 56). Since father and son are considered as one person, it is natural for the son to be the instrument of his father. Hence, the father in solemnly contracting out his son acquires on his own behalf (*Dig.*, bk. 45, t. 1: 39); just as the son, in solemnly promising for his father, acquires for the father (*Dig.*, bk. 45, t. 1: 38, §17) who may be ignorant of the whole affair (l. 18, l. 19, Pact. d. §4 d. l. 130). 'The father's voice is considered as the son's, just as the son's voice is considered as the father's in those things which are acquired for the father.' Again if the son concludes an agreement 'that he may not be requested from his father', this exception is acquired as the father's right (*Dig.*, bk. 2, t. 14: 17, §7). Again if the son concludes an agreement '*that he may not accede to a request for himself*', this personal pact is also to the father's benefit (*ibid.*, 19, §1). Again, if the son concludes an agreement concerning something which has been contracted with himself or with his father, this exception is acquired as the father's right (*ibid.*, 18). It follows, then, from the same unity of person that children have nothing of their own and cannot acquire anything for themselves.

Everything they acquire, they acquire for their father as the head of the family and master of the house, even if he is unaware of what is happening. Even when they take possession of something, they do so in the name of the father who is considered to will this (*Dig.*, bk. 41, t. 1: 10, §2 and 53; and t. 2: 1, §5 and 4). It follows that the father can dispose as he wills of anything which comes to the children under any title whatsoever (*Dig.*, bk. 41, t. 1: 10, §1; and *Cod.*, bk. 6, t. 61: 6, and bk. 8, t. 47: 2; and *Caj. Inst.*, bk. 2, t. 1, §10). And this is true even if the children have married. The reason is that children cannot institute any civil action in their own name, even if the father is willing (*Dig.*, bk. 49, t. 7: 39). Roman law makes certain exceptions (*Dig.*, bk. 44,

t. 7: 9). According to Roman right (*Inst.*, bk. 2, t. 12) a son cannot make a will, and a father can substitute for his son as for a ward (*Dig.*, bk. 28, t. 6).

Such unity of person is present only if there is a question *of acquisition*, not in the case *of obligation*. A father is not held to the son's obligation; the son alone is held, both civilly (*Dig.*, bk. 46, t. 4: 8, §4) and criminally (*Inst.*, bk. 4, t. 8, §7; *Dig.*, bk. 44, t. 7: 5, §5; and bk. 15, t. 1: 3, §11). If, however, the son has private property from some other source, his father is responsible for this property (*Dig.*, bk. 41, t. 2: 1, §5 and 4). Again this unity gives rise to the fact that children, as heirs of their father, necessarily succeed to every right of the dead person. This is the real reason why in natural right the consent of the parents is required for the marriage of their children lest an heir be forced upon an unwilling father. As I said, father and son are not considered as one person 1. if the son puts himself under obligation; 2. if a third party, such as a promisee, takes upon himself the son's obligation (because children are naturally obliged to the father) (*Inst.*, bk. 3, t. 20, §4); 3. in public trials where the son can judge his father (*Dig.*, bk. 5, t. 1: 77; bk. 1, t. 6: 9) (*Disert. Proem.* 12, bk. 3, c. 4, sect. 2: 159).

More recently, Roman Right decreased *patria potestas* even with respect to goods, leaving to the children's disposition *private property* (*peculium castrense* and *quasi-castrense*), *maternal goods, the benefits arising from marriage and espousals* and all *adventitious goods* (*Cod.*, bk. 6, t. 61). Moreover, the fathers' faculty for acquisition through their children was restricted to determined cases (*Instit.*, bk. 2, c. 9).

12. (1529).

The first-born and the older children dominate wherever domestic society is strong. There are many reasons for this:

1. The *moral reason*, which supposes that the eldest has more knowledge and experience. Hence, the general respect for old age. This respect was greater in primitive times when everything was learned through experience and tradition, and individual activity was little developed.

2. A reason dependent upon *individual Right*, that is, the child who comes first into the world is the first to occupy with his father the family goods.

3. A reason dependent upon *domestic-social Right*, that is, which originates from a dynastic feeling according to which a father sees his line assured in the first-born. In the East, such a feeling was elevated to the order of religious feelings in the following way. Filial piety pushed to extremes deified the ancestors. Descendants thought they fulfilled a religious duty by giving existence to a child who would perpetuate the line of their predecessors, now accepted as domestic gods. Entirely taken up with the thought of satisfying the feeling of dynasty which they imagined subsisted in their dead ancestors, they forgot that they were satisfying their own desire of succession. Indians who did not satisfy such a religious obligation were condemned to hell.

In the *Mânava-Dharmasâstra* (bk. 9: 105), it first says:

> At the death of the father, the eldest son, if he is sufficiently virtuous, can take possession of the entire patrimony. The other children must live under his tutelage as they lived under that of their father.

The condition, 'if he is sufficiently virtuous', indicates the *moral reason*, which varies according to the quality of the eldest brother. Then follows the domestic-religious reason:

> At the moment of birth of the first-born son, even before the child has undergone the sacred rite, the man becomes father and has paid his debt to the ancestors. The eldest son must, therefore, have everything. The son, through whose birth the man pays his debt and obtains immortality, was generated to fulfil a duty. The sages consider other children to be born of love.
> (bk. 9: 105–106).

Where such a value is put on the first-born, families easily remain united and grow into tribes. The Indian legislator continues to describe the duty of the first-born, at the death of the father, to govern his brothers (as long as they are united) with paternal love and prudence, and to determine the advantages that fall to him in the case of division (bk. 9: 107, 126).

Index of Biblical References

Numbers in roman indicate paragraphs; numbers in italic indicate footnotes. Bible references are from RSV (Common Bible) unless marked †. In these cases, where the author's use of Scripture is dependent solely upon the Vulgate, the Douai version is used.

Index of Persons

Numbers in roman indicate paragraphs or, where stated, the appendix (app.); numbers in italic indicate footnotes.

General Index

*Numbers in roman indicate paragraphs or, where stated, the appendix (app.);
numbers in italic indicate footnotes*